# Caught in
# Cr⊕ssfire

## Civilians in
## Conflicts
## in the
## Middle East

**Edited by**

P. R. Kumaraswamy

DURHAM MIDDLE EAST MONOGRAPHS

*To Jayanthi and Ravi Mama*

**CAUGHT IN CROSSFIRE**
*Civilians in Conflicts in the Middle East*

*Published by*
Ithaca Press
8 Southern Court
South Street
Reading
RG1 4QS
UK

www.ithacapress.co.uk

Ithaca Press is an imprint of Garnet Publishing Limited.

First Edition

Hardback ISBN: 978-0-86372-331-5
Paperback ISBN: 978-0-86372-334-6

British Library Cataloguing-in-Publication Data
A catalogue record for this book is available from the British Library

*Typeset by* Samantha Barden
*Jacket design by* David Rose
*Cover photo* © Lynsey Addario/Corbis

Printed by Biddles, UK

# Contents

----

# Contributors

Stuti Bhatnagar is a doctoral candidate at the School of International Studies, Jawaharlal Nehru University, New Delhi, India.

Dr Dalia Gavriely-Nuri lectures in the Department of Political Studies, Bar-Ilan University, and in Hadassah College, Jerusalem.

Amira Hass is a journalist for the Hebrew daily *Ha'aretz*. She covers the Gaza Strip and the West Bank.

Dr N. Janardhan is a Research Analyst for the Ministry of State for Federal National Council Affairs, Dubai, UAE.

Professor Samir Khalaf is Professor of Sociology at the American University of Beirut, Lebanon.

Professor P. R. Kumaraswamy teaches Middle East Politics at Jawaharlal Nehru University, New Delhi, India.

Dr Meron Medzini was a senior aide to Prime Ministers Levi Eskhol, Golda Meir and Yitzhak Rabin and since 1973 has been Senior Lecturer in Political Science at the Rothberg International School of the Hebrew University of Jerusalem.

Professor Girijesh Pant teaches at the Centre for West Asian and African Studies, Jawaharlal Nehru University, New Delhi, India.

**Dr Avraham Sela** is the A. Ephraim and Shirley Diamond Professor in the Department of International Relations, the Hebrew University of Jerusalem.

**Professor William Haddad** is Professor of History at California State University, Fullerton, USA.

# Introduction

*P. R. Kumaraswamy*

*Tens of thousands of bones will become ashes*
*when one general achieves his fame.*

**Chinese proverb**

Unarmed civilian populations are the principal victims of inter-state, intra-state and internal wars, conflicts and other violent upheavals. The evolution of international norms and codification of laws proscribing deliberate targeting of civilian populations has somewhat minimized large-scale violence against civilians and non-military targets. Pre-meditated attacks on civilians are increasingly unacceptable to the international community and states which resort to such practices face widespread condemnation, sanctions and even isolation. Actions by non-state actors and groups are also becoming less tolerated, particularly when non-combatants become the prime victims; yet, caught in crossfire, civilians continue to suffer more than men and women in uniform. Their true suffering should not be measured merely by the number of civilians killed during conflicts. Both during and after wars, their lifestyles are dislocated and they face irreparable personal and emotional damage. Their suffering is a prolonged agony and often is bequeathed to the next generation.

The Middle East is no exception to this general trend and civilian populations have borne the brunt of various conflicts and wars that have haunted the region since the early 20th century. Besides inter-state conflicts, the people of the region have had to endure the twin problems of imperialism and decolonization. European power politics drove major powers, especially Britain and France, to expand their colonial possessions overseas. Their expansionist ambitions came into conflict with the Ottoman Empire that ruled over most of the Middle East. As a result, during World War I, the European powers were not only seeking to defeat the Islamic empire but were also scrambling for post-war spoils. It was this colonial drive for territories that resulted in the British conquest of Jerusalem in December 1917 and its promise for a Jewish national home under the Balfour Declaration a month earlier.

The post-Ottoman political order in the Middle East created more problems than is commonly recognized. The vast area was parcelled into different states and countries, reflecting colonial interests and calculations. In most cases, the process of decolonization and state formation ran counter to the conventional logic of nations aspiring to statehood. The European concept of political entities rooted in territory-based loyalties challenged the prevailing Arab and Islamic identities that revolved around clan and religion-based allegiance.

Thus, while carving out independent political entities, the colonial powers simultaneously sowed seeds of a deep division over national identity.[1] The territorial boundaries of these newly formed post-Ottoman states in the Middle East were arbitrary and artificial. In most cases, they also undermined the ethno-national homogeneity. Either different ethnic or national groups were clubbed together under one political entity (modern Iraq) or the same group of people were dispersed into different states (Kurds). In Lebanon, on the other hand, France created a multi-religious state by expanding the territorial limits of the Maronite entity. Because some of the new states were created explicitly to serve or further imperial interests, they were accompanied by imposed leadership from outside. Great Britain, for example, installed the two sons of Sharif Hussein of Mecca as the ruler of Transjordan and the King of Iraq. Until the late 1960s, Britain had a military presence in and political control over the littoral states of the Gulf.

While most of these newly independent states of the Middle East eventually regained political control over their territories and economic resources, the political divisions of peoples were harder to overcome. In some cases, the divisions continue to run deep. The formation of the State of Israel in 1948, for example, divided the Palestinians into three distinct categories: those Palestinians who became Israeli citizens in 1948; the residents of the West Bank and Gaza, occupied by Israel in the June 1967 war; and the Palestinian refugees scattered in countries such as Lebanon, Syria and other parts of the Middle East and beyond.[2] Elsewhere, internal tensions in Lebanon, the Kurdish regions of Turkey,

Iran and Iraq, and the ongoing sectarian violence in Iraq can all be traced directly to the arbitrary division of populations.

Such divisions and amalgamations not only generate divided loyalties and tension but also prevent these nations and ethnic groups from functioning normally. Otherwise normal events like family functions, cultural events and social interactions become problematic and politically controversial. For example, divided between Israel and Syria since the June war, the Druze of Golan Heights travel to third countries to meet members of their divided families or to solemnize marriages. In post-Saddam Iraq, the relatively heterogeneous central province has became a battleground for sectarian violence between Shias and Sunnis.

As if the colonial legacy was not bad enough, since the end of World War II, the Middle East has become a battleground for numerous wars, conflicts, hostilities and civil strife. It has also witnessed innumerable domestic upheavals, military coups, putsches and violent attempts to overthrow unpopular leaders and regimes. During the Cold War years, ideological rivalry between the United States of America and the Union of Soviet Socialist Republics (USSR) was played out across the region. Through a steady supply of weapons to their respective clients, both the superpowers ensured a heightened state of alert and tension in the region. The enormous wealth generated by oil-rich countries of the Middle East since the early 1970s thus was funnelled back to the great powers in the form of massive arms exports.

Thus, the Middle East region has witnessed a number of major conflicts, including the prolonged Arab–Israeli conflict, which burst into full-scale wars in 1948, 1956, 1967 and 1973, Israel's Lebanon wars in 1982 and 2006 and the two Palestinian uprisings of 1987 and the al-Aqsa intifada. The civil war in Lebanon, which began in 1975, continued until 1989 while the US invasion of Iraq in 2003 set in motion prolonged sectarian violence. The Iraqi invasion of Iran in September 1980 led to an eight-year long war between the two neighbours, and a similar adventure by Saddam Hussein in August 1990 ended in a US-led military campaign that expelled Iraqi forces from Kuwait. In 1979, a popular revolution led by Ayatollah Khomeini overthrew the notorious rule of the Shah in Iran. Then there is the prolonged strife in Turkey involving its Kurdish ethnic minority and Islamist-led violence in Algeria. Above all, since the 1970s the Middle East has become the principal playground for international terrorism, where various militant groups explicitly target civilian populations in pursuit of their political agenda.

Important as they are, focusing on military leaders, national interests, strategies and weapons systems, etc does not convey the true impact and magnitude of wars. Rather, violence in the Middle East leaves behind an irreparable imprint and repercussions for the unsung heroes: civilians. While men and women in uniform can return or retire to civilian lives, such options are not available to civilians. In times of crisis, they are expected to rally behind the state, its army, ideals and war objectives. Political miscalculations and shortsighted personal ambitions often drive nations to wars with brutal consequences. In victory or defeat, civilians are expected to pay a high price, in terms of rearmament, re-construction of a war-torn country or other forms of social reconstruction. How do wars affect the daily lives of civilians in the Middle East? How do civilians get involved in conflicts and shape their course? Or, conversely, is it the war that shapes the destiny of civilians?

## Casualties

Despite growing international concerns, nations and groups have often not hesitated to launch military action deep into civilian locations. Wars in the Middle East, like other parts of the world, have been carried out in densely populated areas, away from traditional 'battlefields'. In smaller countries, the entire national terrain can become the battleground, leaving little distinction between front and rear. As a result, intentionally or otherwise, civilians account for a large portion of war casualties in the Middle East.

According to *B'tselem*, a leading Israeli human rights group, during the first intifada (1987–93) as many as 1,346 Palestinians were killed, including *at least* 276 civilians. Between September 2000 and September 2007 over 4,000 Palestinians, a large portion of whom were civilians, lost their lives in the al-Aqsa intifada. Out of these, as many as 854 were identified as children or minors.[3] Israeli civilians have also been badly affected. In its conflict with neighbouring Arab states in 1948, the nascent Israeli state lost about one per cent of its total population. As of April 2007, the number of civilians killed in Israel during wars and other terror attacks since the foundation of the state was estimated at 1,635. Out of these, 874 were killed since the outbreak of the al-Aqsa intifada in September 2000.[4] Nearly one fifth of the civilians killed since 1948 were children.

During the eight-year Iran–Iraq war, between one and two million people were killed or maimed. Following the US-led invasion of Iraq in March 2003 and until September 2007, over 81,000 civilians lost their lives.[5] According to one estimate, "67,365 civilians (most of them Iraqi citizens) . . . have been reported killed or wounded during the first two years of the ongoing conflict, up to 19 March 2005."[6] The number of Palestinians killed during the civil-war-like situation in Jordan in 1970 remains hazy. The pros and cons of the Hashemite crackdown on the Palestinian guerrillas and the expulsion of the PLO leadership to Beirut are well known. However, the actual number of Palestinians who lost their lives during the Black September massacre still remains guesswork and estimates range from 2,000 to many thousands. The ethnic conflict in Turkey is estimated to have claimed thousands of lives, most of them Kurdish civilians. War casualties, however, also include indirect and prolonged side effects. As highlighted by the Iran–Iraq war, there can be a number of long-term effects such as malnutrition, health hazards, physical handicaps, large-scale disability and children becoming orphans.

On a number of occasions, armies and groups have directly targeted civilian populations. This was more pronounced during the Arab–Israeli conflict of 1948 when the demarcation between civilian and combatant remained blurred. The war also witnessed some of the worst pre-meditated violence against civilians. For example, weeks before the formation of Israel, on April 9, 1948, a small contingent of Jewish underground group members from Irgun and the Stern Gang attacked the Arab village of Deir Yassin overlooking the Jerusalem–Tel Aviv road. In the ensuing battle, a large number of unarmed Palestinian men, women and children were killed by the Jewish forces, contributing to Arab fears and their large-scale fleeing from their homes. A few days later, a convoy to the Hadassah Hospital on Mount Scopus in Jerusalem was ambushed near the Arab village of Sheikh Jarrah. In this attack dozens of Jews, mostly doctors and nurses working in the hospital, were killed. This was seen as an Arab retaliatory attack for the Deir Yassin massacre. In both cases, despite the international uproar, no one was ever brought to justice.

Similar events unfolded in September 1982 after the assassination of Lebanese President-elect Bashir Gemayel. Believed to be carried out by Palestinians, this killing angered the Phalange militia affiliated to Gemayel's political party and their members entered the Palestinian refugee camps in Sabra and Shatila on the outskirts of Beirut. Despite being aware of the prevailing mood for revenge, the Israeli army, which was in control of the areas at the time, did not prevent the entry of the Phalange forces into the refugee camps. During September 16–18, hundreds of unarmed Palestinian men, women and children in these refugee camps were massacred. While Israel was condemned for its failure to anticipate and prevent the killing of unarmed civilians, no member of the Lebanese militia was ever tried, let alone convicted for the massacre.

Excessive use of airpower has greatly exposed the civilian population. With aircraft and missiles capable of deep penetration into enemy territories, warfare is no longer confined to border areas. During the Kuwait war of 1991 for example, Iraq was able to send Scud missiles over 600 miles to strike Israel's population centres. Though the actual number of casualties was minimal, for the duration of the war normal life in Israel came to a standstill and Israelis were often confined to their sealed bunkers. During the final stages of the Iran–Iraq war, both countries indulged in what was known as the 'War of Cities' whereby they pounded each other's population centres. Their less-than-accurate missiles could not be used effectively against military targets. Therefore, they settled for attacking major cities of the other with the hope of terrorizing the non-combatants. In one such attack, the historic mosque in Borujerd in Iran was destroyed by an Iraqi missile attack.

Militant groups such as Hamas and Hezbollah frequently resort to premeditated targeting of civilians. Their low-range and usually inaccurate missiles have limited military value and are not capable of striking at valuable military targets. In the second Lebanese war in 2006, for example, Hezbollah used Katyusha rockets as an effective tool against Israel's civilian population. Its leader Hassan Nasrallah repeatedly threatened that even the city of Tel Aviv in the centre of Israel would not be free from Hezbollah targets. During the 42-day conflict, Hezbollah launched over 2,500 missiles.[7] Some of these missiles reached as far as the port city of Hadera, about 70 miles south of the Israel–Lebanon border. For similar politico-strategic reasons, since February 2002 Palestinian Islamic groups in Gaza have been striking at Israel with low-range Qassam rockets, especially against the southern Israeli town of Sderot. While the actual military usefulness of these short-range rockets is minimal, they cause havoc and panic among ordinary civilians and disrupt their daily routine.

For its part, Israel has often targeted the Lebanese civilian population and infrastructure as a means of exerting popular pressure against Hezbollah. The actual number of civilians killed during the second Lebanese war remained relatively small: about 600 in Lebanon and 57 in Israel. However, according to one Israeli account, over 5,000 were injured, with almost 40 per cent of the injuries being "psychological rather than physical".[8] As will be discussed, the destruction of infrastructure on both sides has been substantial.

Widely popularized during the operation to liberate Kuwait from the Iraqi occupation, 'collateral damage' is the Siamese twin of modern wars. This innocent sounding expression presents wars in gentler terms, hiding the cruel manifestations of death and destruction. This has been used effectively to explain and at times justify the large-scale killing of civilians or the deaths of children. This is most clearly manifested in the Palestinian territories, especially the Gaza Strip. Every major Israeli strike against militants has been accompanied by death and destruction of civilian lives. Victims are often blamed for being there in the wrong place and at the wrong time.

Inaccurate or false intelligence or malfunction of weapons systems have caused some of the brutal killing of civilians. During *Operation Desert Storm* in 1991, a bunker in Baghdad was identified as the command and control centre of the Iraqi Republican Guards and was bombed. Subsequently it was revealed that dozens of women and children who were taking refuge in the shelter had been killed by the Allied attack. Such incidents became more frequent following the US invasion of Iraq in 2003.[9]

Similarly, during the Grapes of Wrath Operation in 1996, an Israeli artillery shell landed in the compound of the United Nations Interim Force in Lebanon (UNIFIL) in Kfar Qana, north of the Litani River, with disastrous consequences. Over one hundred Lebanese civilians who had been taking refuge in the compound were killed. The village once again came under Israeli attack during the second Lebanese war, when dozens of civilians were killed on July 30, 2006.

Lacking an effective military strategy against militant groups, Israel responds to threats by targeting civilian infrastructure that supports these militant groups. The periodic escalation of tensions in the 1990s between Israel and Hezbollah saw both sides explicitly targeting the civilian population. Following the Israeli launching of the Grapes of Wrath Operation in April 1996, an estimated 400,000 Lebanese civilians were forced to flee from the south towards the northern part of the country. Similarly, the second Lebanese war in 2006 witnessed an exodus of over 300,000 civilians from northern Israel to safer areas in the south. The war has expanded along a "line that would run roughly from Haifa to Afula and Tiberius", thereby affecting the lives of about 1.5 million people unable to maintain their ordinary routines.[10]

Enumerating the destruction caused by Israel during the Second Lebanese war, a report by *Amnesty International* observed:

> The Israeli Air Force launched more than 7,000 air attacks on about 7,000 targets in Lebanon between 12 July and 14 August, while the Navy conducted an additional 2,500 bombardments. The attacks, though widespread, particularly concentrated on certain areas. In addition to the human toll – an estimated 1,183 fatalities, about one third of whom have been children, 4,054 people injured and 970,000 Lebanese people displaced – the civilian infrastructure was severely damaged. The Lebanese government estimates that 31 'vital points' (such as airports, ports, water and sewage treatment plants, electrical facilities) have been completely or partially destroyed, as have around 80 bridges and 94 roads. More than 25 fuel stations and around 900 commercial enterprises were hit. The number of residential properties, offices and shops completely destroyed exceeds 30,000. Two government hospitals – in Bint Jbeil and in Meis al-Jebel – were completely destroyed in Israeli attacks and three others were seriously damaged.[11]

This is equally valid for the destruction caused by militant groups, which explicitly target civilian infrastructure. Hezbollah, for example, came under widespread criticism for its attacks against the civilian population in Israel.[12]

## Cost

Human casualties are a major consequence of wars. However, irreplaceable as they are, human lives are not the only costs involved in wars. Reminding readers that there are no 'free wars' in the Middle East, an editorial in Israel's leading daily *Ha'aretz* observed:

Wars cost a lot of money, and they cause economic damage to the state and its citizens, whose scope is impossible to estimate while it is happening. Consumer activity declines sharply during wartime, even in areas where no missiles have fallen, and this is liable to cause the economic collapse of families and businesses. The economic price of the current war will become clear one day, but meanwhile, it is impossible to avoid providing immediate answers to those whose lives have changed overnight and are unable to earn a living or support a family.[13]

This is equally true for the Lebanese civil war, Iran–Iraq war, Kuwait war and the US-led invasion of Iraq.

Since the outbreak of the first intifada in 1987, Israel has frequently resorted to closures whereby Palestinians are prevented from entering Israel for work, education or medical needs. Such restrictions are also extended to east Jerusalem, which was captured by Israel in the June 1967 war and was subsequently annexed. These restrictions apply to both people and goods, and hence they are not as harmless or 'defensive' as one tends to believe. As the World Bank pointed out in 2003, "Even assuming no physical damage, losses from closure and curfew would still amount to some US$5 billion of an estimated total of US$5.2 billion."[14] According to its estimates, by 2002 Israel had inflicted severe damage to the infrastructure of the already impoverished Palestinian National Authority to the tune of over a billion dollars.[15] Because much of the Palestinian infrastructures were built with outside aid and donations, the international community will eventually have to bear the cost of re-building the destroyed public buildings and facilities.

Even Israel was not immune from the economic cost of the Palestinian uprising. As one World Bank study highlighted,

Israel is also paying a heavy economic price. The Israeli economy has experienced a 9 per cent decline in real GDP per capita between September 2000 and December 2002, and the Bank of Israel recently estimated that the costs to the Israeli economy of the *intifada* in 2002 amounted to between US$3 and US$3.6 billion, a figure well in excess of total Palestinian economic losses in the period . . .[16]

Israel has also been slowly coming to terms with the cost of intifada. In 2002 the Bank of Israel disclosed,

In its first year, the *Intifada* hit mainly tourism, construction, agriculture, and exports to the Territories. Its effects expanded to other areas in 2002, among them private consumption, in the wake of the entrenchment of individuals' assessments that the *Intifada* was not a passing phase, but an ongoing situation with far-reaching repercussions on income and taxes, adding up to a fall in permanent disposable income . . . The *Intifada* caused the loss of between 3.0 and 3.8 per cent of GDP in 2002 measured against a benchmark scenario in which it would end in 2001 . . . This loss exceeds that incurred due to the slowdown in world trade, and the slump in the high-tech industry in particular.[17]

The Palestinian uprising and the resultant tension and uncertainty also affected the flow of foreign investment into Israel, which dropped from US$11.5 billion in 2000 to US$3.5 billion in 2002. Likewise, the budget deficit rose from 0.7 of the GDP in 2000 to 5.6 per cent in 2003.[18] Unlike the Palestinian areas however, Israel could easily sustain the war cost primarily because of the larger size of its economy, estimated at about US$100 billion.

A much more devastating picture of war cost can be found in the Gulf. The economic cost of the eight-year-long Iran–Iraq war was astronomical. Apart from the terrible human tragedy, the economic cost of the war was estimated at US$542 billion for Iran and US$524 billion for Iraq.[19] Their rich oil resources were spent wastefully on the war and post-war reconstruction. The liberation of Kuwait in 1991 was also a costly affair. The cost of the military operation alone was estimated at over US$75 billion.[20]

The UN-backed economic sanctions against Iraq also affected a number of other countries.

Turkey lost revenues associated with Iraq's oil pipeline through Turkey. Egypt lost foreign remittances from workers in Gulf countries, Suez Canal tolls, proceeds from exports to Iraq and Kuwait and tourism revenues. In total, Egypt's losses were estimated at over $3 billion. Syria, Jordan, Pakistan and several other countries incurred similar costs.[21]

On the flipside, as part of *Operation Desert Storm* the United States wrote off Egyptian debts to the tune of $7 billion while Arab state forgave $7 to $9 billion debts owed by Egypt. Cairo also received $10 billion additional loans for its role in securing the Arab League's backing for the military campaign over Kuwait.

The second Lebanese war caused widespread destruction and damaged about 30,000 housing units in Lebanon.[22] Following the August 2006 ceasefire, the Lebanese government disclosed that rebuilding the infrastructure would cost US$1.5 billion and take between a year to 18 months. The rebuilding of buildings destroyed in Israeli attacks would cost an additional US$2 billion.[23] A spokesperson for the UNDP put the overall economic loss "at least US$15 billion, if not more".[24] In January 2007, a number of countries met in Paris and pledged $7.6 billion towards the reconstruction of war-torn Lebanon. Whichever figure one accepts, for a country that was slowly recovering from a 15-year-old civil war, destruction to Lebanese infrastructure was considerable. Israel also faced a similar problem. *Amnesty International* reported that between 350,000 and 500,000 Israelis living in the north "fled their homes and became internally displaced".[25] Others suggest that around 16,000 houses and vehicles were damaged during the war and about 90,000 claims would be filed for compensation.[26]

In many countries, wars and conflict situations severely undermine the tourism industry. Not only Israel but also countries like Egypt, Jordan, Morocco, Turkey and the Gulf region have faced the sudden drying up of tourists, which has an adverse effect upon local communities. Sudden cancellation of charter flights, hotel reservations and other economic activities brings enormous loss to those who depend upon tourism for their livelihood. Some of the wars also caused irreparable damage to the ecological system. In the closing stages of the 1991 Gulf War, nearly 800 Kuwaiti oil wells were set alight deliberately by the retreating Iraqi army. Not only could these wells not be used until the fires were fully under control, but also huge quantities of carbon dioxide engulfed Kuwait and its neighbouring countries, creating problems of visibility, breathlessness and long-term disease and ailments.

## Refugees

As vividly highlighted by the Arab–Israeli conflict, refugees are the most visible manifestation of wars in the Middle East. The establishment of the state of Israel ended the centuries of Jewish exile and statelessness. Prolonged suffering and subjugation gave way to statehood and sovereignty.

However, what was an historic accomplishment for the Jews also brought about a major catastrophe for the Palestinians. For over sixty years, the international community had continued to debate over the origin of the problem: whether the Palestinians were forcibly expelled from their homes by the Jewish forces during the 1948 war as claimed by the Arabs and revisionist historians in Israel, or whether the refugee problem was merely the result of hostilities during which basic human instincts compel people to flee from war zones.

For the thousands of Palestinians who became refugees in 1948, deprived of their homes, property and above all identity, the subject is not an academic debate. It is a problem that they and their descendants have had to endure. From an estimated 800,000 at the end of 1948, the number of Palestinian refugees passed the four million mark in March 2003.[27] The Palestinians faced another catastrophe in 1967 when Israel captured vast Arab territories including the West Bank and the Gaza Strip. Some of the Palestinians who had fled their homes in what became Israel to the West Bank in 1948 ended up becoming refugees for a second time in their lives.

Currently most of the Palestinian refugees are scattered in Jordan, Syria, Lebanon and other parts of the Middle East, as well as in the West. While they managed to find a temporary refuge, their living conditions in most refugee camps managed by the United Nations Relief and Works Agency (UNWRA) are barely liveable. These camps are not only highly crowded but also lack many basic conditions like running water, sanitation, health and education facilities.

Their real problem, however, is much larger: loss of identity. From the very beginning, Arab states hosting these refugees refused to grant them citizenship. Bestowing immediate citizenship or through the gradual process of naturalization would have meant absolving Israel of its responsibility for the refugee problem. Jordan has been the sole exception to the general Arab policy on Palestinian refugees. Following the 1948 war, the Hashemite Kingdom sought to integrate territories west of the Jordan River that it had captured. In so doing, it granted full citizenship to the Palestinians, including rights to political participation. Over the years, a number of Jordanians of Palestinian origin have been appointed to different official positions, including Prime Ministers and cabinet ministers. It is widely accepted that Jordanians of Palestinian origin or West Bankers account for more than half the population of Jordan.

The situation of Palestinian refugees in other Arab countries is pitiable. In times of regional crisis, the stateless, homeless and often powerless Palestinian refugees become prime targets for political or military reprisals. Gulf States, especially Kuwait and Saudi Arabia, were angered by the pro-Saddam stand taken by the PLO leadership during the Iraqi invasion of Kuwait in 1990.[28] Hence, following the liberation of Kuwait by the US-led Allied forces, the Gulf rulers targeted the Palestinians. Within the next few months, nearly 400,000 Palestinians were expelled from Kuwait and other Gulf states. Most of the Palestinians returned to Jordan, a country with few natural resources.

The Lebanese army, which could not act against Hezbollah or disarm its militants, was quick to respond when in May 2007 a splinter Palestinian group challenged the authority of the state. Their location within the dense Nahr al-Bared refugee camp in the coastal city of Tripoli did not inhibit the army from striking against Fatah al-Islam, believed to be linked to al-Qaeda. This campaign, which lasted for over 100 days, enjoyed the support of all major political forces in Lebanon, including Hezbollah. The use of heavy weapons by the army led to 40,000 refugees fleeing to nearby Beddawi camp.[29] When the confrontation eventually ended in September 2007, the refugee camp was in shambles and needed large-scale reconstruction. The overwhelming support for the government over this issue compelled even the Palestinian leadership both inside and outside Lebanon to support the army action. Thus, devoid of the protection of a state, Palestinian refugees are often at the mercy of their hosts.

Moreover, most of the Palestinian refugees in Syria and Lebanon dwell in dilapidated and crowded refugee camps. In return for this 'hospitality', the host countries have imposed a number of political, economic and social restrictions. The situation of Palestinian refugees in Lebanon is a case in point.[30] For over four decades, they could undertake only manual and clerical jobs. Granting access to other sectors of the economy was viewed as a 'prelude' to their permanent settlement in Lebanon and, in order to maintain their 'foreigner' tag, they were excluded from over 72 professions in that country.[31] Due to constant internal pressures, in June 2005 the Lebanese government liberalized its employment rules and declared: "From now on Palestinians born on Lebanese land and registered officially with the Lebanese Interior Ministry will be allowed to work in the jobs previously unavailable to them."[32] In practical terms, this will benefit the bulk of the 400,000 registered Palestinians living in the 12 refugee camps in the country, as nearly 90 per cent of these refugees were born in Lebanon.

Palestinians, however, are not the only refugees who endure the consequences of wars and conflicts in the Middle East. The US-led invasion of Iraq has created a major humanitarian crisis with large-scale population displacement and exodus. At the time of the US-led invasion of Iraq, it was hoped that a large number of Iraqis who fled during the reign of Saddam Hussein would return and contribute to the democratic experiment in that country.[33] Not only did this not happen but also a large number of Iraqis fled and took refuge in neighbouring countries. The impoverished Kingdom of Jordan alone houses over 750,000 Iraqi refugees, while Syria hosts about 1,200,000 Iraqi nationals.[34] "The 2003 war and its continuing aftermath", *Human Rights Watch* concludes, "brought new waves of Iraqis to Jordan, at least doubling their number by 2006. Amman's population is estimated to have grown by as much as one-third since the war began."[35] Likewise, in September 2007 the UN High Commission for Refugees (UNHCR) put the total number of displaced Iraqis at over four million.[36]

The same sense of disappointment prevails in the Palestinian territories. A number of Palestinians who had returned to the territories administered by the Palestinian National Authority in the 1990s were forced to go back. Their hopes for returning to their homes were short-lived. The harsh realities of post-Saddam Iraq and the post-Oslo Palestinian territories do not offer them any hope of ending their exile and starting a new life in their homelands.

In the wake of the Israeli strikes against Lebanese infrastructure in 2006, Syria opened its borders and accepted an estimated 250,000 Lebanese and other refugees who were fleeing the war zone, while another 750,000 Lebanese were identified as "internally displaced".[37] The prolonged military campaign by the Turkish army against Kurdish militants has also resulted in large-scale displacement of Turkey's Kurdish population.

Finally, even conflicts beyond the region have resulted in the Middle East hosting a large number of refugees. At the height of the crisis in Afghanistan following the Soviet invasion, for example, Iran found itself hosting as many as 810,000 Afghan refugees.[38]

**Terrorism**

More than wars, it is terrorism that has become a major menace to the Middle East's civilians. Terrorism not only threatens the lives of civilians but by bringing wars to the streets also undermines civilians' right to pursue a normal daily routine. The perennial controversy – terrorist vs. freedom fighter – has prevented the international community from adopting a universal definition but the impact of terrorism continues to be brutal. Since the early 1970s, terrorism has become a highly prominent manifestation of the Arab–Israeli conflict. While it does not pose an existential threat to their state, it has exposed Israeli civilians to profound uncertainties as they go about their daily lives. Such acts have increased since the onset of the Middle East peace process. Indeed, more Israeli civilians have been killed since the signing of the Oslo Agreement in September 1993 than before. Such attacks have not been confined to the occupied territories but have also been carried out within the June 1967 borders of Israel. A host of locations and means of transport used by the civilian population have become targets for attacks, often carried out by suicide bombers. Buses, cafeterias, street crossings, shopping centres, railway stations and other public places where people gather have frequently came under terrorist attack.

Individual hopelessness, a strong sense of injustice, hatred for the other, anger at international indifference and religious extremism and indoctrination have all contributed to scores of young men and women disregarding their own lives and taking the lives of others. Widespread religious sanctity associated with such actions has bestowed a degree of social acceptance and even respectability for suicide bombers and transformed them into martyrs in the cause of Islam.

Such attacks, however, have not been directed only against Israel. Much of the ongoing sectarian violence in Iraq clearly falls into the category of terrorism. While resistance against foreign occupation has been internationally recognized, most of the violence does not fall into this category. The resistance against occupation carried out by different groups inside the country has been sporadic, disjointed and lacks any coherent national agenda. While operations against Allied military targets, power centres or infrastructure can be considered 'resistance', assaults directed against the support system of the US-backed Iraqi government fall into a distinctly grey area.

However, periodic attacks against religious places, community gatherings, market places and other explicitly 'soft' non-military civilian targets cannot really be considered 'resistance'. These attacks explicitly target civilians and are aimed at instilling fear and insecurity among ordinary Iraqis. By attacking the vulnerable civilian population, which has no military value or motive, these groups have succeeded in terrorizing the vast majority of the Iraqi public. *Human Rights Watch* admits the difficulties in making an accurate assessment of casualty figures due to the "chaos of the conflict, the partial functioning of Iraqi institutions and the unwillingness of the United States to keep statistics on civilian deaths". At the same time it concludes, "all evidence suggests that insurgent attacks in Iraq have killed many more civilians than combatants."[39]

A number of Shia and Sunni places of worship have come under attacks by rival groups. For example, in August 2003 massive car bombs outside the Shrine of Imam Ali Mosque in al-Najaf, the most holy site for Shia Muslims, killed more than 85 people. Mosques in different parts of the country have come under attack and large numbers of Shia pilgrims were killed while performing *Ashura* or other religious duties. On scores of occasions, buses have been waylaid by militants, passengers separated along sectarian lines, and members of the wrong community brutally killed. Such attacks have been carried out primarily by militants belonging to the Sunni minority to generate panic and helplessness among different sections of the population. Afraid for their personal safety, many individuals have been forced to organize themselves into smaller militia or flee to safe havens within or outside Iraq.

A number of other countries of the Middle East have also faced the menace of terrorism. While some of the violence is explicitly directed against the West and Israel, other attacks are homegrown and are directed against their respective governments. Anti-American violence in Morocco, Saudi Arabia, Jordan and other countries often poses a far more serious threat to the regimes of those countries than to the Western interests. For over a decade Algeria has been riddled with protracted political violence, which is primarily domestic in nature. Terrorism against tourists in Egypt killed more Egyptians than foreigners. The phenomenon of Afghan Arabs often takes its toll in Jordan and other Arab countries. Turkey has endured PKK-initiated violence. In recent years, Lebanon has witnessed numerous terror attacks against individuals and groups who are critical of Syria. Of late, even Syria is no longer safe from the scourge of terrorism.

Some of the terror attacks in Saudi Arabia, for example, have claimed the lives of expatriate workers who came to the kingdom in search of a decent living.

Terrorism is not just violence per se but also a form of psychological pressure against the non-combatants. In the 1980s, a number of westerners were taken hostage by various militia groups operating in Lebanon. Kidnapped individuals were often used as pawns to settle political differences between various groups or their patrons in the region. Though most were released, their experiences had a traumatic effect on these individuals. The kidnapping of two soldiers by Hezbollah from inside Israeli territory in July 2006 led to the prolonged Lebanese conflict that lasted 42 days. The kidnapping of BBC journalist Alan Johnston in the Gaza Strip lasted for over 100 days until the Hamas government secured his release in July 2007. A large number of kidnapped victims have not been so lucky, however. The sectarian violence in Iraq has been accompanied by the kidnapping of a large number of Iraqi, Arab and western nationals. Various militant groups and armed bandits have resorted to this tactic. Some of the hostages have been brutally killed and their gruesome executions posted on the internet.

Terrorism thus does not distinguish between friends and foes. Even people who come to the Middle East to offer humanitarian assistance, present unbiased media coverage or even identify and empathize with the suffering of the people of this region have been taken hostage and killed by their captives. These victims were not only far removed from the war, but also were in the region merely to play a part in the peaceful resolution of the problem, or to present Arab voices to the wider world.

Lamenting on this sad state of affairs, one Israeli commentator observed:

> The encounter with foreign countries, at least those that are not part of the Third World, is like a blow to the consciousness: In many states, people go about their daily life without Qassam or Katyusha rockets or terror attacks. There are places in the world where civilians are not exposed to news about the security situation from morning to night. There are nations that do not live with the constant moral unease deriving from the occupation of another nation. There are societies that are not surrounded by incessant

violence. Public life in most developed states is not suffused with feverish preoccupation with fateful questions about their national survival.[40]

Thus, ordinary Israelis going to malls, Egyptians in holiday resorts, Yemenites visiting historic sites, Moroccans on the beaches and Iraqis praying in mosques have all been victims of terrorism. It does not distinguish between religious faiths, political ideologies or rights of individuals. Terrorism creates a sense of uncertainty, fear and anxiety in the minds of scores of ordinary individuals who are merely going about their daily routine.

## Social Fallout

The real social problems of wars begin only after the guns fall silent. Both the victor and the vanquished, even if they can be clearly identified, bear the cost long after the cessation of hostilities. The death and destruction caused by the eight-year Iran–Iraq war is a vivid reminder of the social consequences of wars. Almost every Iranian family was directly affected by the prolonged war and in the process suffered because of it. The presence of a large number of physically handicapped men and thousands of war widows in Iran are directly linked to the war.

War not only destroys the lives and limbs of soldiers but also physically and psychologically cripples the healthy. The desire to secure victory at times drives nations to pursue insane paths. Devoid of sufficient mine-sweeping equipment, for example, Iran's Ayatollahs sent thousands of child soldiers to the battlefield to 'clear' mines laid by their Iraqi enemy. Ayatollah Khomeini and his colleagues presented this cruel decision as a divine mission. Children were assured that, by sacrificing their lives in such brutal operations, they would become martyrs in the cause of Islam. The soldiers even carried a symbolic key to heaven. Thus, a whole generation of Iranian children and young boys became human minesweepers and perished in the battlefield.

Religious sentiments and places of worship are becoming less sacrosanct in wars. President Anwar Sadat of Egypt launched the October war of 1973 on the holiest day in the Jewish calendar, Yom Kippur. This offensive also coincided with the Islamic holy month of Ramadan. While it gave him a great strategic surprise over Israel, the date selection generated huge resentment over Sadat's insensitivity. More than two dozen Israelis were killed in March 2002 while sharing the *Pessah* (Passover) meal in a hotel in Netanya. In November 2001, the United States carried out a major offensive against al-Qaeda in Afghanistan during the holy month of Ramadan. The sectarian violence in Iraq no longer recognizes the sanctity of places of worship as both Shia and Sunni mosques have been frequently targeted by rival sects. The Temple Mount/Harem al-Sharif area of the old city of Jerusalem has often been a battleground for Israelis and Palestinians. In February 1994, Israeli settler Baruch Goldstein gunned down 29 Muslim worshippers in the Ibrahmi Mosque in Hebron, also known as Tomb of the Patriarchs.

Wars and conflicts also affect and at times poison the relations between different groups within a country. Its prolonged conflict with the Arab world, for example, undermines Israel's ability to treat its Arab population on an equal footing. Apprehensions over their loyalty towards the Jewish State have resulted in Israel perceiving its minority Arab population through the prism of security rather than democracy. The civil war in Lebanon was primarily the outcome of the internal tensions and rivalry between the three principal groups in the country, namely, Maronites, Sunnis and Shias. The willingness of these groups to maintain private militia in defence of their respective sectarian interests eventually plunged the country into a civil war. Likewise, the determination of Hezbollah to pursue an independent foreign policy and resist any attempt to disarm its militia eventually culminated in the second Lebanese war that brought scores of deaths and much destruction to both Lebanon and Israel.

Other groups also faced a similar fate. The war with Iran undermined the status of Kurds in Iraq. Though their relations with the central authority in Baghdad have always been problematic, their situation worsened in the later stages of the war. Apprehensions that they might join forces with Iran and work towards an Iraqi defeat led to a widespread military crackdown against Kurds. The use of chemical weapons in the Kurdish town of Halabja took place while Iraq was fighting Iran. The Shia uprising following the Kuwait war of 1991 also led to similar Iraqi offensives in the southern part of the country.

Sudden eruptions of violence in the Middle East entangle a number of third countries and their citizens. Following the Iraqi invasion of Kuwait in August 1990, thousands of citizens belonging to a number of countries were caught in the crossfire. Partly to prevent any western military campaign President Saddam Hussein sought to use these foreign citizens as 'human shields' and scattered them into different parts of Iraq. Securing the safe release of their citizens thus became a major pre-occupation for a number of foreign countries. At the time of the Iraqi invasion of Kuwait for example, thousands of Indian nationals were trapped in both these countries and ensuring their safe evacuation became a political as well as logistical nightmare for the government of India. Between August and October 1990 India carried out the largest airlift since the end of World War II and brought home nearly 160,000 Indian expatriate labourers from Kuwait and Iraq.[41] Such a massive human tragedy also resulted in India adopting a blatantly pro-Saddam position during the early stages of the Kuwait crisis.

Evacuation of third-country nationals is possible only if both the warring sides are prepared to provide safe passage. This was poignantly highlighted during the second Lebanese war when scores of Arab, western and other nationals were caught in the crossfire between Israel and Hezbollah. Even when Israel was prepared to offer a safe corridor, getting a host of foreign ships to the Beirut port and evacuating their respective nationals proved to be an ordeal. As a result, while most of the western nationals were taken to Cyprus by their respective navies, a large number of foreigners opted for circuitous and dangerous land routes to Syria and Jordan. Because of the destruction of many bridges, they had to travel by narrow and dangerous mud roads to escape from Lebanon.

## Outline of the Present Volume

Taking these broad developments into account, in this book a group of diverse and established scholars examine civilian lives during various wars in the Middle East. The Arab side of the Arab–Israeli conflict forms the focus of the chapters by Avraham Sela and Amira Hass. Examining the role of the Arabs in the 1948 war, Sela highlights the challenges faced by the Arab population and the internal differences that existed between the local Arab communities and external fighters who came to Palestine in their defence. Looking at the al-Aqsa intifada, Hass offers a moving human portrayal of the suffering of the Palestinians. Even though Jewish Israeli civilians also suffered during the uprising, it was the Palestinians who bore most of the sufferings and Hass captures their plight through her first-hand accounts.

Israeli society forms the focus of the chapters by Meron Medzini and Dalia Gavriely-Nuri. Examining the June 1967 war and October 1973 respectively, they reveal the fears and trepidations experienced by Israeli citizens during the days running up to the conflicts. The civilian sense of helplessness was also accompanied by a growing public distrust of the government and its ability to handle the mounting threat.

The civil war in Lebanon and its impact upon different segments of the population is the subject of Samir Khalaf's chapter. The remaining four chapters are devoted to wars in the Gulf and their impact. Stuti Bhatnagar examines the popular nature of the Islamic revolution in Iran and its aftermath. The impact of the Iraqi invasion upon Kuwaiti citizens forms the core of the chapter by N. Janardhan. The chapter by William Haddad deals with the devastating consequences of the UN-mandated economic sanctions upon Iraq, while Girijesh Pant presents a poignant picture of the ongoing internal violence in Iraq and its impact upon different segments of the population.

## Acknowledgements

This volume would not have been possible without the active cooperation of the contributors. Despite their other pre-occupations, they took time off to explore a new area. I remain grateful to them for their labour of love and patience with my endless demands. Special mention is reserved for Sreeradha who has been a great source of inspiration ever since the volume was conceived. In numerous ways I have been blessed with the loving care of Appa, Sreedhar and Lin. All these years I enjoyed the love and affection of Ravi Mama and Jayanthi, to whom I dedicate this volume.

## NOTES

1 P. R. Kumaraswamy, 'Who am I? Identity crisis in the Middle East', *MERIA*, Vol. 10, No.1 (March 2006), pp. 66–76 [Text: http://meria.idc.ac.il/journal/2006/issue1/Kumaraswamy.pdf].

2 For recent discussion see *Palestinian Refugees and the Politics of Peace Making*, ICG Middle East Report No. 22 (Brussels, International Crisis Group, 2004).

3 *B'tselem*, http://www.btselem.org/English/Statistics/Casualties.asp, accessed on October 6, 2007

4 Ruth Sinai, 'NII: 66 terror fatalities in past year, 1,635 since establishment of state', *Ha'aretz*, April 21, 2007.

5 Iraq Body Count, www.iraqbodycount.org, accessed on October 2, 2007.

6 A Dossier of Civilian Casualties, 2003–05, *Iraq Body Count*, 2005, http://www.iraqbodycount.org/analysis/reference/pdf/a_dossier_of_civilian_casualties_2003-2005.pdf, accessed on September 23, 2007.

7 Written statement submitted by Human Rights Watch to the Second Special Session of the (UN) Human Rights Council, August 10, 2006, http://www.hrw.org/english/docs/2006/08/10/lebano13955.htm, accessed on September 23, 2007.

8 Ruth Sinai, 'NII: 66 terror fatalities in past year, 1,635 since establishment of state', *Ha'aretz*, April 21, 2007.

9 *Off Target: The Conduct of War and Civilian Casualties in Iraq* (New York: Human Rights Watch, 2003).

10 'There are no free wars', Editorial, *Ha'aretz*, July 26, 2006.

11 Amnesty International, *Deliberate Destruction or 'Collateral Damage'? Israeli Attacks on Civilian Infrastructure* (London, August 23, 2006), http://web.amnesty.org/library/index/engmde180072006, accessed on June 7, 2007.

12 Amnesty International, *Israel/Lebanon: Under Fire: Hezbollah's Attacks on Northern Israel* (London, September 14, 2006), http://web.amnesty.org/library/index/engmde020252006, accessed on June 7, 2007.

13 'There are no free wars', Editorial, *Ha'aretz*, July 26, 2006.

14 World Bank, *Twenty-Seven Months – Intifada, Closures and the Palestinian Economic Cost: An Assessment*, (Washington DC, 2003), p. 9.

15 World Bank, *Four Years – Intifada, Closures and the Palestinian Economic Cost: An Assessment* (Washington DC, 2004), p. 10

16 Ibid., p. xv

17 Cited in Ibid, p. 10n

18 Neill Lochery, 'The politics and economics of Israeli disengagement, 1994–2006', *Middle Eastern Studies*, Vol. 43, No. 1 (January 2007), pp. 12–13.

19 Kamran Mofid, 'After the Gulf War II: The cost of reconstruction', *The World Today*, March 1989, p. 49.

20 Katsuaki L. Terasawa and William R. Gates, *Burden Sharing in the Persian Gulf: Lessons Learned and Implications for the Future* (Monterey: US Naval Post-Gradaute School, 1993), p. 15, http://web.nps.navy.mil/~brgates/documents/research/13-gulfpaperfinal.doc.

21 Ibid.

22 Osama Habib, 'Report says Lebanon's GDP will fall 1 per cent', *The Daily Star*, August 26, 2006.

23  Lysandra Ohrstrom, 'CDR: Rebuilding infrastructure will take at least a year, cost $3.5 billion', *The Daily Star*, August 17, 2006. Hezbollah, whose kidnapping of two Israeli soldiers triggered the violence, accused the government of inflating the estimates for political purposes and put the cost at US$1.5 billion. Michael Bluhm and Osama Habib, 'Hezbollah questions government's estimates on cost of reconstruction', *The Daily Star*, February 16, 2007.

24  'War wiped out 15 years of Lebanese recovery – UNDP', *The Daily Star*, August 23, 2006.

25  Amnesty International, *Israel/Lebanon*.

26  Eli Ashkenazi, 'War hasn't ended for homeowners in the North', *Ha'aretz*, August 16, 2006.

27  *Palestinian Refugees and the Politics of Peace Making*, p. 2.

28  For background discussions see among others, George T. Abed, 'The Palestinians and the Gulf crisis', *Journal of Palestine Studies*, Vol. 20, No. 1 (Winter 1991), pp. 29–42; and Lamis Adnoni, 'The PLO at crossroads', *Journal of Palestine Studies*, Vol. 21, No. 1 (Autumn 1991), pp. 54–65.

29  Rym Ghazal, 'Army goes back on offensive against Fatah al-Islam', *The Daily Star*, June 6, 2007.

30  Rosemary Sayigh, 'Palestinians in Lebanon: Harsh present, uncertain future', *Journal of Palestine Studies*, Vol. 25, No. 1 (Autumn 1995), pp. 37–53; and Julie Peteet, 'From refugees to minority: Palestinians in post-war Lebanon', *Middle East Report*, No. 200 (July–September 1996), pp. 27–30.

31  Simon Haddad, 'The Palestinian predicament in Lebanon', *Middle East Quarterly*, Vol. 7, No. 3 (September 2000), http://www.meforum.org/article/68.

32  Rym Ghazal, 'Lebanon to let Palestinians obtain work permits', *The Daily Star*, June 28, 2005. See also Mohammed Zaatari, 'After 20 years Palestinians are finally allowed to work', *The Daily Star*, June 28, 2005.

33  In 1996, for example, four million Iraqis were living outside their country and out of them 600,000 were considered to be refugees. UNHCR figures quoted in Geraldine Chatelard, *Iraqi Forced Migrants in Jordan: Conditions, Religious Networks and the Smuggling Process*, EUI Working Paper 2002/49 (Robert Schuman Centre for Advanced Studies, Italy), p. 5.

34  *Statistics of Displaced Iraqis Around the World, April 2007*, UN High Commission for Refugees, http://www.unhcr.org/cgi-bin/texis/vtx/home/opendoc.pdf?tbl=SUBSITES&id=461f7cb92, accessed on September 23, 2007.

35  *'The Silent Treatment' Fleeing Iraq, Surviving in Jordan* (New York: Human Rights Watch, 2006), p. 20.

36  *The Daily Star*, September 14, 2007.

37  *UNHCR Global Report 2006, The Lebanon Situation*, http://www.unhcr.org/home/PUBL/4666d244e.pdf, accessed on September 23, 2007.

38  *UNHCR Global Appeal 2007 The Islamic Republic of Iran*, http://www.unhcr.org/home/PUBL/455443aa0.pdf, accessed on September 23, 2007.

39  *A Face and a Name* : Civilian Victims of Insurgent groups in Iraq, (New York: Human Rights Watch, 2005), p. 4.

40  Uzi Benziman, 'A look outside the local pond', *Ha'aretz*, June 5, 2007, http://www.haaretz.com/hasen/spages/867516.html, accessed on June 6, 2007.

41  P. S. Jayaramu, 'India and the Gulf Crisis', in A. K. Pasha (ed.), *The Gulf in Turmoil: A Global Response* (New Delhi: Lancer Books, 1992), p. 153.

# 1

# Arab and Jewish Civilians in the 1948 Palestine War

*Avraham Sela*

## Preface

Hostilities between Arabs and Jews erupted following the United Nations resolution on the partition of Palestine into two separate Jewish and Arab states, in November 1947. During the period between November 30, 1947 and May 14, 1948 when the State of Israel was proclaimed, the two ethnic communities became engaged in an ever expanding and intensifying conflict parallel to the incremental withdrawal of the British military and civil administration.[1] The inter-communal conflict culminated in the military and political collapse, social disintegration and mass displacement of the Palestinian-Arab community, especially urban Arab society which had been almost entirely wiped out, turning about 250,000 people into refugees. The echoes of the Palestinian Arabs' disaster among the neighbouring Arab-Muslim societies, the anticipated official end of the British Mandate and the proclamation of the State of Israel, all triggered the invasion of Palestine by four Arab regular armies and the beginning of the 'official', or 'international' Arab–Israeli war.

The inter-communal war was the culmination of an escalating Arab–Jewish conflict over the land of Palestine which the British government failed to settle. In the aftermath of World War II, economically exhausted and badly in need of American financial aid and strategic cooperation, Great Britain came under renewed and contradictory regional and international pressures in support of both Arab and Jewish claims to Palestine. With the failure of the 1946–47 diplomatic efforts to forge an American-backed political settlement of the Palestine conflict, the unbridgeable gap between the Arab and Jewish positions regarding an agreed-upon post-Mandatory political settlement, and British interests in preserving Arab and Muslim 'good will' led Britain to refer the issue of Palestine to the United Nations. Finally, in view of the growing international support for the partition of Palestine and the establishment of a Jewish state, Britain decided to relinquish the Mandate and withdraw its civil administration and military forces from Palestine.

Though violence and tension between Arabs and Jews had been on the rise since early 1947, the Arab riots that erupted in Jerusalem as a spontaneous reaction to the UN resolution on the partition of Palestine on November 29, 1947 could only develop into a *total* inter-communal war due to the anticipated end of the Mandate and the continuous withdrawal of Britain's forces and administration from the scene, leaving the two communities to face the new reality on their own. Thus, while the British Mandate remained officially in force and continued to bear official responsibility for law and order in the country as a whole until its very last day, in effect the government became increasingly preoccupied with the safe evacuation of its personnel and materiel from Palestine, giving way to a growing societal and political chaos and escalating violence between Arabs and Jews.

The inter-communal war, however, soon got entangled with the growing infiltration into the country of a few thousand irregular and semi-regular volunteers from the neighbouring Arab countries, under the supervision of the Arab League's Military Committee. Regardless of their declared purpose of 'rescuing' Palestine, the entrance of these forces into the Arab-dominated areas and mixed cities was much to the chagrin of the Palestinian leadership headed by al-Haj Amin al-Husseini, who perceived them as competitors representing foreign interests of the Arab rulers. Nonetheless, the Arab states' declared commitment to help the Palestinian Arabs in their effort to prevent the establishment of a Jewish state and the expectation of an intervention by the regular Arab armies in the war had a major psychological impact on the disputant communities whose perceptions had been shaped by a half-century-long conflict.

The perception of the conflict within the organized Jewish community under the Mandate (*yishuv*) was shaped by repeated violent eruptions against Jews in the early 1920s, the massacres of Jews in the 1929 riots, the Arab rebellion of 1936–39, and a perception of the British administration as a supporter of the Arabs. Hence, the UN Resolution on partition was received with mixed feelings – as a realization of the Jewish people's long dream for statehood yet as a sure recipe for an all-out war with the Arab world, hoping that the British would not abandon the Jews to their fate "alone and defenseless in a sea of Arabs".[2] The ensuing war for statehood was generally understood as the only guarantee of physical and political survival.

As for the Arab community, however, the intended partition of their country confirmed their worst fears of the Zionist project and was utterly unacceptable as an abhorrent injustice. Moreover, the very premise that about 400,000 Arabs would have to live within a Jewish sovereign state seemed politically and religiously inconceivable, a perception that had been strongly encouraged by the neighbouring Arab societies.[3] Practically, however, large segments of both the urban and rural Arab population were well aware of their collective weakness and refrained from active involvement in the conflict. Yet, the complex nature of the conflict and the course of events were beyond the capacity of this society, which soon found itself swept into the abyss.

## A Historical Overview

By the end of 1947, the total population in Mandatory Palestine was 1,970,000, two-thirds of which was Arab. Despite this numerical advantage, in the ensuing inter-communal war the Arabs of Palestine demonstrated an inherent disorder, fragmentation and poor capability of national mobilization, all of which accounted for their collapse and disintegration. Of the 826,000 Arabs who lived in the territory that became the State of Israel only 146,000 were included in the first Israeli census in late 1949 while the rest, around 670,000, became refugees in the Arab-dominated parts of Palestine, namely the Gaza Strip and the West Bank, or in the neighbouring Arab countries.[4]

The demographic results of the war underlined the disaster that befell the Palestinian-Arab society. Apart from the immense territorial and material losses, and the destruction of the social, economic and political structures of about half of its members, Palestinian society also sustained a serious blow to its fragile identity as a distinct political community, the disintegration of its national leadership and the disappearance of its political centre. Conversely, despite the immense death toll suffered by the Jewish community – six thousand, or one per cent of its population, mostly civilians – the Jews prevailed and managed to win international recognition for their newly established state, repel the invading regular

Arab armies and significantly expand the territory allotted to it by the UN partition plan. Thus, for Arabs the war became remembered as the '*Nakba*' (disaster), while Israelis coined it the 'War of Independence'.

The results of the 1948 Palestine war highlighted the huge gap between the Arab and Jewish communities in Palestine in terms of their respective social, economic and political organization and the effectiveness of their political institutions. Unlike the steady development of the '*yishuv*' as a 'state in the making', whose social, political and military institutions won the legitimacy and compliance of the vast majority of the *yishuv*,[5] the Arab community was led by notables and marked by deep social and geographical fragmentation and a lack of an effective political centre. These notables and the new urban middle class were largely oblivious of the existential difficulties of the peasants and workers who constituted the vast majority of the population and who were rapidly undergoing processes of dispossession, proletarianization and disintegration. The notions of identity of this population were rooted in locality, kinship and religion rather than in abstract nationalism.[6] This type of identity could hardly help the leadership's efforts towards national mobilization, and would determine the atomistic behaviour of this population during the war strictly on the basis of family and clan.[7]

Moreover, the Arab struggle against the Mandate and the Jewish community, especially the 1936–39 rebellion, which turned largely against itself, further aggravated the existing fragmentation and disintegration of the national elite, resulting in the social and economic exhaustion of the rural population and deepened enmities and mistrust among rival groups. Adversely, since the mid-1930s, and especially during World War II, the *yishuv* underwent unprecedented demographic, economic and military growth. This was largely due to the Zionist movement's successful diplomacy and ability to identify and seize opportunities for the continuous growth of the Zionist enterprise.

Arab–Jewish relations on the eve of the 1948 war were marked by almost total political, economic and social separation between the two communities, with no significant partnerships of private firms or individuals. Nonetheless, Arabs were employed in Jewish agriculture, construction and services, and much of their agricultural produce was marketed to Jews.[8]

The Arab–Jewish cleavage was also discernible in their total geographic separation in the rural areas, and almost entirely separate neighbourhoods in the mixed cities (Jerusalem, Haifa, Safad, Tiberias), resulting mainly from the 1929 Arab riots against their Jewish neighbours.[9] With the exception of Jerusalem and some isolated settlement pockets around the city, the Arab–Jewish geography left much of the eastern part of the country, namely the mountainous area stretching from Jinin to Bir al-Sabi' and the Negev, completely Arab. Conversely, the area allotted to the Jewish state constituted a mosaic of mixed Arab–Jewish cities, Jewish towns and blocks of settlements, and Arab villages. This geography meant that communication lines between Jewish towns and settlements could be controlled by nearby Arab villages and that many Jewish settlements faced the threat of being cut off from the main Jewish areas on the coastal plain. The necessity of securing logistical and military links with these isolated Jewish communities required a tremendously complex military and civilian coordinated effort, but mainly effective institutions and compliance on the part of the Jewish civilians.

The inter-communal war witnessed two main phases distinguished by their relative scope and intensity of violence. The first phase, from early December 1947 to mid-March 1948, was marked by limited and sporadic fighting, mainly along the dividing lines between the two populations in the mixed cities of Jerusalem, Haifa and Tel Aviv-Jaffa. The limited nature of the war derived from the parties' insufficient preparations for war, lack of weapons and organized forces. In addition, during this period the British army was still present in most parts of the country and continued to fulfil much of its active duties which prevented an all-out Arab–Jewish confrontation. Despite its limited scope, the first three months of the civil war witnessed an increasing exodus of Arabs from the country, mainly from the mixed cities. At the same time, Jews left their neighbourhoods along the border lines with the Arab neighbourhoods in their quest for security.

The last two months of the inter-communal war constituted the second phase, which saw a discernible escalation of the fighting across the country due to the entrance into the country of new Arab commanders and volunteers both in the south and east. The Arab-Palestinian irregulars initiated attacks on Jewish supply routes and levelled heavy blows against *Hagana* (the *yishuv*'s secret armed force) convoys, especially to Jerusalem and the Etzion Block. In early April 1948 the *Hagana* began its offensive known as 'Plan D' (a military plan originally aimed at occupying all Jewish-inhabited areas and roads accessing them), first along the road to

Jerusalem and later in other parts of the country. The *Hagana* offensive led to the collapse of the Arab-Palestinian military force in the Jerusalem area and the defeat of the 'Army of Salvation' (*jaysh al-inqadh*) following its failed attempt to capture Mishmar Ha-'Emek. The 'Plan D' offensive resulted in a mass exodus and displacement of the Arabs from the mixed cities and villages.

## The Jewish Community

### National Institutions and Preparations for the End of the Mandate

Although the *yishuv* lacked the status of a sovereign government, during the Mandate it developed into a voluntary framework of a political community with limited governing responsibilities. The voluntary nature of the *yishuv* and the accumulated experience of its institutions, both abroad (the World Zionist Organization) and in Palestine, were crucial for an effective process of human and material mobilization. Moreover, unlike the Arab case, the *yishuv's* representative institutions enjoyed legal status and formal recognition from the Mandate government which enabled them to develop their activities through continuous cooperation with the government. In addition to the national institutions, the *yishuv* developed numerous political, social and economic sub-centres which provided services to specific organized sectors; most conspicuously, the *Histadrut*, the General Federation of the Jewish Workers in Palestine, established in 1920 by the labour movements. By the mid-1930s the *Histadrut* came to fulfil semi-governmental functions in the *yishuv* and, with the rise of the Labour movement to leadership in the Zionist community, into a key base of the Jewish 'state in the making'.[10]

As of the late 1920s the Jewish Agency, which had been accorded recognition in the Mandate Charter as the representative of the Jewish people, functioned as the *yishuv's* political centre, especially after its expansion in 1929 to include powerful non-Zionist organizations, mainly of American Jewry. The demographic and economic growth of the *yishuv* in the early 1930s, coupled with the 1936–39 Arab revolt, led to a dramatic rise in the national centre's resources and legitimacy and strong communal solidarity and identification with the national institutions. A significant development in this context was the reorganization of the *Hagana* and its transformation into a national organization subordinate to the national centre, according it greater financial resources and enabling it to rapidly grow in manpower.[11] By the mid-1930s the centre of gravity of Zionist decision-making had moved from Europe into Palestine, expediting the consolidation of the *yishuv* as an institutionalized political community with a strong political centre.[12]

As of April 1947, anticipation of the partition of Palestine put the Jewish national institutions on a path of preparation for the inevitable war and seizure of the Mandatory government's functions in the areas allotted to the Jewish state. Meanwhile, military preparations, especially the transformation of the *Hagana* into a regular army, were supervised personally by David Ben-Gurion, Chairman of the Jewish Agency.[13] The Agency's main concern was to secure the uninterrupted functioning of basic civil services such as land and maritime transportation and communication, finance, fuel, and food supplies. Aware of the modern nature of the Jewish economy, Ben-Gurion stated that an economic collapse meant a political collapse.[14] It was only in October 1947, however, that a national 'Situation Committee' was established and began active planning, appointing professional committees for each governmental function and allocating resources for this mission.

The preparations necessitated various measures of centralization of food stores and systems of supplies, including rationing, to overcome scarcity and ensure sufficient quantities for emergency situations. One of the first measures adopted by the 'Situation Committee' was a ban on sales of food to Arabs, close control of flour mills and bakeries as well as of the purchase of beef.[15]

## Jewish Civilians in the War

The eruption of hostilities in early December 1947 encouraged increasing numbers of Jewish residents in the mixed cities to leave their homes near the Arab neighbourhoods in search of a safe haven. In early March the number of Jewish refugees who evacuated their homes bordering with Jaffa reached 12,000 and by the end of April the total number of refugees in the larger Tel Aviv area had grown to 20,000. Similar phenomena were discerned in Haifa and Jerusalem, with about 6,000 refugees in Haifa prior to the conquest of the city in late April. In Jerusalem, until April about 8,000 people left their homes in dangerous neighbourhoods and moved into the homogeneous Jewish parts of town. The difficult situation in Jerusalem led to the exodus of some additional 5,000 Jews – half of whom were officials of the national institutions and the Mandate government and their families – from Jerusalem to Tel Aviv, which then became the location of the Jewish central authority.[16] In Tiberias, by early April almost all the Jewish residents had left their homes in the old city, where they had constituted a small minority, and moved to the new Jewish neighbourhoods. This process forced the *Hagana* to take over and establish itself in this part of town and isolate its Arab residents from the rest of the city.[17]

The spread of Jewish settlements from the northern Negev in the south to the upper Galilee in the north, many of which were accessible only by passing through Arab-dominated areas, posed a major security dilemma to Jewish decision-makers. From a purely strategic military viewpoint, there was little logic in maintaining such a dispersed network of settlements – investing in their fortification and reinforcing them with combat forces – especially in view of the *yishuv*'s limited capabilities. The traditional Zionist approach, however, conceived these frontier settlements as strategic assets which not only marked the boundaries of the Jewish space but were also necessary outposts for the defence of the inner core of the Jewish population. Hence, the policy adopted by the Zionist leadership maintained that settlements on the outskirts of the Jewish state (northern Negev) or out of the partition boundaries (Etzion Block and Western Galilee) must be reinforced and fortified.[18] Once hostilities escalated, however, the *yishuv*'s leadership had to respond practically to the critical situation that befell these settlements. This dilemma became a crucial test of authority and accountability for the Zionist leadership on the one hand, and of the level of legitimacy and acceptance of its authority by the Jewish community, on the other. Indeed, it is in this context that the gap between the Jewish and Arab leaderships' political effectiveness and responsiveness to their constituencies was of primary significance in shaping the collective behaviours of each of the warring communities.

The Jewish decision-makers were placed on the horns of the dilemma shortly after the eruption of hostilities in December 1947. Suggestions for abandoning settlements located south of the Gaza–Bir al-Sabi' road so as to better prepare for a possible Egyptian invasion were rejected by Ben-Gurion, who adhered to the Zionist traditional line and ordered the strengthening of these settlements and their transformation into military outposts. At the same time, he left open the option of evacuating the non-combatant population under conditions of existential danger, which was soon to be implemented, first in the case of Etzion Block in mid-January 1948, and a month later in other isolated places such as Ben-Shemen, near Lydda, and Atarot, north of Jerusalem. A similar policy was orderly implemented in dozens of Jewish settlements, especially those located along the anticipated routes of the invading Arab armies north of the Dead Sea and the Galilee toward the end of the Mandate.[19]

Yet not all Jewish communities were willing to stay put and endanger their lives, especially in localities out of the Jewish state's boundaries defined by the UN Partition Plan. Especially among private, non-organized Jewish communities (such as the farmers' colonies or the pre-Zionist 'old *yishuv*'), whose links and subordination to the political center and the *Hagana* were minimal or non-existent – hence, their feeling less secure – the decision whether to stay or move to a safer place was made independently. Thus, residents of Neve Ya'acov north of Jerusalem began leaving their homes as early as December 1947. Similarly, about 300 out of a total population of 1,900 residents of Nahariya in the western Galilee (which was to be included in the Arab State) left the town. The national institutions attempted to resolve the hardships of the Jewish 'internal' refugees by establishing temporary camps and, as the exodus of Arabs from their homes in cities and villages continued, by inhabiting the abandoned Arab property with Jewish refugees, which the latter often undertook anyway in an effort to return to normal life.

The case of the Jewish community of Safad demonstrates the crucial role played by the *Hagana* as a symbol of the central Zionist authority amidst extremely desperate conditions endured by the civilian population. The Jewish community in Safad – about 2,000 people out of a total population of 13,500 – was, by and large, comprised of traditional, 'old *yishuv*' residents whose approach to the nucleus organization of the *Hagana* in town was marked by mistrust and condescendence. As of mid-December 1947, the Jewish community became increasingly disconnected from the Arab part of town and from the nearby Jewish settlements. Amidst growing Arab military pressure, these settlements lent the *Hagana* command and manpower in town an increasing significance in the decision-making of the local 'situation committee' over the community's general conduct and the practical organization of daily life and civil defence of the Jewish quarter.[20]

The dependence on the *Hagana* became all the more fateful when the British force in Safad withdrew from the city on April 16 at short notice and almost a month in advance of the original date set for this exit. The news about the imminent withdrawal of the British force, coupled with the accumulated hunger, physical fatigue and sense of despair at what seemed the abandonment of the community by the national institutions, led most members of the 'situation committee' to support the British proposal to evict the Jewish women, children and elderly before their departure, as they had done with the Arab populations of Haifa and Jaffa. A major argument justifying acceptance of the British suggestion was the precedent of such evacuation from Etzion Block and other kibbutz communities. Some of the 'situation committee' members warned that evacuating the women and children would constitute a serious blow to the morale of the quarter's defenders and would lead to the fall of Jewish Safad because the defenders would no longer be motivated to fight in defence of their families. Yet it seems that despite the temptation to accept the proposed British evacuation, all understood that no decision on this matter could be made without the approval of the *Hagana* headquarters. Indeed, the latter's instructions – given by the *Hagana* district command – unequivocally forbade acceptance of the British proposal. Though the decision was uneasily accepted, there was no attempt by the local leadership to challenge it. The ethical responsibility towards the wellbeing of the Safad community, however, came in the form of the arrival that same night of a *Palmach* unit (elite unit of *Hagana*) to the Jewish quarter, which saved the Jews of Safad and helped sustain them until the capture of the city as a whole was completed on May 10.

The daily life of civilian Jews during the inter-communal war differed from one place to another according to social cohesion, economic strength and proximity to the front lines. The administration of civil life was in the hands of 'situation committees' which had been established in the Jewish towns as well as in the mixed cities and consisted of both civilian and *Hagana* representatives. These committees functioned as local governments and handled all civil affairs, in conjunction with security needs, in an attempt to enable as normal a flow of life as possible. They fought various manifestations of lawlessness, such as crime (which at times assumed Arab–Jewish collaboration), the 'black market' economy (including attempts by certain traders to exploit the scarcity of goods by raising prices), and tax evasion.[21]

Undoubtedly, the situation of Jewish Jerusalem was the most difficult, because it was the most isolated of all the large Jewish towns in

Palestine. In February and March 1948 the city's Jewish population sustained a series of three heavy bombings in public places and buildings which were "clearly designed to shock the Jewish population and break its morale".[22] These bombings took place while the British army and police were widely present in the city, though according to some Jewish accounts they had been perpetrated by British police and military personnel in collaboration with the Arabs.[23] While the impact of these bombings on the spirits of Jerusalem's Jewish population was limited, as of March 1948 there was a very real threat to the sustainability of the Jewish city as a result of the increasingly acute shortage of food and water.

According to the UN partition plan, the city was to constitute a 'Corpus Separatum' under international supervision. Surrounded by a large Arab population on all sides, as of mid-March 1948, its link to the coastal plain became subject to frequent attacks by villagers along that road, resulting in a growing food and water shortage parallel to the escalating hostilities in the city itself. With nearly 100,000 Jews living in the city – about one sixth of the total Jewish population in Palestine – maintaining a constant line of supply to the besieged city became a top priority for the national institutions. This entailed, however, an immense effort to mobilize (or confiscate) hundreds of drivers and trucks, the concentration and control of food stores, and other necessary means to equip repeated convoys with military escorts all the way to the city, many of which were attacked and never reached their destination.[24] The anguish of Jewish Jerusalem necessitated the appointment by the Jewish Agency of an emergency committee headed by Dov Joseph as a civil governor of the city. The committee supervised the rationing of food and water – a bucket of water per person every two or three days. "Bread, vegetables, sugar, milk, eggs, and other foodstuffs were strictly rationed and were distributed to families under a system of food coupons . . . Drugs and medical supplies had almost run out." The daily shelling and insecurity of going out to the street to receive one's ration during the months of the siege created a deep sense of continuous horror and weariness amid the constant death of innocent people.[25]

Administering daily life was easier in the purely Jewish town of Rehovot, the core population of which was comprised of affluent farmers. These farmers employed many Arabs from the neighbouring villages and were highly driven by private economic interests, especially the harvest of the citrus, traditionally implemented by Arab workers. Hence, Arab work in the town's orchards and farms continued until late March, despite occasional armed clashes and casualties. During this period, tensions surfaced in the relations between the civil and military figures in town over policies and priorities. While the former were interested in continuous stability and the employment of Arab workers, the military saw these Arabs as a menace and did their utmost to drive them out of the town and region. As time went on, and as the sporadic hostilities developed into a full-scale war, the military's voice prevailed and dictated the policy toward the Arab neighbours. During these months the mobilization of civilians for collective purposes such as building fortifications and civil defence transformed from being on a voluntary basis to being legally supported acts, including the use of disciplinary measures to impose authority.[26]

## The Arab Community
### National Institutions and Preparations for War
The state of weakness and disarray of the Palestinian-Arab community surfaced toward the end of World War II, with the renewal of the political, economic and military Arab–Zionist struggle for Palestine. In the absence of the primary Arab leaders from the country, especially al-Haj Amin al-Husseini and his close aide Jamal al-Husseini, the present Arab elite failed to forge a broadly agreed-upon national leadership due to personal and factional struggles over the control of financial and political resources. Despite the rise of new social and political forces, represented by the new leftist intelligentsia and the growing sector of loosely organized workers, urging political reforms and participation in the national institutions, the traditional leadership of notables prevailed, largely thanks to the intervention of the Arab League in shaping the Arab-Palestinian leadership.[27]

In June 1946, the Political Committee of the Arab League decided to appoint the Mufti al-Haj Amin al-Husseini – who had just returned to the Middle East from exile in Europe – as the head of the resumed Arab Higher Committee (AHC). In view of the Palestinian Arabs' weakness and driven by competing particular interests, however, the League subordinated the Palestinian national institution to its authority, thereby reducing it to one of its apparatuses. Henceforth, the Palestinian-Arab leadership became dependent on the League for financial and military support from the Arab governments. The appropriation of the Palestinian-Arab cause by the League was a culmination of over two decades of growing interest from the neighbouring Arab societies and states in the Palestine question which, in the wake of World War II, became the top issue on the collective Arab agenda.

Though the Palestinian leaders still enjoyed freedom of action within their own community, in effect they faced serious obstacles. The British ban on the return of al-Haj Amin and some of his senior lieutenants to Palestine clearly complicated the task of national organization of the Palestinian community and preparation for the anticipated showdown with the *yishuv*. Worse still, the deep factional cleavages between the Husseinis and their opponents and fresh memories of their bloody internal strife in 1936–39, especially the fear of the Mufti's terrorist methods, rendered the AHC's attempt at institution-building almost impossible. Nonetheless, the return of the Mufti to the Middle East sent waves of excitement – but also fear among his rivals – and a sense of urgency among the Arab public calling for preparation for the ensuing Arab–Jewish showdown. This was indicated, among other things, by the rising demand for arms among Palestinian Arabs and the development of a black market in personal arms smuggled from the neighbouring Arab countries, which were sold for staggering prices.[28]

Indeed, the 1946–47 period witnessed an intensive effort on the part of the AHC to develop national organizations. This endeavour was marked by an uncompromising urge, including the use of personal terror against political rivals, for exclusive and centralized control of all public sectors – economic, military and political – especially those controlled by non-Husseini figures or groups. The following examples illustrate not only the failure of these late efforts but also the irreparable damage they caused to the prospect of an organized collective Palestinian action, both of which were to affect the conduct of Palestinian civilians in the war.

In early 1946, following the League decision to employ a total boycott of the Jewish economy in the Arab states and Palestine, the AHC established a central boycott committee to oversee its implementation through local committees in every town and large village. Soon, however, the efforts to enforce the boycott, often undertaken by local youth associations, turned into an instrument of threat and extortion and at times also assumed violence against traders maintaining commercial ties with Jews. Yet despite the bullying methods used to impose the boycott, in practice it survived only for short periods of time.

Another example was the effort to take over the only semi-military Arab organization, *al-Najada*. The organization was established by a non-partisan lawyer from Jaffa, Muhammad Nimr al-Hawwari, in 1945 and within a short time established a countrywide presence with 5,000 to 6,000 registered members. As of the summer of 1946 the AHC waged an open campaign aimed at gaining control of *al-Najada* by establishing its own paramilitary organization (*al-Futuwwa*) and employing threats and violence against the former. In June 1947 an agreement was reached to merge the two organizations into a new one entitled the Arab Youth Organization, which was meant to be a framework for the Palestinian-Arab army. As a commander of the new organization the Mufti appointed a former Egyptian officer whose links to the Muslim Brotherhood and Nazi Germany led the Mandatory government to deport him from Palestine after a short while. The end results were the loss of the opportunity to establish a nucleus of an Arab militia and demoralization in the ranks of existing paramilitary groups, which was well indicated by the poor response towards volunteering in the irregular combat groups established in Syria as of October 1947.[29]

A major trait of the Palestinian national movement throughout the Mandate was its weak or non-existent capabilities of financial mobilization. In May 1946 the AHC decided to establish the Arab Treasure House (*Bayt al-Mal al-ʿArabi*), whose main task was to collect indirect taxes and charges as well as contributions from the Palestinian-Arab community and also to administer funds raised in the Arab world. Yet the implementation of this decision stretched over a whole year mainly due to difficulties in naming the notables to the new institution's councils and executives. During the first year of operation (April 1947–March 1948) the Treasure House assigned 50 per cent of its revenues towards 'redeeming' Arab lands about to be sold to the Jews and only 11.4 per cent toward national organization, which apparently included military preparations.[30] Practically, although the institution managed to collect around 168,000 PL, one-third of which was raised on November 29, 1947 in the city of Jaffa alone, the Palestinian public as a whole remained reluctant to contribute to the new treasury, which was closely identified with the Mufti's faction. In any case, the eruption of violence in late November

1947 seriously impeded the fundraising efforts and soon brought them to a halt. The poor financial condition of the AHC and the factional characteristics of the use of the limited resources that it received from the Arab League were clearly indicated by the marginal role it played during the war.

### Arab Civilians in the War

The conduct of the Palestinian-Arab population during the war was largely shaped by the perception of being an indivisible part of the larger Arab-Muslim world. This perception had been nurtured by the Palestinian-Arab national leaders since the end of World War II and increasingly by Arab nationalist and Islamic movements in the Fertile Crescent and Egypt, leading to the regionalization of the Palestine cause. This was demonstrated in growing manifestations of popular solidarity in the neighbouring Arab countries and strong public and official rhetoric in support of the Palestinian Arabs' struggle against Zionism and the Mandate. Indeed, since the early 1920s the Palestinian-Arab elite systematically endeavoured to mobilize regional Arab and Muslim support for its cause and practically demonstrated the perception that the emerging Arab states were obliged to mobilize their resources in support of their Palestinian brethren. The traditional social and economic links between Palestinian elite families and their counterparts in the neighbouring Arab countries assumed a growing public and official political dimension of support as of the Arab rebellion of 1936–39 and the welcoming of thousands of Palestinian Arabs, mostly of the urban elite families, who sought a temporary refuge from Mandatory persecution or clashes with rival Arabs. This precedent further reinforced the perception of a culturally and socially familiar haven at a short distance, all of which made the option of a temporary departure to the neighbouring countries both appealing and practicable, especially to those who could afford it financially.

It is difficult to evaluate the impact of this perception on the collective behaviour of the Palestinian-Arab population during the 1948 war. It is more than likely, however, that the long absence of the national leadership from Palestine, the public commitment of the Arab states for the Palestine cause and its supervision by the Arab League, all combined to create a state of psychological dependency on the neighbouring Arab countries as a supportive hinterland. Thus, in May 1946 the Palestinian leadership issued rumours about the evacuation of women, children and elderly to the neighbouring countries ostensibly in preparation for a military rebellion against the recommendations of the Anglo-American Committee of Inquiry and their implementation.[31] Similarly, the League's Political Committee at its meeting in Sofar in September 1947 called on its members to open their gates to any children, women and elderly of the Palestinian Arabs who might seek haven in the event of an armed conflagration.[32] Though such a call meant that men were expected to remain and fight, and in fact many Arabs, especially in the rural areas, preferred to send their women and children to a safe haven – often a nearby village or even to the olive orchards outside the village itself – as a means of protection, it often turned into a demoralizing factor which weakened the men's sustainability.[33]

The gap between the Jewish and Arab communities in terms of effective institutional action and political institutionalization was strongly exposed when beginning in December 1947 the Mandatory government started withdrawing from homogeneous Arab and Jewish areas and handing over the responsibility of administration and security to their respective communities. In the absence of an effective central authority and with a lack of self-governing experience the Arab community was hardly capable of replacing the government's authority and facilities, enforcing law and order, supplying food, fuel, electricity and clean water and providing basic services such as health, education and public transportation. The growing disruption of daily life was particularly salient in the mixed cities where the escalating clashes, ambushes, sniping and other sorts of indiscriminate attacks on civilians had increasingly prevented Arab farmers from marketing their fresh produce in town, especially to the Jewish population. The disturbed routine and food shortages, and failure of the AHC and its representatives to regulate the distribution of funds and food products led to the development of a 'black market' and aroused much criticism of, and resentment towards, the Palestinian-Arab leaders, especially due to their absence from the country.

The literature on the inter-communal war emphasizes the impact of Arab attacks on Jewish transportation, especially to isolated areas, some of which resulted in heavy Jewish losses, especially in the last week of March 1948. Yet at the same time Jewish attacks on Arab vehicles on major routes such as Jaffa–Gaza, Jaffa–Jerusalem, Haifa–Acre, Haifa–Nazareth, Lydda–Jerusalem and Bethlehem–Jerusalem, forced Arabs to minimize their use of vehicles on those roads, and increasingly use boats between Jaffa and Gaza and Haifa and Acre, or travel in armed convoys. The reduced scope of passengers on bus companies, also affected by the reduced labour market in the cities and rising gasoline prices, caused heavy losses to Arab bus companies and led to a reduced scope of Arab transportation.

One of the first results of the loosened British authority was a sharp rise in crime – violence, robbery and theft – within the Arab community itself, conducted by criminal gangs, many of them Bedouins who also committed criminal activities in the Jewish sector, presenting them as 'national'. While a similar phenomenon in the Jewish sector was stemmed by employing the *Hagana* as a law-enforcement mechanism, in the absence of a centralized authority and militia capable of implementing the leadership's instructions, the AHC's scarce financial resources and narrow factional approach, the result was increasing social disintegration and quests by individuals and families to ensure their own security. The sense of insecurity and disarray was all the more aggravated by the allocation of arms and funds in accordance with political loyalty to the Mufti, whose ardent supporters had been traditionally located in the Jerusalem area and its vicinity, between Bir Zeit, Zurif and 'Azariyya.[34]

It is hard to underestimate the responsibility of the notable elite in general and the AHC in particular for this state of affairs, which was aggravated by the distant residence of the Mufti and other salient figures of the Palestinian-Arab national leadership. Much has been written about the early departure of the elite families from the country as of December 1947, which turned increasingly into a broad and hasty exodus in the following months. The exodus of public figures and representatives in political institutions, as well as of owners of commercial and manufacturing businesses and services firms all contributed to the growing economic chaos, demoralization and sense of insecurity among Arab residents, especially in the mixed cities and villages within the areas allotted to the Jewish state.[35]

The Mufti's appeal to the Arab League's Political Committee in February 1948 to establish a provisional Palestinian-Arab government was indeed refused, due to strong opposition from Iraq and the then Transjordan, sworn enemies of the Husseini faction. Yet even if such a government had been established it would have made little difference in the course of events at this late point in the inter-communal war, which had witnessed the exodus of tens of thousands of the notable and the urban elite families. In addition, the Mufti's concerns that a competitive political power might rise in his absence, his deep suspicion toward his close aides and partners and extreme centralization of power and resources, all but created an authoritative and institutional void thus reinforcing the existing tendencies among Arab civilians to focus on their narrow local and family interests in response to the uncertainties and existential threats caused by hostilities.[36] Cooperation among neighbouring villages was the exception and so was the phenomenon of reinforcements from relatively safe areas to the battlefield, which was conspicuous among the 'Holy Struggle' combatants in the Jerusalem area and the role played by the militia of Lydda in the rural periphery.[37]

A succinct description of this situation was provided by the Egyptian Consul General in Jerusalem in those days:

> In July 1947 only three AHC members stayed in Palestine and after a short period of time only two remained there . . . The two AHC members who remained in Jerusalem, Ahmad Hilmi 'Abd al-Baqi and Hussein Fakhri al-Khalidi were aged and bereft of authority. They lacked sufficient funds for necessary purposes and knew nothing about arms that the Mufti had sent to combatants. They had to refer to the Mufti in Cairo in every small matter . . . [T]he few arms that were purchased and delivered to dubious elements was the very little positive thing done by the AHC.[38]

The repercussions of this institutional void and political fragmentation were not limited to the local sphere. Even after hostilities became a countrywide phenomenon, some of the opposition leaders secretly endeavoured to persuade the Arab governments to refrain from providing the Mufti with funds and arms out of fear these might be directed against them. These leaders, representing traditional anti-Mufti foci in Haifa, Nablus and Hebron, also refrained from mobilizing young Arab volunteers from their areas to the semi-regular forces that were to be trained and organized in Syria under the League's supervision as part of the 'Army of Salvation'. The abyss of hostility between the Mufti and his rivals was also apparent in the general reluctance of the urban well-to-do population to donate to the Arab Treasure House even after the eruption of hostilities. This reluctance turned all the more obstinate in response to the Husseinis' efforts at pressuring and intimidating potential donors of the bourgeoisie, most of whom were urban dwellers who had not been among the Mufti's supporters.[39] The poor collective mobilization of the Palestinian Arabs was represented by the strikingly minute scope of military recruitment to the war effort. At best, the scope of those Arabs taking part in mobile forces – apart from those tied up with the local defence of their own village, neighbourhood or town, or involved in the occasional rush (*faz'a*) to join an attack on, or looting of, a Jewish convoy – hardly exceeded 2,500 at any given time.[40]

### The 'National Committees' as a Case in Point

The inter-communal war reiterated the socio-political causes of fragmentation and poor institutionalization of the Palestinian-Arab community once the AHC embarked on a policy of establishing 'national committees' (*lijan qawmiyya*) in all cities and large towns to operate as its local representatives and take full responsibility for civil and military affairs with the latter's financial and military support. The national committees were in fact given emergency powers that superseded the local government – levying taxes, administering local security, allocating funds and arms and assigning military roles. The AHC's decision came in the wake of Britain's announcement on October 26, 1947 that in the absence of an agreement between the Arab and Jewish communities it would withdraw its forces and administration from Palestine, underlining a growing awareness of the imminent total Arab–Jewish confrontation.

The idea of establishing 'national committees' was reminiscent of the 1936 Arab rebellion when such committees were spontaneously established in many Arab towns and villages and functioned as popular self-imposed governing institutions. Yet the process of establishing national committees dragged on and on, despite having started shortly before the UN resolution on partition was made. By early December 1947 only three national committees had been established, a far cry from the 24 committees the AHC had initially instructed be established in the major cities and towns. Especially in the mixed cities (Haifa, Jerusalem, Tiberias, Safad) and Jaffa (which was to remain an enclave surrounded by the Jewish state), where such committees were absolutely necessary for the efficient conduct of the war effort, the process of establishing those committees faced difficulties as a result of social cleavages, both vertical (between the AHC and local notables) and horizontal (among competing figures, families and associations). Precisely because the national committees involved control of financial and administrative power, in addition to social prestige, their establishment entailed bitter competition and power struggles underlining existing family feuds, political factionalism and generational gaps. The disagreements accompanying this process often necessitated an active involvement of the AHC's offices in Jerusalem and Cairo which had to invest much energy in mediating these disputes among rival factions and individuals.

Thus, it was not until the end of January 1948 that Arab Jerusalem had a national committee while Tiberias remained without one till the beginning of March. A more successful case was the national committee of Lydda, a purely Arab town where the powerful and sustainable local leadership manifested autonomy and creativity in preparing the city's population for the ensuing war and conducting its military and civil affairs during the war.[41]

Setting up and operating the national committees was accompanied by a deep sense of frustration among the bourgeoning middle class, including young educated men, traders, leaders of social associations and youth clubs, at the socio-political immobility represented by the national committees. These new professional elites kept protesting and complaining to the AHC about misconduct in establishing the national committees, especially their practice of excluding representatives of important social sectors and the new political groups that emerged in the 1940s, the poor functioning of the existing committees, and calling for the appointment of an external military command. Indeed, military commanders were often appointed not due to their military skills but rather by their social status.[42]

A major weakness was the poor distribution of funds by national committees due to excessive financial commitments and expenditures, especially for salaries to clerks, guards, fortifications and the acquisition of arms, which were beyond the limits of their own resources. Appeals to the AHC to cover extra expenses, including from groups that were not to receive any funding, could hardly be met due to the limited funds available to the AHC itself, the absence of the Mufti and the weakness of the AHC in Jerusalem. Even when the AHC did intervene in matters concerning the national committees, its impact was often insignificant or temporary at best.

The national committees reflected the traditional pattern of power politics and competition for prestige along family and faction lines.

In many cases national committees abused their authority in order to accumulate private material benefits. Thus, despite the clear general policy adopted by the AHC regarding the duty of men to remain in place and fight, with the growing urge of Arab citizens to flee, some national committees imposed financial charges on those wishing to leave in the form of permits for them to do so. The Arab urban population was also affected by the state of competing allegiances among militia groups and local leaderships and fragmented military commands and civil authorities. This was mainly the result of the presence in most Arab cities, as of January 1948, of foreign Arab volunteers mostly subordinated to the Military Arab Committee in Damascus. In Jaffa, for example, a number of local militias competed with each other and operated without coordination, while the Mufti's appointed representative subverted the authority of consecutive military commanders appointed by Damascus. In Haifa and Jaffa, where relations between the Mufti's loyalists and the local leaderships had been deeply affected by past rivalries and mistrust, views as to the desirable level of involvement of Arab civilians in hostilities remained unresolved, which had a negative effect on the AHC's financial and military allocations to these cities. In Tiberias, the appointment of a national committee in March failed to resolve rivalries over military decision-making among local leaders, making it inefficient and short-lived.

Relations between the local civilian population and the Mufti's militias were quite different, especially in the villages and towns identified with the Husseini elite and hence favoured by the AHC as far as arms and funds were concerned. Yet even in the Arab neighbourhoods of Jerusalem, which were typically under control of the 'Holy Struggle' militia, in the wake of bombings of the police building (Saraya) in Jaffa by the Irgun Zva'i Le'umi (IZL – the main Jewish dissident organization) and of Smiramis Hotel in the Jerusalem Arab neighbourhood of Qatamon by the *Hagana*, Arab civilians of these cities, especially the social elite, took self-defensive measures such as closing the entrances and exits of the neighbourhood and hiring guards. These steps, however, soon became insufficient and the residents appealed to the AHC to protect them, only to hear about the serious shortage of arms and funds suffered by the AHC. Even when Arab militiamen of the Holy Struggle had been deployed in the prestigious neighbourhood of Qatamon in late March and further reinforced by an Iraqi unit, the latter's presence was insufficient to alleviate the Arab residents' fears and prevent their flight before the neighbourhood was captured by the *Hagana* in early May.[43]

In many other cases, however, tension and mistrust between the Mufti and certain village and town leaderships prevailed as a result of abused funds collected from the local population for arms procurement by the AHC which had never been fulfilled. In many cases this grievance resulted in the refusal of villages to allow the entrance of the Holy Struggle militiamen – and even more so of foreign volunteers – into their vicinity. These villagers were not necessarily confident of their own capability but primarily feared that any presence of outside combatants would expose them to Jewish reprisals. Indeed, it was this fear of Jewish reprisal that motivated the inhabitants of the Khalda village near Latroun to flee their village in the wake of an attack by the foreign volunteers on a Jewish convoy, though the villagers themselves had no role in the attack, before any Jewish retaliation took place.[44]

### The Impact of Foreign Arab Volunteers

The deployment of foreign volunteer units in the cities, especially the mixed ones, turned out to be disastrous for the Arab civilian population.[45] Undoubtedly, given the minute scope of self-mobilization of the Palestinian Arabs towards the war effort they did need help from other Arabs. However, the deep hostility between the Hashemite regimes in Iraq and Transjordan and the Mufti, and the mistrust and fear with which other Arab elites perceived the Palestinian leader led to the Arab rulers rejecting the Mufti's call for exclusive control of military activities in Palestine. Instead, they decided to divide Palestine into three main sectors, with only the central and most populated sector, stretching from Jerusalem to Jaffa, remaining under the command of his loyalists, known as the 'Holy Struggle' (*al-jihad al-muqaddas*).[46] The northern and southern sectors were assigned to the 'Army of Salvation', under Fawzi al-Qawaqji's command, and the Egyptian volunteers, mostly of the Muslim Brothers, respectively.

The split in military command further aggravated rivalries and competition among commanders of these forces/sectors, especially between those subordinated to the Mufti and Qawaqji. Local commanders of both parties endeavoured to foster close relations with the local population which had already been divided about the Mufti's leadership and role in the war. The presence of these irregular forces, especially in the rural areas allotted to the Jewish state, was sometimes beneficial to the Arab civilians as it elevated their morale and sense of security. However, the foreign volunteers not only became a heavy burden on the villagers' poor economy but, soon after their deployment, they effectively embarked on issuing military restrictions to the local population such as forbidding them to carry arms and arresting or executing individuals alleged to have been collaborating with the Jewish enemy. Despite instructions not to become an economic burden on the local population, the volunteers often issued arbitrary claims for the meeting of their needs in food and services, some committed theft and plundering of cars from local owners and at least one case of rape of a local girl was reported.[47]

Worse still, the growing bitterness of the local population at the conduct and inaction of the volunteers coupled with the competition between the Mufti's loyalists and the Army of Salvation's command pushed the latter to repeated attempts to elevate their prestige by initiating attacks on Jewish settlements, all of which ended in failure. In the case of Qawaqji's failed offensive on Mishmar Ha-'Emek in early April, the Jewish counter-attack resulted in the conquest of a number of nearby Arab villages and the exodus of thousands of their inhabitants from their homes.[48]

In the mixed cities of Haifa and Jaffa the command of the foreign volunteer forces turned out to be largely chaotic. Due to their unfamiliarity with the specific needs of the local Arab population, they often failed to cooperate with the local leaderships and collapsed or deserted the battleground under the first heavy pressure from the Jewish forces, leaving the civilians with little choice but to flee or surrender. In cases such as Jaffa, the growing exodus of civilians from the city was accompanied by mass looting and plundering by the foreign volunteers and their commanders, which expedited the morale crisis of the civilian population and their decision to flee to a safe haven.[49]

The chaotic conditions that dominated the Arab community, especially the absence of an effective and accountable authority, was reflected in the repeated appeals and travels of many mayors and leaders of national committees to the Arab capitals and the Arab League's headquarters in Damascus to raise financial and military aid 'above the head' of the Mufti and contrary to his instructions.[50] The failure to meet these pleas on the part of the Arab governments coupled with fear and mistrust of the national and local leaderships rendered individual citizens unresponsive to public calls by national committees to stay in place, undeterred by financial charges applied on those wishing to leave, or by threats from the Army of Salvation to blow up the houses of those fleeing their homes.[51]

*Local Arab–Jewish 'Good Neighbourliness' Agreements*
During the inter-communal war most of the rural Arab population remained passive and refrained from taking an active part in hostilities. The Arab villagers, about two-thirds of the Arab population, had apparently internalized the lesson of the devastating 1936–39 Arab rebellion and its repression by the British Mandate just as they enjoyed the wartime economic prosperity, which was now terminating along with the end of the Mandate. In addition, after two consecutive years of drought, the winter of 1948 was blessed with precipitation raising expectations for a good harvest, which further minimized the villagers' willingness to jeopardize a good harvest anticipated in the summer by taking up arms against their Jewish neighbours. Nonetheless, with the intensifying hostilities Arab and Jewish crops became increasingly a target in the inter-communal war. Fears of arson and sabotage of the harvest by the other side forced both Arab and Jewish rural communities to secure their crops through ad-hoc accords or by attacking the other's ripening crops as a deterrent or retaliatory measure. So vital and irreplaceable were the crops for Arab farmers that they repeatedly tried to return and harvest their fields even after they had been captured by Jewish forces.[52]

In many cases rural Arab communities prevented and at times chased out combatants of the Holy Struggle in the Jerusalem area, or foreign volunteers of the Army of Salvation in other parts of the country. Moreover, in many cases village and urban neighbourhood leaders sought to ensure ad-hoc peaceful relations with their Jewish neighbours to secure their work at the latter's orchards and avoid a disaster to their own economy. Though these agreements, mostly informal, were short-lived and collapsed as soon as the *Hagana* embarked on its 'Plan D' offensive in early April 1948, it clearly indicates the broad interest, especially of the Arab rural sector in the areas allotted to the Jewish state and beyond, in avoiding taking an active role in the war and contenting themselves with a defensive position on the narrow local basis of one's immediate village or neighbourhood.

Local efforts at striking ad-hoc deals between neighbouring Arab and Jewish communities drew on historical records of good neighbourly relations and were generally motivated by a mutual quest for security and a smooth seasonal harvest. A major mutual interest in preserving peaceful Arab–Jewish relations was the need to secure an uninterrupted harvest of the citrus fruits during the first three months of 1948, based primarily on Arab manual work, especially in the central coastal plain. Good neighbourliness agreements were, by and large, the result of approaches by local Arab leaders to their Jewish neighbours, representing the former's awareness of their military inferiority, economic anxiety and mistrust of their national leadership. In some cases, local Arab leaders threatened the AHC that they would seek protection from their Jewish neighbours unless their requests in arms and funds had been met.

On the Jewish part, local peace agreements between Arab and Jewish communities were often initiated or mediated by the Arab Department of the leftist labour movement of *Ha-Shomer Ha-Tza'ir*, which employed its connections with village leaders and communists who supported the UN Partition resolution and represented organized Arab workers. The efforts to attain 'peace' agreements between local Arab and Jewish localities were backed by the *Hagana*'s national command till late March 1948 as part of the Jewish Agency's attempt to reduce the scope of the inter-communal war and its negative impact on the international community's support for the implementation of the UN Partition resolution.

Yet despite dozens of agreements reached between local Arab and Jewish communities they proved to be inherently fragile. Apart from the temporary motivation underpinning many of those agreements, as the Mandate approached its end they came under political and military pressures, on both local and national levels, which they could not withstand. The rapidly changing political and military conditions surrounding the inter-communal war, particularly the growing intervention of foreign Arab forces and interests – even before the invasion of Palestine by Arab regular armies – and the determination of the Jewish political and military leadership to secure control of the areas allotted to the Jewish state, all worked against those local agreements, turning them increasingly anachronistic.

A case in point was the village of Deir Yassin on the western outskirts of Jerusalem, which became the scene of the most notorious massacre of innocent Arab civilians in the whole 1948 war. The horrendous atrocity, in which almost one hundred of the village inhabitants were killed and partly mutilated, including women and children, became the most significant event in the war in terms of its repercussions on Arab civilians. Moreover, due to the deliberate publicity of the massacre by the Palestinian-Arab leadership,[53] it became a major trigger of panic and demoralization amongst the Palestinian Arabs, resulting in the mass flight of Arab civilians from their homes, not only in the Jerusalem area but in the country as a whole. Tragically, Deir Yassin was a peaceful village which had reached an accord of good neighbourliness with the Jewish residents of the neighbouring Jewish village of Giv'at Sha'ul. Moreover, the peaceful conduct of Deir Yassin was recognized by the Jewish military commander of Jerusalem, David She'alti'el, who also approved of the attack on the village by the nationalist splinter groups of Irgun and Lehi.[54]

Thus, as the Arab community collapsed and a military intervention by the Arab states seemed realistic, Arab civilians opted for exodus from their homes even when their Jewish neighbours – with or without an agreement of good neighbourhood – appealed for them to stay. The urge to leave could have been the result of panic, despair at their own leadership, a rejection of the very idea of living under a Jewish government, instructions from an outside national or inter-Arab authority, or fear lest their exceptional stay might be considered an act of treason. The most conspicuous case in this respect was the mass exodus of the Arabs of Haifa following its conquest by the *Hagana* forces on April 22, 1948, despite the appeals of the local Jewish leadership and the *Hagana* command to the Arab leadership not to leave and promises to secure their equal rights under Jewish sovereignty.[55]

Indeed, the fragility of the local agreements was a reflection of the multiplicity of armed factions, weak central authority, and local and external provocateurs determined to prevent any peaceful implementation of the UN Partition resolution. On the Arab side, supporters of the Mufti, local rivals of villages' leaders and most of all, foreign volunteers of the 'Army of Salvation', often managed to drag villages and towns into the fray against their best wishes. On the Jewish side, despite the relatively centralized authority of the *Hagana* and its interest in reducing violence and stemming the tide of Palestinian refugees, this policy was not always applied. Though the splinter groups of Irgun and Lehi undertook the lion's share of attacks on Arab civilian transportation and urban targets, local *Hagana* commanders were also responsible for similar attacks, all of which contributed to the escalation of hostilities and panic among the Arab civilian population.[56]

## Conclusion

The results of the inter-communal war in Palestine reflected the huge gap between the two communities' social and political development. In particular, the efforts of both national leaderships in preparing and mobilizing their communities underlined the huge advantage exercised by the Jewish national institutions whose effectiveness – the result of long experience before the war – and ability to secure a broad complicity and responsiveness from its constituency was in direct contrast to the Palestinian-Arab factionalism and poor national institutions. Although the weakness and disarray within the Palestinian-Arab community on the eve of the war was also a result of years of exhausting struggle against Britain and the *yishuv*, the extreme fragility it demonstrated during the war highlighted primarily the anachronistic and chaotic national leadership of the Husseinis and the self-interested involvement of inter-Arab actors, whose main representatives during the period under discussion were the no less chaotic Arab volunteers of the Army of Salvation.

The tragedy that befell the Palestinian-Arab society in the war claimed its price mainly from innocent Arab civilians, urban and rural alike, who had little to do with the deteriorating conditions which led to a total inter-communal war. It was also the mass flight of Palestinian-Arab civilians, many of whom arrived as refugees in neighbouring Arab countries, which triggered the public empathy and solidarity that played a major role in the Arab League's decision on the collective Arab military invasion of Palestine, thus beginning the second part of the war, the Arab–Israeli war.

# NOTES

1 This part of the war is described elaborately in David Tal, *War in Palestine 1948: Strategy and Diplomacy* (London: Routledge, 2004), pp. 41–143.
2 Amos Oz, *A Tale of Love and Darkness* (Orlando: Harcourt, Inc., 2003), p. 343.
3 Said K. Aburish, *Children of Bethany, The Story of a Palestinian Family* (Bloomington and Indianapolis: Indiana University Press, 1988), pp. 92–93, p. 123; Michael Gorkin, *Days of Honey, Days of Onion: The Story of a Palestinian Family in Israel* (Boston: Beacon Press, 1991), p. 112.
4 Charles S. Kamen, 'After the Catastrophe 1: The Arabs in Israel, 1948–51', *Middle Eastern Studies*, Vol. 23 (1987), pp. 453–57; Gad Gilbar, *Trends in the Demographic Development of the Palestinians 1870–1987* (Tel Aviv: Tel Aviv University, Dayan Center, 1989), p. 3 (Hebrew).
5 Dan Horowitz and Moshe Lissak, *Origins of the Israeli Polity: Palestine under the Mandate* (Chicago: Chicago University Press, 1978).
6 Yehoshua Porath, *The Emergence of the Arab-Palestinian National Movement* (London: Frank Cass, 1974); Issa Khalaf, 'The Effect of Socioeconomic Change on Arab Societal Collapse in Mandate Palestine', *International Journal of Middle East Studies*, Vol. 29, No. 1 (February 1997), pp. 93–112.
7 'Arif al-'Arif, *The Disaster: The Disaster of Palestine and the Lost Paradise* (Sidon: 1956), p. 172 (Arabic).
8 On the 'dual' economy in Palestine, see J. Metzer and O. Kaplan, *Jewish Economy and Arab Economy in Palestine: Produce, Employment and Growth in the Mandate Period* (Jerusalem: 1990), pp. 155–59 (Hebrew). A limited degree of economic cooperation existed, especially in Haifa, see Ya'acov Salomon, *In My Own Way* (Haifa: The Gillie Salomon Foundation, 1982), p. 102.
9 On the impact of these riots, see Yehuda Slutzki et al. (eds.), *The Hagana History Book* (Tel Aviv: Ma'arakhot, 1972), Vol. 2, Part I, p. 195, pp. 313–40 (Hebrew); *Report of the Commission on the Palestine Disturbances of August 1929* (London, March 1930), Cmd. 3530, pp. 63–66.
10 Horowitz and Lissak, pp. 70–72.
11 Slutzki, ibid., pp. 416–434; Meir Pa'il, *Min ha"Hagana" le-Tzva Hagana* (Tel-Aviv, 1979), Ch. 1–3.
12 Horowitz and Lissak, pp. 64–66.
13 Tal, pp. 24–34.
14 Quoted by Yehonatan Fein, 'The Organization of the Jewish Rare toward the War of Independence', in Alon Kadish (ed.), *Israel's War of Independence 1948–1949* (Tel Aviv: Ministry of Defense, 2004), p. 682.
15 Ibid., pp. 686–87.
16 Arnon Golan, 'The Shaping of the Formerly Arab Space', in Kadish, *Israel's War 1948–1949*, pp. 904–05.
17 Tamir Goren, 'The War on the Mixed Cities in the North', in Kadish, ibid., pp. 177–78.
18 Golan, p. 905.
19 By July 1948 the total number of non-combatant evacuees reached 11,000 from 74 settlements, about one-third of the Jewish rural communities in Palestine, ibid., p. 914.

20 The story of Safad's Jewish community is based on Shmaryahu Ben-Pazi, *A Community at War: The Jews of Safad 1947–1948* (Jerusalem: Ariel, 2006), pp. 13–52.
21 For example, Ben-Pazi, pp. 32–36; Fein, pp. 686–88.
22 Dov Joseph, *The Faithful City* (New York: Simon and Schuster, 1960), p. 36.
23 Ibid. pp. 36–37.
24 Joseph, pp. 41–42. For a vivid description of hastily organizing one such convoy, see Larry Collins and Dominique Lapierre, *O Jerusalem* (New York: Simon and Schuster, 1972), pp. 251–52.
25 Oz, p. 361, pp. 365–66.
26 Nimrod Hagil'adi, 'The Colony of Rehovot between Mandate and State: Patterns of Authority and Violence', in: Alon Kadish and B. Z. Kedar (eds.), *A Few against Many? Studies in the Quantitative Balance of Powers in the Battles of Yehuda Ha-Makabi and the War of Independence* (Jerusalem: Magnes Press, 2006), pp. 131–40.
27 An Arab regional organization established in 1945 by Egypt, Iraq, Syria, Saudi Arabia, Lebanon, Transjordan and Yemen which, regardless of its Pact's stated purposes, became a symbol of shared pan-Arab national identity and cooperation.
28 Aburish, p. 95; Khalil al-Sakakini, *That is How I Am, O World, the Diaries of Khalil al-Sakakini* (Beirut: The General Association of Authors and Journalists, 1982), p. 367.
29 Bayan Nuwayhid al-Hout, *The Palestinian Leaderships and Institutions 1918–1948* (Beirut: 1981), pp. 508–13 (Arabic); Haim Levenberg, *Military Preparations of the Arab Community in Palestine 1945–1948* (London: Frank Cass, 1993), pp. 126–54.
30 S. Hamoud, 'The Palestinian Fund Raising: History and Analysis', *Shu'un Filastiniyya*, No. 6 (January 1972), pp. 133–34 (Arabic).
31 Ahmad al-Shuqayri, *Forty Years in Arab and International Life* (Beirut: 1969), p. 268 (Arabic).
32 Iraq, *Report of the Parliamentary Committee of Inquiry in the Palestine Question* (Baghdad: 1949), pp. 75–76.
33 Akram Dayri, 'The Fall of Nazareth and the Galilee: The Role of Hittin-Ajnadin Battalion', *Shu'oun Filastiniyya*, No. 21 (May 1973), p. 90 (Arabic); Nafez Nazzal, *The Palestinian Exodus from Galilee 1948* (Beirut: The Institute of Palestine Studies, 1978), p. 57, p. 66.
34 Aburish, p. 105.
35 al-Hout, pp. 623, 632–37; al-'Arif, pp. 259–63, 308–10, 323–24.
36 Al-'Arif, p. 172.
37 Aburish, pp. 108–09, 112, 117, 120; Isbir Munayyir, *Lydda in the Eras of the Mandate and Occupation* (Beirut: The Institute of Palestine Studies, 1997), p. 59 (Arabic).
38 Ahmad Farraj Tayi', *Folded Pages on Palestine* (n.p.; n.d., n.p.), pp. 65–66 (Arabic). See also Sakakini, p. 384.
39 Khaldun Sati' al-Husri (ed.), *Memoirs of Taha al-Hashimi, Pt. II, 1942–1955* (Beirut, 1978), pp. 156–58 (Arabic); Khayriyya Qasimiyya (ed.), *Palestine in the Memoirs of al-Qawaqji, 1936–1948* (Beirut: 1975), pp. 130–31 (Arabic).
40 Avraham Sela, *The Question of Palestine in the Inter-Arab System 1945–1948* (Unpublished Ph.D. dissertation, submitted to the Senate of the Hebrew University, Jerusalem, 1986), p. 491 (Hebrew).

41  Munayyir, pp. 49–82.
42  Aburish, pp. 104–05.
43  Sakakini, pp. 379–80, 384–85; Collins and Lapierre, pp. 306–09.
44  Alon Kadish, 'Who Attacked the Hulda Convoy (31.3.1948) and why it is Interesting?', in: Haim Nir'el (ed.), *'Uzi Narkis, Papers that Remained on the Desk . . .* (Jerusalem: The Zionist Library, 2000), pp. 255–63.
45  This is the conclusion of the Palestinian historian 'Arif al-'Arif, p. 459, as well as of pro-Mufti Muslim Brothers. See for example, Kamil Isma'il al-Sharif, *The Muslim Brothers in the Palestine War* (Cairo: Wahaba Library, 1951), p. 38.
46  According to Aburish, p. 104, the units and their emblems deliberately avoided exclusive Islamic symbols so as to attract Christians as well.
47  al-'Arif, p. 459. The case of rape is recorded in Elias Shoufani, 'The Fall of A Village', *Journal of Palestine Studies*, Vol. 1, No. 2 (1972), pp. 108–21. On punishing alleged collaborators, see Gorkin, pp. 116–17.
48  Al-'Arif, p. 183.
49  Hani al-Hindi, *The Army of Salvation* (Beirut: Dar al-Quds, Markaz al-Abhath al-Filastiniyya, 1974), pp. 116–17 (Arabic); al-Hout, pp. 630–33; Wasfi al-Tal, *Essays on Arab Affairs* (Amman: 1980), pp. 267–68 (Arabic).
50  Husri, *Memoirs of Taha al-Hashimi*, pp. 198–200.
51  Yoav Gelber, *Palestine 1948: War, Escape and the Emergence of the Palestinian Refugee Problem* (Brighton: Sussex Academic Press, 2001), p. 112; Walid Khalidi, 'Why did the Palestinians Leave?', *Middle East Forum*, Vol. 35, No. 7 (1959); and his 'The Fall of Haifa', ibid., Vol. 35 (1959), pp. 22–32.
52  Benny Morris, *1948 and After* (Oxford: Oxford University Press, 1990), pp. 173–81; Gorkin, p. 115.
53  See for example, Gelber, pp. 98–99. On the impact of the publicity given to the event by the Palestinian leaders, see Collins and Lapierre, p. 281; Shuqayri, p. 289; al-'Arif, p. 174.
54  Collins and Lapierre, p. 272.
55  On the case of Haifa, see Gelber, pp. 102–05; D. J. Bercuson, 'The Haifa Arab Refugees: A Documentary Essay', *Middle East Focus*, Vol. 10, No. 4 (Summer 1988), pp. 20–21. For a different viewpoint, see Khalidi, Walid, 'The Fall of Haifa', *Middle East Forum*, Vol. 35 (December, 1959), pp. 22–32.
56  Gelber, p. 22, p. 62, p. 98.

# 2

# Israeli Civilians in the 1967 Six-Day War[1]

*Meron Medzini*

Few people paid much attention when the Chief of Staff of the Israel Defence Forces, General Yitzhak Rabin, leaned over and handed Levi Eshkol, Israel's Prime Minister and Defence Minister, a note. It contained an intelligence report saying that overnight and early morning, in broad daylight, long columns of Egyptian soldiers and armour had been seen streaming across the Suez Canal into the Sinai Peninsula. All this took place on the reviewing stand in the stadium of the Hebrew University campus in Jerusalem on Monday morning, May 15, 1967, as Israel celebrated its 19th Independence Day with a modest military parade. Thus began the longest and most fateful month in the short history of the State of Israel, the consequences of which were still being felt nearly four decades later.[2]

In a hastily convened consultation later that day, it was decided to wait for additional information to properly assess the meaning and intent of this unexpected Egyptian move. Most Israeli decision makers were aware of the intelligence estimates presented to the Prime Minister and Minister of Defence in early April 1967 saying clearly that if war was to break out, the earliest it could be expected was 1970. The United States, when contacted, also saw no room for undue alarm. It was decided, therefore, not to call up the reserve forces, but to move additional tank units to the Egyptian border, and place the air force on alert. By early the next morning some two hundred Israeli tanks were deployed near the border.[3]

A few understood the reasons for the blatant Egyptian move. Indeed, tension along Israel's borders had been rising since the middle of 1966, but mainly along the armistice demarcation line with Syria in the north. Tensions reached a climax on April 7, 1967, when Israeli jet fighters shot down six Syrian MiGs, two of them over Damascus.

The Soviet Union, then Egypt's superpower patron and military supplier, for reasons not yet clarified until today, led President Gamal Abdul Nasser of Egypt to believe that Israel was massing troops in the Hula valley, below the Syrian Golan Heights, in preparation for an attack aimed at toppling the Syrian regime. They cited a number of speeches by Israel's Chief of Staff, General Yitzhak Rabin, that could be interpreted as calling for regime change in Damascus.[4]

The atmosphere deteriorated further when King Hussein of Jordan publicly taunted Nasser and claimed that Egypt was just posturing rather than taking meaningful steps to rescue Syria from an impending Israeli attack. He chided Nasser for hiding behind the skirts of the United Nations Emergency Force (UNEF) that had been stationed along the Israel–Egypt armistice lines since the conclusion of the 1956 Sinai-Suez War.

The Israeli public was not aware that something was amiss. The newspapers reported Egyptian troop concentrations in Sinai, but official sources sought to allay the growing unease and expressed the hope that this crisis would soon blow over. But the mood in Israel became sombre. Those listening to broadcasts from Arab radio and television stations became alarmed in view of the shrill tone emanating from Cairo, Amman, Damascus and Baghdad. But the more Israeli military and civilian spokesmen attempted to reassure the public that the situation was under control, the more they achieved the opposite effect and the more Israelis felt that something was seriously wrong but could not put their fingers on the problem.[5]

Two days later, emboldened by the absence of a decisive Israeli response to Egypt flooding the Sinai Peninsula with troops, Nasser made his second move. He demanded the withdrawal of the United Nations Emergency Force from the entire Sinai Peninsula and asked that they should be stationed only in the Gaza Strip. This, he wrongly assumed, would not be considered by Israel as *casus belli* and would silence his critics who still rebuked him for not doing enough to help ease the pressure on Syria. The Israeli unease was demonstrated in the course of a meeting of the Knesset's Foreign Affairs and Defence Committee. The hero of the 1956 Sinai war, Moshe Dayan, now a Knesset member representing *Rafi*, a breakaway faction from the ruling *Mapai* party, accused Eshkol of causing a serious deterioration in the situation. Eshkol adhered to the IDF intelligence assessment that Egypt had no intention of starting a war against Israel and that the crisis would soon abate. Rabin, however, was becoming highly concerned and won the approval of the Prime Minister to start calling up reservists including many pilots. The call up started on Thursday, May 17, 1967. It was done by telegram, messengers sent to the homes of reserve soldiers and by radio. Each unit had a code name which was broadcast on the Israeli radio. Reservists started making their way to their bases, some by car, the majority by bus and some even hitch-hiked. Few believed the country was facing war. By May 19, some 40,000 reservists had been called up. Most of them assumed that the crisis would be over within a week. Those who had not yet been called up carried on with their lives as planned. Over the first weekend of the crisis, football matches were held, beaches were packed with families enjoying the first days of the swimming season, and hikers crammed walking trails throughout the country. Nature reserves and national parks reported brisk business.[6]

However, a decision taken in New York, which proved to be a fatal mistake, worsened the crisis. U Thant, the Secretary General of the United Nations, when faced with the Egyptian demand to limit the deployment of UNEF only to the Gaza Strip, away from the Straits of Tiran leading to the southern Israeli port city of Eilat, told Egypt that it must decide if it wanted the entire force to remain in place or to ask for its total withdrawal. Nasser was left with little choice, lest he be ridiculed by the other Arab countries for hiding behind what some of their leaders called the skirts and aprons of UNEF. He demanded the entire force be withdrawn and it started leaving on May 18.[7] On that day Israel mobilized additional reserve soldiers and tension began to mount.

Most Israelis still did not understand what had brought about this sudden crisis and the government was not much help in informing them what was happening. It, too, was in the dark. By then there were close to 80,000 Egyptian troops in Sinai with some 800 tanks and hundreds of pieces of artillery. Israeli leaders and diplomats who reviewed the 1957 arrangements reached after the 1956 Sinai war that called for the demilitarization of Sinai, stationing of UNEF and the keeping open of the Straits of Tiran, came to the harsh conclusion that within a few days these arrangements seemed to have completely collapsed. They now anticipated a third move, the re-imposition of the naval blockade on the Straits of Tiran. For Israel this would be a *casus belli*.[8]

From May 21, calls were heard among Israeli politicians that the IDF be authorized to strike a preemptive blow at Egypt. The Israeli public was completely unaware that on May 18 a stern warning arrived from President Lyndon Johnson: The United States would vigorously oppose any unilateral Israeli action taken without prior consultation with Washington. The message was clear: Israel was told not to preempt. Eshkol ordered additional mobilization of reserve forces. The War Room in General Headquarters in Tel Aviv was activated. The issue now on the minds of a growing number of Israelis was not if there would be a war, but rather when it would start, who would fire the first shot and could Israel win American support for a pre-emptive strike?

By the end of the first week of the crisis, Israel had mobilized some 80,000 reserve soldiers. By then, the total number of Israelis in uniform, both regular army and reserve soldiers, stood at 200,000. Of a total population of 2,770,000, of whom 2.3 million were Jews, this meant that close to ten per cent of the population was in uniform and away from economic activity and other daily pursuits. Obviously those mobilized were the youngest, productive and contributing members of the Israeli society and a key factor in its faltering economy. The massive call up became starkly evident as main streets emptied and public transportation thinned out since hundreds of buses had been pressed into military service. At night the large cities looked like ghost towns. Those who had not yet mobilized but who had cars were asked to transport those without any means of transport. Cultural activities and nightlife came to a halt. Movie theatres continued to screen films to empty houses. It looked as though the country was on the verge of economic and cultural paralysis. Schools found themselves without teachers. Parents were asked to help and retired teachers were called back to the classroom. Universities closed down as students and faculty members were now in uniform. The only educational institutions functioning properly were kindergartens that were maintained by women teachers assisted by parents.[9]

Increasingly the key question on everyone's mind was how long would this crisis last and who would break the deadlock? The dramatic events of May 1967 were a climax in a series of developments that had been plaguing Israel since the end of 1965. In that year there had been a split in the ruling *Mapai* party which resulted in the establishment of a new party called *Rafi*, headed by the legendary founder of Israel David Ben-Gurion and supported by Shimon Peres, Moshe Dayan and Teddy

Kollek. That party had been able to win only 10 seats in the Knesset elections held in October 1965. Prime Minister and Defence Minister Levi Eshkol had been able to build a coalition that had the support of 75 out of the 120 Knesset members. In that year Israel entered an unprecedented economic recession as the government thought the economy was overheating. But the planned recession soon verged on a depression. Unemployment reached ten per cent of the labour force (or some 100,000 unemployed) and for the first time in its history the Israeli government was paying unemployment compensation. Home prices plummeted, there was a major decline in foreign investments in Israel, and in 1966 alone prices went up by eight per cent. Israel's annual rate of economic growth that in previous years had been between 8–10 per cent fell to 4 per cent and in 1966 there was virtually no economic growth registered. Store owners reported a drop of 30 per cent in purchases by Israelis. There was a growing sense of loss of trust in the country's economic leadership. The Prime Minister, who was known to have played a key role in Israel's economic growth, now seemed to have lost his touch. Israel appeared to have lost its attraction to world Jewry. In 1966 fewer than 16,000 immigrants arrived, the smallest number since 1954. It was believed that there were more Israelis leaving the country and emigrating abroad than there were Jews immigrating to Israel.[10]

The mood of many Israelis was bleak. In the newly built development towns, populated mainly by Sephardic Jews, there was no visible economic growth. Tensions between veteran Ashkenazi Israelis, descended from Europe, and the Sepharadi sector that descended from North African and Middle Eastern countries, widened. So did the growing social, economic and cultural gap between the Jewish majority and the 12 per cent non-Jewish Arab minority in Israel. They felt totally alienated from Israeli society. For them the defeat of the Arabs in 1948 was still an open wound. The general mood was expressed by a series of satires whose butt were the Prime Minister and his cabinet. One common joke requested that the last Israeli to leave the country turn off the lights at the airport.

Since the beginning of 1966 there had been some 120 terrorist attacks carried out mainly by the newly established Palestine Liberation Organization headed by Ahmed Shukeiri with its headquarters in Cairo. These caused the death of 11 Israelis, but the seemingly low figure did not hide a sense of impending major military problems. A number of retaliatory raids failed to allay the growing anxiety of the population. In November 1966 military service for men was extended again to thirty months.

Therefore the current crisis found the country at one of its lowest ebbs since its establishment in 1948. Many Israelis were wondering what had happened to the Zionist dream, to the great hopes and to the Israel that was created as a peaceful haven for world Jewry bent on rebuilding its national homeland. For many who were called up after May 17, this would be the third war they would be fighting in less than twenty years. The first, the 1948 war or the War of Independence in popular Israeli parlance, was the longest. It lasted a year and a half and cost the country some 6,500 dead, almost one per cent of the total Jewish population. The second was the lightning Sinai War that took 100 hours and cost 171 dead. Now this would be the third time. For thousands who fought in World War II, this would be their fourth. Many of those called up were holocaust survivors who could not shake off the terrible memories of this cataclysmic event in Jewish history. If Israel was once again threatened with annihilation, what have we achieved in building the Jewish state and fighting two wars to defend it, they asked.[11]

Already on May 21, there was more open talk of the danger of a looming war. The flooding of Sinai with Egyptian troops and the removal of UNEF created a threatening situation for Israel. The public was now waiting to see what would be the next Egyptian move and how Israel would respond. At this stage, and certainly during the first week of the crisis, there were no visible signs of panic, but there was growing concern verging on fear among most Israelis. They did not get much comfort or solace from their own leaders who, at the time, were already in the midst of a major domestic political crisis focusing on the ability of the Prime Minister, who was also the Defence Minister, to handle the crisis. During the first few days of the crisis, from May 15 to 23, 1967, the average Israeli citizens attempted to carry on with their normal lives. While there were only temporary food shortages, there was no run on the banks, and there was no panic buying of food and other basic goods. Israelis restrained themselves and did not engage in massive purchases apart from masking tape to place on windows and paint to blacken their cars' headlights. They also bought black cloth to ensure that blackout, when proclaimed, would be observed completely. The distribution system of the country coped well with new situation. There were no gasoline shortages and no long lines near filling stations. Officials estimated that Israel had emergency food supplies to last it for some months and fuel for at least 120 days. And now Israel was at its best – Israelis who were not called up began to volunteer their services. High-school children started delivering mail and helping out in hospitals. Others dug trenches. Long lines stretched near *Magen David Adom* (the equivalent of the Red Cross) stations to donate blood. Among them was a British journalist, Winston Churchill, the grandson of the great British wartime leader. Foreign students at Israeli universities volunteered their services at the post office, in hospitals, homes of the elderly or in digging air raid ditches. It appeared as though Israelis were learning how to cope with the new emergency. But above all people wondered how long Israel's economy could sustain the extensive call up before it collapsed.[12]

It was becoming clear to Israelis what they knew well from past experience: the country could not sustain a long period of almost total mobilization but rather had to achieve a quick and decisive military victory. Few knew that the IDF had many 'drawer plans' ready for such an eventuality. What the average Israeli citizen felt during those tense days and very long nights was the seeming paralysis that many thought had gripped the nation's leadership. This sense of the absence of a steady hand at the steering wheel seeped down to the rank and file. The general mood was not improved by what appeared to be the hesitancy of the government to act decisively.

Various options were considered. On May 22, the cabinet decided not to embark on a military campaign as suggested by General Rabin. It still preferred to pursue a diplomatic solution. That afternoon, the Prime Minister addressed the Knesset and declared that Israel was willing to participate in any effort to restore stability and promote peace in the Middle East. But he warned Egypt not to blockade the Straits of Tiran.

The Egyptian response came the next day when Nasser announced the re-imposition of the naval blockade in the Straits of Tiran. Eshkol was now convinced that this meant war. But he still sought to win superpower and chiefly American support. The US had once again, a day earlier, urged Israel not to preempt. Britain and France announced that they were no longer committed to any party in the Middle East. The war of words intensified. On May 26, 1967, Nasser declared: "The blockade of Sharm el-Sheikh means our waging an all-out war against Israel. This is going to be a total war. Our fundamental aim is the annihilation of Israel."

In those days there were no public television broadcasts in Israel and Israelis got their information from newspapers and radio broadcasts. The three leading newspapers launched a major campaign against the Prime Minister questioning his ability to lead the country at such a critical time. The *Rafi* party was headed by former Prime Minister Ben-Gurion, former Deputy Defence Minister Shimon Peres and former Chief of Staff Moshe Dayan, all heroes of the 1956 campaign. Ben-Gurion embarked on a wide-scale campaign directed at discrediting Eshkol. They were joined by the leader of the *Gahal* party and founder of the nationalist *Herut* party, veteran politician Menachem Begin. The government failed to launch a public relations campaign to assure the population that things were under control. For the first time in the history of the country, there were serious doubts in the minds of its citizens about the competence of the Prime Minister who also held the portfolio of Defence Ministry. Few knew how painstakingly he had prepared the Israel Defence Forces. Few knew how the instrument called the IDF had been honed and its strength almost doubled in the period since Eshkol had become Defence Minister in 1963.

The image of Eshkol however, was that of a well-meaning but faltering old man and a decent but doddering grandfather. Most of his ministers had an even less flattering image. There was a growing groundswell to replace the Prime Minister. Many young Israelis saw the members of the government as a collection of relics from the Diaspora where Jews did not fight against those who perpetrated pogroms against them. Many native-born Israelis even wondered if the IDF had lost its deterrent power, that element which was fundamental to Israel's defence strategy and on which tens of thousands of Israelis were educated and motivated during their military service. Instead, they read a great deal of the Arab threat to destroy Israel and throw the Jews to the sea.[13]

From sparse newspaper reports, but mainly from rumours that spread like wildfire, Israelis understood that in a series of meetings among the leaders of the various political parties, a number of proposals were raised – all of them aiming to at least replacing Eshkol as Defence Minister. In the background there was the warning from Ben-Gurion expressed to General Rabin in a meeting held on May 22, that Israel must refrain from engaging in war at this time. It must seek the support of at least one major power (as Israel did in 1956 when it was supported by both France and Britain). Ben-Gurion suggested to Rabin that he fold up the tents and send the troops back home to wait for a more opportune moment. Rabin also consulted Dayan and the leader of the National Religious Party Moshe Chaim Shapira. Both advised him to wait for better times and warned him not to preempt. Rabin sought the advice of Golda Meir, then Secretary General of the ruling *Mapai* party. She told him there was no other way but to fight. She was also determined not to allow the creation of a national unity (or national emergency) cabinet or to agree to the replacement of Eshkol as Defence Minister.[14]

The next day the Chief of Staff suffered a nervous breakdown and was confined to his home for forty-eight hours. It was described as 'nicotine poisoning' since Rabin was a heavy smoker. But the news travelled fast and created much confusion and concern among Israel's leaders. Initially they had grave doubts over the Prime Minister's ability to handle the situation. Now the Chief of Staff too had caved in to the unbearable pressure. Who would lead the country, they asked in the newly constructed tent cities along the borders that housed the soldiers, in the cities, in the kibbutzim and *moshavim* and in virtually every Israeli home.

The average Israeli citizen now became frightened. Listening to the radio was now the national pastime. Virtually every soldier had his own transistor radio. In those days no one had mobile phones and even public telephones were a rare instrument. Israelis, soldiers and civilians alike became addicted to reading newspapers. From these two sources they heard and read the stream of Arab threats and invective against Israel. In the absence of a steady voice and a sense that the reins of Israel were in solid hands, the Israeli citizen was wondering what would become of his family, children and the future of Israel, barely nineteen years old. Rumours circulated that in Tel Aviv, parks had been prepared as mass burial grounds capable of interring thirty thousand casualties. Rumours described how a number of generals, among them Chief of Operations Ezer Weizman and Chief of Training Command Ariel Sharon, had accused Eshkol of playing with the future of the country. It was reported they told Eshkol that every day that passed there would be more casualties if and when Israel finally decided to shoot first. The rumours were also fanned by the opposition parties supported by the three leading newspapers. One editor even showed Ben-Gurion an anti-Eshkol editorial he was about to publish the following day, an unprecedented event in the history of journalism. It was reported that Begin called upon his arch-rival Ben-Gurion and suggested that he replace Eshkol as Prime Minister. Ben-Gurion wisely refused. It was evident that he was too old and was a prisoner of the past.[15]

A growing sense of impotence gripped many Israelis who were not aware of the IDF war plans. Among them were hundreds of thousands of holocaust survivors. For them Israel was the last and ultimate haven. And now, barely twenty-two years after the end of World War II and the holocaust, Israelis were facing another holocaust and once again the world remained silent. There was a growing feeling of despair; twice in one generation Jews were being led to slaughter and could do nothing, as their fate was already sealed. Would Israel become another Auschwitz or Treblinka, some wondered. The betrayal of the world only added more poignancy to this feeling. Many interpreted the repeated calls on Israel by the UN and the great powers to restrain itself as confirmation that the world had not yet come to terms with the existence of a Jewish state and that Israel still did not deserve to live a normal life like any other nation.[16] The average Israeli citizen also felt that the right to self defence was denied to him because Israel was a Jewish state. Those Israelis who had television sets watched with growing alarm live broadcasts of Egyptian military parades and the bellicose speeches of Nasser and the leaders of Syria, Iraq, Lebanon and even of King Hussein of Jordan.

Nine days before the war there were already some signs of panic. People began to hoard food. Jerusalemites who remembered the 1948 siege were the first to make a run on food shops that soon emptied out. Part of the problem had to do with the dislocation of distribution networks as many drivers and their trucks were called up to the war fronts. Some Israelis decided to leave the country and seek refuge in safer places until the crisis abated. Planes were arriving empty and leaving full. Curiously, those called up failed to understand the panic that began to grip those Israelis who remained behind at home. In their bases they were very busy going over the war plans and acquired a sense of quiet confidence in the ability of the IDF to protect the country. But they failed to transmit this sense of reassurance to their families at home.

Parallel to the panic, there was also a growing mood of defiance. Israel was not going to become a new version of Czechoslovakia, sacrificed by the western powers in 1938 to appease Nazi Germany. The basic sentiment was, 'there is no one we can trust. Our fate is in our own hands. There will not be another holocaust. This time we have a state and an army.' But, many wondered, when would 'they', meaning the government ministers, finally order the army to act?[17]

The only ray of hope and meaningful help came from world Jewry that mobilized itself to support Israel financially to an even greater extent than during Israel's War of Independence. Jews understood that if Israel was destroyed, there was no hope for the continued existence of the Jewish people. Israel's war became their own. Thousands of volunteers began to make their way to Israel to help in any way they could, mainly in kibbutzim and *moshavim* that were on the verge of collapse as most of the men had been fully mobilized since May 17.

If, during the first week of the crisis, there was a comparative sense of calm, the second week witnessed a major change in the general mood. Much of it had to do with the reporting of the media on the evolving crisis. As stated above, the average Israeli citizen had to rely for news on the state-run radio station called 'The Voice of Israel', the army-run IDF Radio and the many daily newspapers that apart from the three leading dailies, *Ha'aretz, Ma'ariv* and *Yedioth Ahronot*, were owned by political parties and echoed their ideology and party line. There was strict military censorship on the Israeli mobilization, operational plans, deployment, arrival of weapons and spare parts or any information that could help raise the sinking national morale but there was no censorship on news from the Arab states. Thus Israelis were constantly treated to reports of massing Egyptian troops in Sinai, threats of annihilation emanating from Damascus, Amman, Baghdad and even Beirut. Those who had television sets could see and hear the shrill war cries and the military preparations made by Israel's enemies. The sense of impending doom grew.[18]

At the same time, Israelis were not getting any solace, guidance, sense of direction and certainly no leadership from their own government. They perceived that there was an ongoing struggle between those who wanted to launch a preventive war at once, and those who still relied on diplomatic solutions and the task of obtaining the support of at least one major power. By the end of the second week of the crisis, most of the IDF reserve soldiers were mobilized and in place along the armistice demarcation line with Egypt. Many who had not been called up came any how. Few wanted to miss what was seen as a major struggle for national survival. But the massive call up did not evolve without its own cost. There was uncertainty how long the country could withstand a prolonged mobilization. Professionals who closed their offices and small business owners were afraid that their businesses and practices would collapse. Many left their wives and children with little cash in hand.

In the rest of the country there were evident signs that Israel was facing a major war: school hours were curtailed as teachers were called up and students were pressed into service delivering mail, newspapers and milk. Others dug shelters and air raid trenches. Home shelters were readied and cleared of bicycles, toys and the excess furniture that was normally stored in them. The amount of garbage piles grew. Many factories were reduced to shorter work hours and abandoned night shifts as men were called up, and raw materials did not arrive as shipping companies were afraid to have their vessels docked in Israeli ports.

Many Israelis watched with growing trepidation as the few tourists who were in Israel left. About 8,000 foreign visitors left on May 24–25. Some hotels were readied to serve as emergency hospitals. Foreign embassies were advising their nationals to leave the country. Some even offered to evacuate their nationals and those included Israelis who had foreign passports. Overseas relatives and friends of Israelis offered to take their children for the duration of the crisis. All this added to the growing sense of national isolation and impotence. Many Israelis were asking a simple question: What happened to our deterrent power on which we based our national strategy. Weren't we told that the IDF was strong enough to deter any attack on the homeland?[19]

On May 24, the deeply divided government decided to send Foreign Minister Abba Eban to Paris, London and Washington in order to ascertain the intentions of these three powers and find out what their advice to Israel would be. For Israelis this meant that at least until his return on May 27, there would be no war. Nerves were frayed throughout the country.

Eban set off on his fateful mission. In Paris President Charles De Gaulle warned him against Israel firing the first shot. He feared a global conflict involving the Soviet Union and suggested that the crisis be resolved by a four-power international conference. In London, Prime Minister Harold Wilson effectively told Eban that Britain could do nothing and suggested that the key was in Washington. In the American capital the Chiefs of Staff told Eban that the IDF could smash the Arab armies within six to ten days. But he became alarmed when a frantic cable reached him from Tel Aviv: the key issue now was not the naval blockade but the presence in Sinai of close to 100,000 Egyptian troops, some 1,000 tanks and a similar number of cannons. He was also told that an Egyptian attack was imminent. Eban did not know what to make of the cable that spelled doom and gloom verging on panic, which he thought gripped both the IDF and the government. President Lyndon Johnson asked Israel to give him two more weeks in which to resolve the crisis either by diplomatic means or by organizing an international flotilla that would sail through the Straits of Tiran and lift the blockade. This later became known jokingly as the Red Sea Regatta.[20]

Eban hastily returned home on May 27, was rushed to a tense cabinet meeting and informed his colleagues of the results of his mission. The ministers, by a vote of nine to nine (with the casting vote of the Prime Minister), decided to give the United States the time it requested. The ministers were told by Eshkol that a few hours earlier, at 2 in the morning, the Soviet Ambassador to Israel delivered to Eshkol what amounted to a threat: do not fire the first shot or be ready to bear the consequences. Some recalled a similar Soviet threat in 1956 when in a blunt letter, Soviet leader Bulganin threatened Ben-Gurion with a missile attack on Israel if it refused to accept a ceasefire in Sinai and withdraw its forces from the Peninsula.

Sunday, May 28 was a fateful day for the embattled Prime Minister of Israel. In the morning a message arrived from President Johnson counselling against a pre-emptive strike. Later that day, the cabinet, by an overwhelming majority, voted to accept the American request. Eshkol was asked to tell the nation what the decision was. A tired Prime Minister decided to broadcast live to a nation whose nerves were on edge. Israelis were told to prepare for a message by the Prime Minister. Tension rose dramatically. Many reservists had been in uniform for almost two weeks and wanted to know what was in store for them and their families and above all, whether they could trust their government and the Prime Minister. The entire country, civilians and soldiers alike, officers and enlisted men, remained glued to their radio sets at home, and to their transistors in their bases or on the borders. The Prime Minister started reading a statement prepared by his aides which included corrections that were inserted in handwriting. There were some eerie pauses when he stumbled over words as he tried to make sense of the corrections and asked his aides for clarification – all this on a live broadcast.[21]

The entire nation was stunned. Some people wept, others swore aloud. Was Israel going to be led to war by an old, tired, stuttering, wavering, hesitant and uncertain political leader? From the radio station, and unaware of the brewing public storm, Eshkol returned to his office to meet with and explain the decision to the IDF generals. They were furious. 'Don't you realize that with every day that passes we are going to sustain very heavy losses?', they asked. Rumours spread describing how one general even threw his insignia on the table in front of the Prime Minister. More Israelis realized that by acceding to the Johnson request for additional time, Israel had placed its very existence in the hands of the United States and lost all possible military initiative. They felt that the United States could not be trusted and feared that the United States would be guided by its own interests rather than those of Israel. They also feared that Nasser would eventually back down having won a tremendous political victory and that in the future Israel would be at his mercy. Whenever he felt like it, he would fill Sinai with troops forcing Israel to call up the reserve and risk an economic collapse.

The impact of that broadcast was enormous. It shocked virtually all Israelis, including those *Mapai* leaders who still felt that Eshkol could lead the country to war. A few of his supporters attempted to shrug off the prime ministerial stutter as a minor incident due to his fatigue and a cold. But the nation was appalled. The next morning the major newspapers openly called for the immediate replacement of Eshkol as Defence Minister. The opposition to Eshkol grew in volume and intensity. But this had to be a decision made by Eshkol's own party. The Labour Party leaders initially opted for Deputy Prime Minister Yigal Allon, a hero of the 1948 war and an avowed opponent of Moshe Dayan, as the more sensible choice. But the Israeli public would have none of this. Letters to the editor, some small demonstrations in front of Labour Party headquarters and growing doubts over the Eshkol style of leadership among the veteran Labour politicians, forced Eshkol to reconsider. All the parties represented in Eshkol's coalition now increasingly felt that Dayan was the right man. The only vociferous opponent of this move was Party Secretary General Golda Meir. She saw no reason to replace Eshkol. She became the target of bitter attacks by many Israelis who saw in her a vindictive woman who failed to grasp the mood of the country and who was driven solely by narrow political considerations, mainly how to preserve the reputation and position of the faltering Prime Minister.[22]

The government realized that it had to regain the public confidence. One decision was to ask former Director of Military Intelligence General

Chaim Herzog to serve as the political-military commentator of the Israel Radio. In a calm voice that carried determined authority he succeeded in making sense of a tense situation and suggested that, knowing the facts, if he had a choice between sitting in an Egyptian plane sent to bomb Tel Aviv and sitting in a house in Tel Aviv, then he would prefer for the good of his health to sit in Tel Aviv. The Herzog broadcasts cast a much needed spell of confidence among Israelis who felt that for the first time since the onset of the crisis they were being told the truth and were being addressed like adults. Another decision was to appoint General Chaim Bar-Lev as deputy Chief of Staff. He returned to Israel from France and coined the following phrase: "We shall hit them fast, hard and elegantly." Another move was to push for the formation of a government of national unity and invite Menachem Begin, the leader of the right-wing nationalist party *Gahal*, to join the government. Begin agreed on condition that Dayan would be asked to become Defence Minister.

The consternation of most Israelis became apparent and the groundswell to expand the government grew when, on May 30, 1967, King Hussein of Jordan flew from Amman to Cairo and signed a defence pact with Egypt, committing Jordan to go to war if Israel attacked Egypt. Hussein also placed his army under the command of an Egyptian general.[23] Most Israelis now felt that the trap was sprung. Israel was now surrounded on all sides by implacable enemies determined to destroy the Jewish state. The adherence of Jordan to the circle of hostility around Israel meant that Jerusalem could become a battleground and that the entire heartland of Israel, including its major international airport, power station, the defence ministry and the IDF Headquarters, could come under artillery fire from the nearby West Bank. The Jordanian adherence to the Egyptian-led military coalition against Israel effectively destroyed the arguments of those who counselled postponing the launching of a preemptive strike. Chief among those opposed to a pre-emptive strike were Ben-Gurion and the leaders of the National Religious Party (NRP). The latter threatened Eshkol that if he did not expand his government and appoint Dayan as Minister of Defence, they would leave the coalition and place Israel in an unbearable political crisis at the very time when its future hung in the balance. Ben-Gurion and the NRP leaders still thought that Dayan would not embark on a defensive war. But they did not realize that the new situation had led to re-thinking on the part of Dayan. He had now become convinced that Israel must strike at once.[24]

Meanwhile, Israel's citizens were being instructed to prepare for war. Seven thousand school children dug trenches in Tel Aviv. Instructions were broadcast and printed in the newspapers on how to ready shelters, what commodities to store in these shelters and how to deal with the elderly and children, how casualties should be handled and even what was the right diet for time of war. All of Israel's hospitals were readied for war, patients who could be sent home were told to go home. Non-emergency operations were postponed. Blood supplies and other emergency equipment were stocked.

Israeli citizens were now at the end of their tethers and their morale sank to its lowest ebb since May 15. They sensed that the country was now surrounded on all sides by implacable enemies bent on destroying it physically. They realized that the arguments used by their government for years that Israel was the strongest nation in the Middle East sounded hollow. If its army was the best equipped in the region, the best led, and the most effective, why did the Arabs embark on what seemed to be a suicidal march of folly? Did the Arab leaders know more than their Israeli counterparts? Were Israelis being told the truth? Were they not told that war, if at all, was to occur at the earliest in 1970? Were not they told that as long as Nasser had some 60,000 troops bogged down in Yemen, he would not risk a confrontation with Israel? Were the assurances given by the powers in 1957 worthless? If so, who could Israel trust if not its own power? But at the crucial time, it seemed that its leadership had failed the test. The time had come for a united, determined and above all inspiring leadership, the last thing Eshkol could provide. And that was his tragedy. He prepared the IDF painstakingly for the coming ordeal, but his affable and easy-going personality failed to impress the desperate Israelis who were now incited by a shrill media and even shriller opposition parties. A number of Israelis also wondered what Israel would do if faced by an attack with chemical weapons. Egypt, they recalled, used gas warfare in the Yemen war. They knew Israel did not possess even rudimentary gas masks. Israeli agents abroad were instructed to obtain gas masks. The only country that responded was Germany. This twist of irony did not fail to be noted. Germany was helping Israel to defend itself from gas.

But as they pondered the future of Israel, the citizens went about their business waiting for the government to make up its mind. Meanwhile, the pace of volunteering gathered momentum. Soldiers with time on their hands in the Negev lent a hand to the kibbutzim to harvest crops. Even Israeli Arabs helped dig fortifications in Jewish settlements. By the end of May thousands of volunteers had arrived from abroad. The majority were young Jews who felt they must lend a hand. A few were non-Jews who felt they must do all to prevent another holocaust. The presence of volunteers was a bright spot for Israelis in an otherwise bleak and dreary situation. Thousands of Israelis continued to form long lines to give blood. Many gave up part of their salaries, even though the government had raised taxes by 10 per cent. While the tens of thousands of reserve soldiers used the time effectively to train, to ready their equipment and go over operational plans, civilians were not as busy as those in uniform and had more time to brood on the future of the country. The question uppermost on the minds of all Israelis was: when would their government give the order?[25]

By June 1, 1967, all this had changed. Moshe Dayan was finally appointed Minister of Defence. Yigal Allon rightly realized that the country wanted only Dayan and no one else and wisely declined the offer to replace Eshkol as Defence Minister. News of the Dayan appointment spread very quickly around Israel and a vast sigh of relief could be heard everywhere. Soldiers and civilians alike celebrated as they greeted this appointment as the best news they heard since May 15. Finally, they argued, our beleaguered leaders have come to their senses and made the right choice. All Israelis knew that this meant war. They were now ready for the supreme test knowing the IDF would be led by a highly daring, courageous and experienced soldier.

A handful of leaders and senior army officers knew that Meir Amit, head of the Mossad, the Israeli intelligence agency, had been sent to Washington to ascertain once and for all what the Americans were intending to do and how serious was the international flotilla idea which Israel had been told would break the blockade on the Straits of Tiran? He met with the head of the CIA and the American secretary of defense Robert McNamara. Both told him there was no flotilla and there was nothing the United States could do for Israel. He was told to go home where he should be. Over the weekend of June 2–3, thousands of reservists were given furloughs. The beaches were packed. In a press conference on Saturday, June 3, newly appointed Defence Minister Dayan hinted that the time was not ripe for war. This led a number of foreign correspondents to pack up their bags and return home, arguing nothing was going to happen. But one American journalist told his editor that the Israeli call up was now Ivory Soap, meaning 99 per cent, and that the country was on the verge of war.[26]

The final decision was taken in the early hours of June 4 in the Jerusalem residence of the Prime Minister. Present were the principal decision makers, among them Eshkol, Dayan, Allon, Eban and Prime Minister's special advisor Yigael Yadin, while Rabin was absent. They were joined by Amit and the Israeli Ambassador to Washington, Avraham Harman. These two flew in from Washington via Frankfurt, where they picked up 20,000 gas masks, which the German government said was the only quantity they were going to supply Israel. Amit reported the new American attitude but still asked for another week to give diplomacy a chance. Dayan had had enough and demanded a decision. He was also aware that the United States was considering sending Vice President Hubert Humphrey to Cairo in a last ditch effort to defuse the crisis. He might have feared that Nasser would then agree to restore the status quo, thereby awarding Egypt an enormous political victory. Israel would have to call off the preparations, fold the tents and send its fighting men, whose number now reached 275,000, home. The decision was taken to strike on Monday morning, June 5, and launch a pre-emptive air strike aimed at destroying on the ground the air forces of Egypt, Syria, Jordan and even Iraq. Operation *Moked* had been honed and practised for many years. The Israel Air Force was confident it would be successful but the task would require virtually every jet Israel had.

The cabinet met on the morning of June 4, and authorized the Prime Minister and the Defence Minister to instruct the IDF to take the necessary steps to defend the country. On that day all hospitals were emptied, the high command reviewed the plans, the reservists went back to their bases, tanks, armoured personnel carriers and other equipment was readied. Israel was like a coiled spring, waiting for the order to repel the looming threat. Interestingly enough, Nasser realized that Israel would hit on Monday morning and cautioned his pilots to be ready. But his advice was not heeded and when the first Israeli jet appeared over the Egyptian airbases in Sinai and in Egypt, the pilots were either finishing their breakfast or on their way to their planes parked in neat rows near the runways. Within less than three hours the war had been effectively decided by the air strike. At 08:10 an air-raid siren was heard throughout Israel. This was the signal for the start of the attack by the ground forces in the south. The code word 'Red Sheet' was now broadcast and Israeli tanks began to move into the Gaza Strip and Sinai Peninsula. The spring was now being uncoiled with all its might.[27]

On the first day of the war, there was some confusion among Israeli civilians as to who should sit in air raid shelters. During the first hours, the IDF imposed strict censorship on what transpired. This left room for many rumours, emanating mainly from Cairo and later Amman. Cairo radio bragged that Tel Aviv was on fire, that Eilat was cut off from the rest of Israel and that Jerusalem was encircled. From the Israeli side there were no denials which only added to the feeling of malaise. At 10:20 in the morning, Jordanian guns and mortars opened fire along the entire Israel–Jordan armistice lines. West Jerusalem was hit by hundreds of Jordanian shells, while Jordanian Long Toms long-range artillery began to bombard Tel Aviv, some 18 kilometres away. In Jerusalem, some twenty civilians lost their lives, mainly because they did not take shelter as ordered by the authorities. Tel Aviv was hit by scores of shells, but there was no visible damage or casualties. In the north, Syrian planes attacked the city of Migdal Haemek next to a major airbase at nearby Ramat David. The Israeli response was paltry. As the major effort was aimed at destroying the Egyptian army, less attention was paid to the other frontlines. On the first day Syrian troops staged a mini-invasion on the northern edge of the Hule Valley but were repulsed.[28]

Jerusalemites began scurrying into air raid shelters, traffic came to a halt, shops closed and streets emptied. A few rescue vehicles were seen speeding along the deserted streets and people noted one car carrying mayor Teddy Kollek who started the first of his many inspection visits, accompanied by foreign correspondents. Jordanian troops entered the Jewish suburb of north Talpiot in an effort to capture that part of the city. They managed to overrun the United Nations Headquarters in Government House and the United Nations commander, the Norwegian General Odd Bull, had to evacuate his staff to the YMCA building in West Jerusalem. Towards evening, the first Israeli paratroopers arrived in the Jerusalem suburb of Beit Hakerem, where they were treated to cakes and soft drinks by the civilian population. They were originally due to jump into Sinai, but were diverted instead to Jerusalem for the hastily planned breakthrough into the Old City. Late that night they stormed a highly fortified Jordanian position called Ammunition Hill. Thirty-seven paratroopers paid with their lives for this attack that opened the way to Mount Scopus, and the next day to the Old City of Jerusalem.

In other parts of the country, on the first day of the fighting, civilians wondered what was happening. There was battle fog, and apart from vague statements by the Prime Minister and the Defence Minister stating that enemy troops had been sighted moving towards Israel and that the IDF had been ordered to repel them, no further details were made available. But rumours began to circulate quickly that the Israel air force had annihilated the entire Egyptian, Jordanian, Syrian and even Iraqi air forces in less than three hours and that Israel had in fact won the war in a stunning pre-emptive strike. Sitting in shelters, many civilians in Jerusalem and Tel Aviv refused to believe the news. They had to wait until after midnight for a confirmation. In a press conference Israelis and the rest of the world were informed that over 400 enemy planes had been destroyed, mostly on the ground, and that Israel was now safe from aerial bombardment.

Over the next five days Israelis avidly followed the advance of their forces in Sinai, the West Bank and towards the end of the week onto the Golan Heights. The climax came on the third day of the war, when on Wednesday, June 7, the paratroopers arrived at the Western Wall, the most sacred place for Jews. The entire country listened as the Israel Radio correspondent accompanying the troops described in a sobbing voice the arrival of the soldiers at the Wall and the sound of the Ram being blown by the Chief Military Chaplain was heard throughout Israel. Thousands wept with excitement. At noon the Defence Minister arrived with the Chief of Staff and senior commanders and stuck a chit into the cracks of the Wall: We have come back to Jerusalem never to leave it again.[29]

Jordan asked for a ceasefire late Wednesday evening when the IDF completed the capture of the entire West Bank. Egypt accepted a ceasefire the next day when the IDF reached the banks of the Suez Canal. The last two days of the campaign were directed at evicting the Syrians from the Golan Heights. A Soviet threat to enter the war, delivered through the United States, convinced the Minister of Defence to accept a ceasefire that went into effect at 1400 GMT on Saturday, June 10, 1967. The Six-Day War was officially over. The recriminations and accusations were temporarily shelved, the political wrangling that was typical of the pre-war period vanished, at least temporarily. All of

Israel was united in view of what was perceived to be a major victory over the Arab forces that had presented Israel with an existential threat.

The despondency that had characterized Israeli civilians and even many soldiers before the war now gave way to a sense of euphoria bordering on religious elation and ecstasy. Many Israelis were convinced that God himself was responsible for their swift victory and that the country had been delivered from an assured annihilation only by divine intervention. The average Israeli did not suffer any privation during the six days of fighting. Supplies had been assured, as was their delivery. There had been no air raid sirens and above all no panic. Israelis had faced the test with calm assurance feeling that after three weeks of dithering and bickering, the future of Israel had been in the experienced hands of leaders who knew what they were doing and who were going about their business in a calm and assured manner. Few Israelis knew of or realized the depth of the arguments and uncertainties that had been present in the cabinet room and in the IDF headquarters throughout the six days of war. These secrets would emerge much later, as would the arguments over who was responsible for the victory. Was it Moshe Dayan who came late and found the IDF a well oiled machine or Chief of Staff Rabin who readied the troops together with the generals, or even the embattled Levi Eshkol who as Defence Minister from 1963 to the eve of the war had made sure that the IDF had what it required?[30]

A few days after the end of the hostilities all Israelis were rudely awakened when the number of casualties was published. Israel had lost 810 dead, thousands wounded and there were even a number of prisoners. It was a very costly victory and the price was paid mainly by reserve soldiers and officers. The stunned country mourned the dead and wondered aloud if this would be the last war. There were no victory parades (apart from the military parade staged in East Jerusalem on the twentieth Independence Day of Israel in May 1968). The country was later deluged with victory albums and the fame of the generals rocketed sky high. This gave rise to hubris for which Israel would pay a devastating price six years later when the Syrians and Egyptians sought to avenge their humiliating defeat in 1967 by launching a surprise attack on the day of Yom Kippur in October 1973.

The Six-Day War was a prime example of how Israeli civilians adjusted quickly to a rapidly changing situation and performed in a stellar manner which few of their leaders had been certain they were capable of. During the week of fighting, the mood in Israel changed swiftly and reflected the new reality on the ground. It was a different Israel, a different Middle East and a different international reality that came about as a result of the Six-Day War, a war that no one had really wanted or planned.

## NOTES

1 Even though the 'June War of 1967' is a neutral expression, this chapter deals with the Israeli domestic situation during the war and hence the expression 'Six-Day War' is being used here.

2 For the most concise work on the Six-Day War see Michael Oren, *Six Days of War, June 1967* (Oxford: Oxford University Press, 2002) and *The Making of the Modern Middle East* (Hebrew version) (Or Yehuda: Dvir, 2004); Tom Segev, *Israel in 1967* (Hebrew) (Jerusalem: Ketat, 2005); Walter Laqueur, *The Road to War* (New York: Macmillan, 1968). See also Asher Susser (ed.), *Six Days – Thirty Years, New Perspectives on the Six Day War* (Hebrew) (Tel Aviv: Am Oved, 1999). See also *Ha'aretz, Ma'ariv, Yedioth Ahronot* and *The Jerusalem Post* for the dates May 14 to June 10, 1967.

3 Yossi Goldstein, *Eshkol – A Biography* (Hebrew) (Jerusalem: Ketat, 2004), pp. 533–42.

4 For the Russian policy see Avraham Ben-Tsur, *Soviet Factors in the Six Day War* (Hebrew) (Tel Aviv: Sifriyat Hapoalim, 1975). For the Israel–Syria border clashes on the eve of the Six-Day War see Yitzhak Rabin, *The Rabin Memoirs* (Hebrew) (Tel Aviv: Ma'ariv, 1979), Vol. I, p. 133.

5 For the Arab war of words see Laqueur, op. cit., pp. 82–108; See also Address to the United Nations General Assembly by Abba Eban, June 19, 1967. For the best description of the behaviour of the civilian population before and during the war see Ruth Bondi, Ohad Zmora and Rafael Bashan (eds.), *Not by the Sword Alone – the Amazing Story of the Heroism of the People of Israel and the Victory in the Six Day War* (Hebrew) (Tel Aviv: Lewin Epstein, 1968).

6 Laqueur, op. cit., pp. 109–21; Segev, op. cit., pp. 245–308.

7 For the UNEF removal see U Thant, *View from the UN* (New York: Doubleday, 1978); Indar Jit Rikhye, *The Sinai Blunder* (London: Frank Cass, 1980); Rosalyn Higgins, *United Nations Peacekeeping 1946–1967, Documents and Commentary* (London: Oxford University Press, 1969), Vol. I, pp. 221–414.

8 For the 1957 arrangements see Abba Eban, *Personal Witness: Israel Through My Eyes* (New York: Putnam, 1992); For US policy during the crisis, see *Foreign Relations of the United States* Vol. XIX, *Arab–Israeli Crisis and War* (Washington, 2004).

9 Laqueur, op. cit., pp. 109–21; Segev, op. cit., pp. 245–308.

10 Segev, op. cit., pp. 31–242; Goldstein, op. cit., pp. 507–32; see also Moshe Dayan, *Milestones* (Hebrew) (Tel Aviv: Edanim, 1976), pp. 391–417.

11  For the domestic scene see Susser, op. cit., pp. 209–54.

12  Segev, op. cit. pp. 245-308; Goldstein, op. cit. pp. 530–53.

13  Laqueur, op. cit., pp. 109–21.

14  On the position of Golda Meir see Meron Medzini, *The Proud Jewess-Golda Meir and the Dream of Israel* (Hebrew) (Tel Aviv: Edanim, 1990), pp. 333–42.

15  See Michael Bar Zohar, *Ben-Gurion* (Hebrew) (Tel Aviv: Am Oved, 1977), Vol. III, pp. 1587–99. For the editorial mentioned see Susser, op. cit., pp. 229–34. For the Rabin breakdown see Rabin, op. cit., pp. 158–60.

16  For the attitude of world Jewry see Eli Lederhandler (ed.), *The Six Day War and World Jewry* (Bethesda: University Press of Maryland, 2000) and Moshe Davis (ed.), *The Nations Identification with the State in the Yom Kippur War* (Hebrew) (Jerusalem: Magnes Press, 1976).

17  Segev, op. cit., pp. 297–358.

18  Susser, op. cit., pp. 209–54.

19  Laqueur, op. cit., pp. 128–32; see also Shmuel Segev, *Red Sheet* (Hebrew) (Tel Aviv: Tversky, 1967).

20  For the Eban trip see Eban, op. cit.; Laqueur, op. cit., pp. 133–39; Gideon Rafael, *Destination Peace* (New York: Stein and Day, 1981), pp. 129–66. For the Johnson-Eban meeting see FRUS, op. cit., pp. 140–46.

21  For the Eshkol broadcast and its aftermath, see Goldstein, op. cit., pp. 556–59.

22  See Dayan, op. cit., pp. 418–32; Moshe Gilboa, *Six Years – Six Days, Origins and History of the Six Day War* (Hebrew) (Tel Aviv: Am Oved, 1969).

23  See Chaim Herzog, *Way of Life* (Hebrew) (Tel Aviv: Yedioth Aharonot, 1997); Susser, op. cit., pp. 161–208.

24  Dayan, op. cit., p. 425.

25  Segev, op. cit., pp. 297–342.

26  For the Amit talks in Washington see Meir Amit, *Head to Head – Personal View on Major Events and Secret Stories* (Hebrew) (Tel Aviv: Hed Artsi, 1999).

27  For the final decision see Dayan, op. cit., p. 425; Goldstein, op. cit., pp. 564–67; Rabin, op. cit., pp. 180–84.

28  For a description of the military moves see Dayan, op. cit., pp. 433–86; Rabin, op. cit., pp. 185–203; Segev, op. cit. pp. 359–438. For the war in Jerusalem see Uzi Narkis, *A Soldier for Jerusalem* (Hebrew) (Tel Aviv: Ministry of Defence, 1991).

29  For the war in the north see Hanoch Bar-Tov, *Daddo – 48 Years and 20 More Days* (Hebrew) (Tel Aviv: Ma'ariv, 1978), pp. 121–48; Segev, op. cit., pp. 406–38; Oren, op. cit., pp. 333–62.

30  For the aftermath and the arguments see Avi Shlaim, *The Iron Wall* (London: Penguin Books, 2000), pp. 244–45; Goldstein, op. cit., pp. 579–607.

# 3

# Israeli Civilians during the 1973
# Yom Kippur War

———

*Dalia Gavriely-Nuri*

## Introduction[1]

On October 6, 1973, Israel came under a surprise attack by a coalition of Egypt and Syria, attacking on Israel's southern and northern borders, Sinai and the Golan Heights, respectively. The Yom Kippur War[2] was Israel's third war since its establishment 25 years earlier. The surprise outbreak fell upon the holiest day of the Jewish calendar, Yom Kippur (The Day of Atonement). According to Jewish tradition, on Yom Kippur, God has all the deeds of all of the living before Him, and he judges them throughout this day. Although Yom Kippur is a religious holiday, in Israel the gravity of the day has gained it respect and observance from most of the population, including the secular sectors. Most Israelis fast for twenty-four hours. Yom Kippur is the only holy day of the year that the broadcasting corporations choose to cease radio and television broadcasts out of acknowledgement of the publicly-accepted solemnity of the day. Streets and highways are almost completely empty of moving traffic, to the extent that children can be seen confidently riding tricycles in the middle of intersections. The combination of the surprise attack and the day it occurred was responsible for the absolute shock of Israeli citizens when the war-sirens were sounded at 2 p.m. Most Israelis heard that first war-siren while resting from their fast at home or while staring down at an open prayer book in synagogue.

However, a few hours before the outbreak of the war the Israeli government intuited that a war was imminent, and sent out an order to recruit all able-bodied men between the ages of 18 and 55. Public and private vehicles were filled with soldiers being transported to the front. Congregations of Yom Kippur prayers were interrupted, and the men filtered out of the synagogues. The military Rabbinate publicly waived the obligation to fast on account of the outbreak of fighting. The Rabbinate of Israel immediately relaxed the prohibition against work on the Sabbath or on religious holidays for anyone engaged in aiding national defence. The doctrine of *pekuach nefesh* (personal succour), a *Halachic* rule which holds that in instances where life is clearly in danger, religious observances may be bypassed, was invoked. Public broadcasting and transportation were operated massively on Yom Kippur for the first time since the establishment of the state.

The Yom Kippur war persisted for 18 days on the front lines, until a ceasefire was accepted by both sides. During this period, the citizens of Tel Aviv, Jerusalem and Haifa, the three largest cities, were instructed to enter their shelters on only a few occasions. With the exception of some missiles that were launched at the northern settlements, little damage was incurred to houses and buildings within the home front throughout the war. Nevertheless, the effect of the war on civilians was enormous, due to the fact that Israel's armed forces constitute a people's army.[3] Of the 300,000 men mobilized for defence, 200,000 were civilians drafted from all walks of life. In peacetime, these civilians held key positions in the economy and all other mechanisms that 'operated' the state.[4] Thus, one of the greatest challenges that home front civilians faced with the outbreak of the war was that of filling the absence of the men who were sent to the front lines.

The following sections will provide an initial mapping of the daily life of Israeli civilians during the Yom Kippur war, via reflection on two realms of home front life: citizens and social institutions. This perspective has hitherto received little attention in the retelling of the Yom Kippur war, despite the fact that people on the home front constituted 90 per cent of the Israeli population at the time. Within the realm of Israeli citizens, this composition will examine the wartime conduct and experience of the home front family, women, youth and children. It will not focus on minority groups (such as Arab-Israelis, Christians who live in Israel, etc.), nor on special groups within the Israeli population (such as orthodox Jews, members of kibbutzim,[5] etc.), since the basic purpose is to reflect the mainstream of Israeli public. Within the realm of social institutions, this chapter will focus on civil institutions in the broader sense: emergency institutions, media, aviation and transportation, volunteering and donations, commerce and industry, and social life and public morale. The overall aim is to shed light on the daily life of Israeli civilians during wartime, rather than to depict or assess the functioning of these institutions. This analysis hopes to contribute to filling the lacuna of research on the Israeli civilian population during wartime.

## Civilians during the Yom Kippur War

### The Family

Israel is a family-oriented society. The war further amplified family bonds between relatives and non-relatives. Maintaining contact between families on the home front and soldiers at the front lines became a national mission. Hundreds of private firms, companies and factories published their phone numbers in the newspaper, and offered themselves as go-betweens to soldiers who wished to convey messages to family members with no telephone. Within the main cities, assigned telephones were operated 24 hours a day by volunteers for the same purpose. Youngsters were not allowed to man the telephone positions since it was considered a very sensitive task to give messages to anxious families. The volunteers were to begin each message with the greeting: 'Sending peace.' Family members who received the regards were always very anxious to know where the soldier was placed.

Personal regards sent by soldiers over the radio to their families often sounded like sentimental love-letters. The majority of the soldiers were 'sons', and the family members on the home front most addressed were 'parents' and 'sisters'. That the 'son' was serving on the front lines was both a source of worry and a great source of pride for the entire family. Even the Prime Minister, Golda Meir, was described as a *Yiddishe Mama* (the proverbial Jewish mother) when she visited and encouraged wounded soldiers.

Families sent care-packages to soldiers that included small items intended for improving their quality of life, such as toothpaste, aftershave, and a personal letter which the entire family took part in writing. Sewing sweaters for the soldier-son turned into a national pastime. On each day of the war an average of 60,000 parcels and 100,000 letters were mailed (as opposed to 60,000 letters in 'regular' times), most of them either sent *from* soldiers or addressed *to* soldiers.

The war had a great influence on familial ceremonies and cele-brations. The Tel Aviv Rabbinate postponed all marriages scheduled for the first week of the war. From a practical point of view, most of the intended bridegrooms had been mobilized. Many personal advertisements announced the postponement of a wedding or a *Bar Mitzvah* (a religious initiation ceremony performed for a boy when he reaches the age of thirteen). In some cases a line was added: 'instead of the planned *Bar Mitzvah*, we decided to contribute the money to the soldiers'.

### *Women*[6]

On October 8, the third day of the war, *Ma'ariv* (a daily newspaper) wrote: "The streets, cinemas, suddenly all these places became so feminine. It is almost a shame for men to walk in town." While this wartime reality could have been an outstanding opportunity for Israeli women to achieve a superior status, instead it confronted Israeli women with the glass ceilings that had hitherto been less transparent. Women realized that they could not fill the empty chairs of the recruited men whom they had served in peacetime in positions of non-professional human resources, such as secretaries, clerics or, at best, minor managers. These non-professional female employees, who constituted a minority in comparison to the majority of women who were housekeepers, could not take the place of men simply because the chauvinistic Israeli society of the early seventies had excluded women from professional arenas and did not provide them with appropriate training.

Quite ironically, a salient example was the functioning of the central emergency organizations, *Melach* (emergency economy) and *Haga* (the Authority of Civil Defence). In times of both war and peace, these organizations relied on a task-force of high-ranking officers and army representatives, most of them men. When the war broke out, the men who operated these organizations had to remain on the home front instead of heading for the front lines, since women had not been trained to take over.

Rather than encouraging women to contribute to the war efforts in much needed ways, the war actually encouraged women to contribute through their traditional roles, for example, by baking and knitting for injured soldiers and caring for their family's basic needs. Thus, the war not only preserved, but also even reinforced women's traditional duties.[7] Tamar Avidar, a well-known journalist, wrote:

> It happened rapidly. The war broke out and suddenly we reverted back to ancient times, when men went to war to protect the tribe,

and the women remained at home, and when the man returns home, her duty is to provide for all his needs and to be accommodating to her man.[8]

The only course of action women could take in order to participate in the war efforts was to volunteer. Outstanding stories of the exceptional war contributions of women were published only in the fish-wrapping sections, as it were. For example, the youth magazine *Ha'aretz Shelanu* (Our Country), a popular magazine for youngsters, published a story about a female electronic engineer who had recently emigrated from the USSR. When she heard a radio broadcast about damages caused by Syrian missiles to settlements on the Golan Heights, she steadfastly drove up to the front to repair damages incurred by electrical circuits. She passed from one settlement to another, and solved all the problems perfectly.[9] Presenting such women as unique and outstanding reinforced the notion of women as a group of non-competent individuals. Hanna Herzog, a contemporary Israeli sociologist, concluded: "Due to the social structure that preceded the war, the war became an immense mechanism that reproduced the traditional gender role-division within Israeli society."[10]

### Children and Youth

The war broke out soon after the start of the school year. On October 7, the second day of the war, the Ministry of Education announced that all schools and day-care would be closed until further notice. A day later the pupils of higher classes were asked to return to schools. For younger pupils, schools opened until 11 a.m. The schools were fully reopened in the second week of the war, interrupting the usual holiday of *Sukkot* (the Jewish harvest festival). The Ministry of Education's policy was that a situation whereby children could be wandering in the streets at times of emergency should be avoided.[11]

Since most of teachers were women, operating schools was relatively easy. One problem faced by the school systems was the transportation of children whose schools were far from their homes. Another problem was that elementary school teachers found it difficult to assume responsibility for the children's safety, particularly in school districts that had no shelters or where the shelters did not have sufficient capacity.[12] Lecturers from universities, students, and soldier-teachers replaced teachers who were recruited. Unlike the schools, all universities postponed the beginning of the new academic year, since many of the lecturers and students had been recruited to the war effort.[13]

In the second week of the war an emergency pedagogical staff was established by the Ministry of Education to debrief school principals and teachers on how to conduct their curriculum during wartime. Teachers were told to maintain their teaching itinerary, but to match the lessons to the occurrences. Pupils were to tune into news broadcasts, and teachers were to dedicate lessons to fully explaining the significance of events occurring on the front lines. The Ministry of Education also organized a crew of psychologists to guide teachers on various topics pertaining to the influences of war.

Contributing to the war effort became the primary after-school activity during this time. Youngsters had spontaneously joined the war effort: they stopped cars on the street and offered to paint their headlights (in accordance with *Haga* instructions regarding the blackout), they helped deliver mail, bake goods in local bakeries, and harvest fruits in agricultural settlements. Children helped to prepare and maintain bomb shelters. *Ha'aretz Shelanu* published the following announcement:

> We too can contribute to the war efforts! Collect transistors, books, games, soaps, and combs, and bring them to the stations of the Soldiers' Welfare Committee in Israel. Enclose a letter to soldiers and tell them about your feelings. You will make them very happy. All those contributions will be sent immediately to the wounded soldiers of the IDF.

This call was heeded by many teenagers who went from house to house collecting the listed supplies, and bringing them to collection stations set up by the Soldiers' Welfare Committee.

Children's magazines of the time clearly reflect the widespread confusion among the children. At the onset of the war children commented that they were very pleased with 'the situation', namely that schools were closed at the beginning of the war, and that the atmosphere in school was less structured than it was in peace-time. These feelings were soon interfused with the children's perceptions of their mothers' and their teachers' anxiety. Many short articles published by youth in *Ha'aretz Shelanu* reflect the mixed feelings that the concept and actualities of the war aroused in the youth. The young writers pondered on the origins of war and about war as a phenomenon. Many youngsters wrote thank you letters to the brave soldiers. Others expressed their fury towards the 'coward Arabs' who had started the war on the day most sacred to the Jews. They expressed their fear of the war sirens. They wrote about their fear for their fathers serving on the front lines, alongside their pride in their brave fathers. Many of them were well up to date with the strategic moves made in the war. A ten-and-a-half-year-old child from Tel Aviv wrote: "I am attached to the radio like the snail is attached to its home." Many children thanked Israeli television for their beautiful programs and films. Many youngsters recounted their adventures as volunteers. Others expressed their hope for peace: "I hope that Arabs will learn the lesson from this war and that me and all the youngsters my age will not have to fight in 4–5 years."

As the war continued and the IDF began announcing the numbers of casualties, youth magazines gradually and increasingly reflected a sharp about-turn in the mood of the teenagers. Now they wrote about how they missed their dead brother or father. They wondered philosophically about life, death and war. Towards the end of the war, youth magazines began to publish letters that children and teenagers had sent to soldiers alongside the replies that they had received. Many Israelis aged 40–50 today have photographs taken after the war of themselves with the soldiers with whom they had corresponded during the fighting.

## Social institutions during the Yom Kippur War

### Emergency Institutions

According to Israeli law, two authorities are responsible for the civilian population during wartime: local municipalities and the Authority of Civil Defence (*Haga*). With a war experience only six years behind them, these authorities were able to mobilize quickly and efficiently. Soon after the outbreak of the war *Haga* began by preparing the population for hostile bombing of major cities. It employed 24 hour-a-day radio broadcasts to convey its messages to civilians: "Fill all available containers with water. Remove all flammable material from your houses and from air raid shelters. Tape up your windows. If possible, prepare a first-aid kit." Citizens were asked to avoid driving their vehicles and making use of their telephones. They were told to teach their children to distinguish between sirens with rising-falling tones that signal to residents to enter their shelters, and sirens with continuous monotone which signal all-clear.

The *Haga* spokesman asked persons with no shelter at home, or with no close public shelter, to dig slit trenches. He placed special emphasis on a total blackout at homes and businesses. Drivers were asked to paint over their car lights (they were allowed to leave a small white square at the center of the headlights). Three information offices were set up in Tel Aviv, to liaise between *Haga* and the public, and to answer public questions regarding preparations for the war.

Just before the outbreak of the war, the government ordered *Melach* (emergency economy), an organization responsible for providing essential commodities to the civilian population, to begin operating. *Melach* was stocked with enough essential commodities for at least for six months. Nevertheless, before seven a.m. on the second day of war, a panic-buying of food began and long queues of housekeepers formed outside supermarkets and groceries. They bought conserves, oil, flour, biscuits or anything else they could get their hands on. In some places people broke shop windows. The panic-buying spread quickly to thousands of people, and the police sent people to restore order. It is noteworthy that a major segment of the Israeli population at the time were Holocaust survivors, to whom starvation and absence of food was still very palpable. The food panic was quieted within a few days. Generally speaking, with the exception of a temporary shortage of specific products (such as batteries and matches) obtaining goods was not a critical problem. The extent to which the supply of food was not a critical problem was evidenced by the fact that *Melach* did not have to open even one emergency storehouse during the entire war.[14] It seems that this fact was of crucial importance in maintaining the public's morale as well as in safeguarding the public's trust in the government.

### *Media*[15]

On the eve of the war, *Galei Zahal* ('The Voice of IDF', the official IDF radio station) went into special alert, by order of the Chief of Staff. Reporters and producers received warning and the officer on duty at the station was handed an envelope with special codes used to call up certain army reserve units over the radio, in the event that it became necessary. Almost immediately after the sirens were sounded, *Galei Zahal* went on the air, announcing that Israel was being attacked by the joint forces of Egypt and Syria. This bulletin was repeated every few minutes, followed by a message of reassurance that the Israeli forces were warding off the enemy.

*Kol Israel* ('The Voice of Israel', the most popular station) and the Israeli television network began broadcasting soon after. Dozens of reporters joined the units at the front. At the end of the first day of the war *Galei Zahal* and *Kol Israel* merged, and began broadcasting the news together.

The radio was the primary source of information for people on the home front. People were continuously tuned in to the radio and were often seen walking in the street, holding transistor radios up to their ears. However, the media's steadfast answer to the call of war was not matched by efficiency in the days to come. In order to assess these broadcasts, one has to take into consideration the unique characteristic of communication channels in Israel at the beginning of the seventies. Israeli television began to broadcast only four years before the war, and offered only one state-controlled channel. The broadcasting was inspected thoroughly by the government. Similarly, the two main radio stations, *Galei Zahal* and *Kol Israel*, as well as the highest circulated newspapers, were controlled in various ways by hegemony. The idea of so-called 'self-censorship' was very common at the time.[16]

In retrospect, supplying the home front with reliable information turned out to be a complete strategic failure during the first days of war. The information received was totally blurred, and camouflaged the harsh reality on the two fronts. The newspapers painted an extremely euphemized and optimistic picture, portraying the Yom Kippur war as the seventh day of the Six Day War.[17] Local defeats of Egypt and Syria were depicted in great detail, while the defeats of the Israeli army were paraphrased and succinct.

However, information which wasn't transmitted via communications technology was soon passed on through the rumour mill, the alternative channel that exposed the shocking realities of the front lines. The plainly harsh realities were all the more shocking when contrasted with the near fabrications that the public had been spoon-fed by the media. As a result, Israelis began tuning in to the BBC and even to the *Voice of Cairo*. But this process took time. Throughout the 18 days of the fighting, the credibility of government spokesmen and of the media remained high and stable. It was only following the end of the war that the full extent of the misinformation came to light. These astounding revelations resulted in unprecedentedly sharp criticism against the Israeli media, voiced by citizens and professional journalists alike. These events proved historical in that they prompted a revision of the function of the media in Israel.[18]

During the war, the misinformation did serve one worthy cause. It enabled the Israeli media to succeed in its other wartime task, the task of easing public tension and strengthening national solidarity.[19] The media had become central to the lives of people who were forced by the circumstances of the war to remain inside their barricaded houses after dark.[20] It appears that the broadcasting authorities felt responsible for the gratification of the social and psychological needs of the audience, most of them women, children and the elderly. The television reformed its programming to include national and international entertainment programs for children and adults. It began broadcasting on Saturdays, the Jewish *Sabbath*, for the first time.

The last mission of the broadcasting authorities was to contribute to solidarity. The television broadcast many shows performed by entertainers before soldiers on the front lines. Showing the singers volunteering prompted feelings of solidarity among the people at home. On the whole, it is clear that the speed of radio made it the preferred medium to receive and transmit information, while television functioned more as a source of entertainment, relief and release, as well as a source of consensus and high national morale.[21]

## Transportation

From the beginning of the war, the roads of the cities were almost empty as most vehicles were recruited to drive supplies to the front. At night, traffic lights were deactivated as part of the blackout. The National Council for the Prevention of Accidents made a public announcement instructing citizen drivers to heed special precautions while driving at night. Many citizen car accidents did in fact occur during the first days of the war, and in response the Tel Aviv municipality ordered that traffic lights be reactivated at five main junctions during the blackout.

On the second day of the war, *Dan*, a central Israeli cooperative of public buses, made the following press announcement: "Dan cooperative requests the public's patience in light of the likely mishaps and the low frequency of some of the [bus] routes." The management of the Israeli railway announced that some routes would be cancelled.

Civil aviation was also greatly affected by the war. When the war broke out 25,000 tourists were vacationing in Israel. They soon found themselves caught in the throes of an unexpected war, with little chance of a regular departure. In the early hours of the second day of the war,

Lod, the central Israeli Airport, became flooded with foreign visitors. Two thousand successfully departed Israel on overnight flights.

While there was a frenzy of tourists clamouring anxiously at the departure gates, there were also many tourists who insisted on staying behind to help. Similarly, thousands of Israelis who were abroad when the war broke out beseeched airlines to fly them back to Israel. Many tourist groups continued to come to Israel, most of them Jews, while many other groups postponed or cancelled their scheduled trips.

As a result of these events, during the first days of war, *El Al*, the national airline carrier, undertook the biggest operation in its history. In the first week of war it surpassed its heaviest regular schedule in any previous week. It also remained the only regular air link with the outside world since Lod Airport was declared closed to civilian air traffic following the outbreak of fighting on October 6. On the fifth day of the war the airport was reopened to routine civilian air traffic. Foreign aviation companies, however, chose not to resume their flights to Israel during wartime.

### Commercial and Industrial Life

Commerce and industry during the Yom Kippur War were naturally affected by the drastic reduction of manpower and motor vehicles. This shortage was greatly pronounced by the sight of desolate shopping centres in the central cities during the first days of the war. The two biggest drugstores in Tel Aviv, *Kolbo Shalom* and *Hamashbir Lazarchan*, were almost empty. The drastic decrease in commercial life was further exacerbated by the Israeli Organization of Merchants, which ordered shops to close their doors by 5.30 in the evening.

With the outbreak of the war, production declined to 40 per cent of its usual rate.[22] Certain branches of industry and production particularly suffered during wartime. For one, construction ceased completely, seeing that most of the workers were Israeli Arabs who feared that Israelis would associate them with the attack of Egypt and Syria. Food production in major factories continued with great difficulty, mostly with regard to delivering supplies to shops. Many factories requested that the shops undertake collecting the goods themselves. For example, *Osem*, one of the biggest food production factories in Israel, had 300 of its 850 workers recruited to the army during the period of the war. As a result, the remaining *Osem* workers were required to work additional hours.

Although the Israeli stock exchange continued to operate during the war, the volume of transactions was low. The value of the dollar inflated as people bought mostly dollars and gold. All bank branches opened on a regular basis from the second day of the war despite the recruitment of many of the workers. Banking institutions continued to receive regular deliveries of currency, but they cut down the types of services offered to customers and concentrated mostly on the release of cash to the public and on dealing with deposits.[23]

Small enterprises and workshops undoubtedly took the full force of the blow. 'For Sale' and 'Wanted' columns in newspapers continued to run in a very condensed manner, advertising apartments, shops and cars. In a sense, these advertisements were not just commercial but cultural as well. Their subtext read: wartime civilian life continues, but to a very limited extent.

### Volunteering and Donation

One of the most moving phenomena of the war was the spirit of volunteering for the war effort.[24] On the first day of the war a wave of volunteers flooded the offices of the municipalities and mostly hospitals. Women, youth and the elderly all tried to find their niche in the war efforts. When the hospitals began admitting wounded soldiers, the influx of volunteers that arrived on the doorstep of emergency rooms was overwhelming, to the extent that they had to be actively turned away. In some cases hospital management was forced to call the police to intervene in organizing the volunteers. Once the initial influx had passed, the volunteers worked along with regular hospital personnel entertaining patients, helping doctors on rounds, filling sandbags, moving beds and distributing laundry.

Volunteers also flooded the halls of the Israeli first aid service, *Magen David Adom*. White collar professionals volunteered as ambulance drivers and took part in duty rotations at the stations while those who could not volunteer their services, volunteered their blood. At *Magen David Adom* stations, more than 17,000 portions of blood were donated throughout the war.

On the 11th day of the war, newspapers reported that more than 4,000 teenagers had been employed as volunteers in Tel Aviv, most of them in hospitals, bakeries and other essential services. They assisted in loading and shipping produce, and in assuring a steady flow of provisions between farms and the metropolitan grocers. About a thousand youngsters spent the days digging trenches in parks and boulevards and putting up sandbags for air-raid shelters. Many girls did babysitting for mothers who operated businesses while their husbands were away at the war front.

In Ramat Gan, a big city next to Tel Aviv, a special initiative was taken whereby the municipality sent requests to citizens asking them to volunteer for specific missions at stations close to their homes. Most of those addressed complied. As a result of this enterprise, the volunteering in Ramat Gan was much more effective than that in other cities.[25] One week into the war, the government erected volunteer manpower centres. Volunteers were officially registered in these offices and referred by these offices to where their services were most needed. Generally speaking, recruiting volunteers ad hoc was inefficient. This inefficiency stemmed from the minimum guidance of the volunteers and from the fact that most volunteers preferred attractive and dramatic duties, such as taking care of wounded soldiers.

One special aspect of volunteering was the volunteering of artists. Israeli and Jewish actors and comedians volunteered to perform before an audience of wounded soldiers in hospitals. Three world-famous Jewish entertainers – the poet Leonard Cohen, comedian Danny Kaye, and singer Enrico Macias – arrived in Israel to visit the wounded in hospitals. A group of 60 painters and sculptors organized an auction of their work, with contributions going to soldiers.

Other than volunteering, the desire of citizens to contribute to the war efforts was expressed in monetary contributions. A stirring announcement was made by the Public Committee of Volunteering, at the beginning of the war:

> Citizens, families, we are in the midst of a difficult struggle, and in order to achieve victory – which we are sure will come – the public must make a special effort. The rulers of Egypt and Syria have forced us into a war on two fronts at one and the same time. The Israeli Defence Forces are at the height of a battle to push back the aggressors. In order to achieve victory and in order, as far as possible, to reduce losses, the IDF must be strengthened while in the midst of war. The IDF must obtain all it needs without delay – in the way of equipment and weapons. All of us, all Israel, must put these weapons into the hands of our army. Each one of us will imagine that his part in the effort will tip the scale of victory . . . we call upon every citizen and every family to respond to this urgent call . . .

Newspapers soon began publishing: "the following have decided to make a personal contribution amounting to one month's salary for the Voluntary War Loan . . ." Dozens of such announcements were published in the following days. Newspapers also published names of wealthy individuals who donated large amounts of money. The newspapers were full of exciting stories of donations, such as that of a disabled Druze man, father of ten, who had contributed his monthly welfare stipend to the IDF.

Another exciting phenomenon was the magnitude of expressions of solidarity with Israel pouring in from all over the world. Amsterdam City Council sent a telegram to the Mayor of Jerusalem, expressing solidarity with Israel. A similar message was sent by the Mayor of Copenhagen. West Berlin Mayor telephoned, asking the endorsement of the Jerusalem Mayor for a solidarity meeting. Jews and non-Jews in Britain donated thousands of pints of blood. On the ninth day of the war, a mass solidarity demonstration took place in Trafalgar Square. Jewish communities all over the world donated money. Baron Edmond D. Rothschild donated six times the amount of funds that he donated to Israel during the Six Day War.

### Social Life and Public Morale

The fact that the war was conducted almost solely on the front lines only technically enabled recreational life in Tel Aviv to resume. The war seemed to de-glorify the morning life of cafés and to sober up the nightlife of clubs along Dizengoff Boulevard (the most lively and trendy street in Tel Aviv). Some cafes which were reopened for business in the evening tried to comply with the instructions by following the blackouts. Catering halls were completely shut down, and a similar situation existed in high-class restaurants. On the other hand, the cheaper restaurants operated almost as usual.[26]

At first, it seemed the show would go on in the cinemas and theatres. Then, during the second week of fighting, the national theatre, *Habbima* in Tel Aviv, announced that scheduled shows would be temporarily cancelled because most of the acting crew had been called away to reserve duty. Other theatres began producing plays that were congruent with the state of the nation. The *Cameri* Theatre staged a production of *Be'Moral Gavoah* ('With High Morale'); the theatre of Haifa announced free entrance to its production of *Be'Sherut Zvayi* ('In Military Duty').

Then, a few days after announcing the cancellation of its shows, *Habbima* reopened with the production *Shalom, Shalom, Ve'Ein Shalom* ("[You say] 'Peace', 'Peace', and 'There is no Peace'").

Movie houses were closed for the three weeks of the war, and when they were reopened, they drew in only 10–30 per cent of their normal occupancy.[27] On the fourth day of war, the Israeli Philharmonic Orchestra, one of the most prestigious orchestras in the world, initiated a special noontime concert. The orchestra was conducted by Maestro Zubin Mehta, with the pianist Daniel Barenboim and the violinist Pinchas Zuckerman as the soloists. Thousands of people arrived and the hall and corridors were full. At first, the orchestra played *Hatikva*, the national anthem. Soon, other orchestras joined the initiative of the Philharmonic Orchestra, and invited the public to special free concerts in the central cities. In these concerts the audience was cordially asked to contribute money to the Committee for the Soldiers. The planned concerts of the Philharmonic Orchestra were conducted according to the plans.

In hindsight, the contrast between the historiography of the Yom Kippur War as the most difficult Israeli war and the public morale during the war was bitterly ironic. It seems that the sobering imminence of the battle days to come was somehow overcome by the intoxication of victory of the Six-Day War (1967). In the first days of the war, the public was not preoccupied with whether Israel would win, rather it pondered on how quickly Israel would win, or how elegant this victory would be. The media, in a sense, enabled and even promoted the public's flight from reality through its very selective reporting.

Eliahu Salpeter, a journalist for *Ha'aretz*, wrote on the third day of the war:

> Opposed to the Six-Day War (1967), at this time there is no emergency atmosphere. There is self-confidence. No one is afraid about the results of the offensive on the home front . . . The feeling of the public is that there is an absolute inferiority to the IDF and it is clear that victory is coming soon.[28]

Questionnaires conducted throughout the war seem to reflect the public morale. The public confidence in the IDF's chances of victory, as exhibited during the first days of the war, was even higher than during the Six-Day War. As the war progressed, public confidence proved to be unfaltering. One low-point did occur on October 16, when the government first announced the high number of casualties. However, the morale shot up again soon after.[29] As reflected in the questionnaires, the public put its faith not only in the IDF, but also in the government. It did not question government announcements nor were the government's strategies of crisis intervention doubted. On the other hand, it seems that the public was very suspicious about Arab broadcasts that reported their battlefield successes.

The most dramatic point reflected in the questionnaire was the public's confidence in Israel's ability to defend itself without international assistance. On this point the public exhibited 'extreme optimism': 84 per cent was absolutely sure that Israel was strong enough to stand alone against its enemy. This belief was especially strong in the first days of the war. It slightly declined in the ensuing days, and then increased once more after the government announced for the first time the number of casualties. This belief reached a peak after the announcement that some units of the IDF had crossed the Suez Canal and were fighting in Egyptian territory.

The Yom Kippur War came to represent a unique unifying force along the many social boundaries within Israel. Young Israeli men, living abroad at the time, boarded flights to Israel, and then caught taxis from Lod Airport to the war fronts. Israeli-Arabs stood in line to donate blood to soldiers. Likewise, many members of the Christian community in Israel offered help.

Even political boundaries became blurred when the dust of war began to settle. Elections for the Israeli parliament (the Knesset) were scheduled for the end of October. In the days prior to the war, newspapers had been filled with the political campaigns of the running parties. However, once the war broke out these advertisements were withdrawn from the newspapers: leaders of the biggest political parties had concurred that election propaganda was inappropriate during war time, and joined hands in postponing election campaigns until after the war.

**The End of the War**
On October 25, *The Jerusalem Post* reported:

> The lights went on again all over Israel last night, after 18 nights of darkness. The end of the blackout was officially announced

over radio and television at about 5.30 p.m. by the National *Haga* Commander. Promptly, blacked-out windows all over the country were flung open, and the home lights – enhanced by the beaming faces of the apartment occupant – shattered the darkness. In Tel Aviv, many who had not heard the announcement started arguing with people who had turned on their lights along Dizengoff Boulevard. Car owners went down to wipe the paint off their car lights. And the traffic lights were a confusing mess for several hours till the Municipal technicians got them all working properly again.

However, the festivities were disappointingly fleeting. Soldiers came home on their first vacation since the outbreak of the war, and for the first time they were able to share the atrocities of war with their families in an uncensored way. For many other Israeli families their soldier-sons did not come home. Whether personally affected or not, the numbers told the story: Israel suffered 2,569 casualties, more than 7,500 wounded soldiers and 314 POWs. Per capita, Israel suffered as many casualties in less than three weeks of fighting as the United States did during almost a decade of fighting in Vietnam. The disparity between the victory songs and the death toll left the Israeli public in a state of shock. Although the figures were unfathomable at first, ultimately they were convincing and conclusive. Optimism was quickly replaced by anger and grief.

Although a ceasefire was announced, battles pursued in moderation on both fronts for a couple of months until approximately May–June 1974, when the separation-of-forces agreement was signed with Egypt and Syria. The ensuing battles, and the fact that only part of the reserves was released, laid a heavy emotional and economic burden on the home front. Small businesses collapsed, payrolls were not kept up and bills were not paid. The situation of the self-employed was perceived as so severe that the government announced the establishment of a fund for rehabilitating businesses.

Four months after the end of the war anti-government protests began, led by Motti Ashkenazi, the commander of the only stronghold next to the Suez Canal not to be captured by Egyptians during the war.[30] The protestors raged against the Israeli government as a whole, and the Minister of Defence, Moshe Dayan, in particular. Shimon Agranat, former President of the Israeli Supreme Court, was chosen to lead the Commission responsible for investigating the events leading up to the war and the setbacks of the first few days.

Although the Yom Kippur War has been considered a military victory, it actually weakened the confidence of Israelis in the military supremacy of their state within the region.[31] This process has a positive side: it eased the ethos of life by the sword that had accompanied the Israeli story since the establishment of the state.[32]

At the same time, the Yom Kippur War cancelled the effect of the great defeat of the Egyptians in the Six Day War and rehabilitated their pride. These two effects served as a comfortable platform for the peace treaty which was signed six years later and ended decades of hostility between Israel and Egypt.

## NOTES

1 Hundreds of academic essays, popular articles and books have been dedicated to the topic of the Yom Kippur War. Surprisingly, few of these compositions have touched upon civilian, quotidian life during the war.

2 Though 'October War of 1973' is a more neutral term, this chapter deals with the domestic situation within Israel where the war is referred to as the Yom Kippur War, hence the use of the expression here.

3 Stuart Cohen, 'Israel's Defense Force: From a "People's Army" to a "Professional Force"', *Armed Forces and Society*, Vol. 21 (1995), pp. 237–54; Uri Ben Eliezer, 'Is a Military Coup Possible in Israel? Israel and French-Algeria in Comparative Historical-Sociological Perspective', *Theory and Society*, Vol. 27, No. 3 (1998), pp. 311–49.

4 About 30 percent of the total civilian labour force was called up, see Baruch Kimmerling (in collaboration with Irit Backer), *The Interrupted System – Israeli Civilians in War and Routine Times* (New Brunswick, New Jersey: Transaction Publishers, 1985), p. 3.; Harold H. Hart, *Yom Kippur Plus 100 Days – The Human Side of the War and Its Aftermath, as shown through the columns of The Jerusalem Post* (New York City: Hart Publishing Company Inc., 1974).

5 Regarding special characteristics of the civilian population in kibbutzim during the war see Mordechai Kaufman, 'Kibbutz Civilian Population under War Stress', *British Journal of Psychiatry*, Vol. 130 (1977), pp. 489–94.

6 References to women were quite marginal both in the newspapers of 1973 as well as in studies that deal with the Yom Kippur War. See Rivka Bar-Yosef and Dorit Padan-Eisenstrak, 'Role System under Stress: Sex Roles in War', *Social Problems* (1977), Vol. 20, pp. 135–45; Hanna Herzog, 'Women in Politics and Politics of Women', in Dafna N. Izraeli et al., *Sex, Gender, Politics* (Tel Aviv: Hakibbutz Hameuchad, 1999), pp. 307–55 (in Hebrew); Hanna Herzog, 'Knowledge, Power and Feministic Politics' in Baruch Kimmerling (ed.), *Sociology of Politics* (Raanana: The Open University, 2005), pp. 387–406 (in Hebrew).

7   Bar-Yosef and Padan-Eisenstrak, 'Role System Under Stress: Sex Roles in War'.

8   *Ma'ariv*, October 16, 1973.

9   *Ha'aretz Shelanu*, October 22, 1973

10  Herzog, 'Knowledge, Power and Feministic Politics', p. 340 (translated by the author).

11  Kimmerling, *The Interrupted System*, p. 64.

12  Kimmerling, *The Interrupted System*, p. 64.

13  Although the academic year began after the cease-fire declaration on October 24, most of the recruited students were still on the front lines. Universities made great efforts to help the recruited students by sending lecture summaries to all soldier-students, by setting additional and flexible examination dates for students who had been recruited, and so on.

14  Kimmerling, *The Interrupted System*, p. 53.

15  Gabriel Weimann, 'What has television broadcasting not learned from the lessons of the Yom Kippur War?', *Otot* (in Hebrew), Vol. 44 (1982), p. 13. For more about media during the Yom Kippur War see Moshe Negbi, *Paper Tiger* (Tel Aviv: Sifriat Poalim, 1985), pp. 87ff.

16  Dina Goren, 'The Press in the Yom Kippur War' in: *Secret, Security and the Freedom of the Press* (Jerusalem: Magnes, 1975), pp. 242–53 (in Hebrew); Tsiyona Peled and Elihu Katz, 'Media Functions in Wartime: The Israeli Home Front in October 1973', in Jay G. Blumler and Elihu Katz (eds.), *The Uses of Mass Communications: Current Perspectives on Gratifications Research* (Beverly Hills: Sage, 1974), pp. 49–69.

17  Harold H. Hart, *Yom Kippur Plus 100 Days – The Human Side of the War and Its Aftermath, as shown through the columns of The Jerusalem Post* (New York City: Hart Publishing Company Inc., 1974).

18  Negbi, *Paper Tiger*, p. 87.

19  Oz Almog, *Farewell to "Srulik"* (Haifa: University of Haifa and Zmora-Bitan, 2004), p. 209 (in Hebrew).

20  Susan Hattis Rolef, 'The Domestic Fallout of the Yom Kippur War', in P. R. Kumaraswamy (ed.), *Revisiting the Yom Kippur War* (London: Frank Cass, 2000), pp. 177–94.

21  Peled and Katz, 'Media Functions in Wartime', p. 55.

22  Kimmerling, *The Interrupted System*, p. 71.

23  Kimmerling, *The Interrupted System*, p. 54.

24  Kimmerling, *The Interrupted System*, pp. 119–43.

25  Yaacov Marcovitz, 'Emergency Economy (Melach) in Municipalities in the Test of The Yom Kippur War', *Leket Maamarim Vidiot Be'avoda Kehilatit*, Vol. 13 (1978), pp. 48–52.

26  Kimmerling, *The Interrupted System*, p. 75.

27  Kimmerling, *The Interrupted System*, p. 75.

28  *Ha'aretz*, October 8, 1973. In the Six-Day War, Israel conquered a large mass of territories and enlarged the territories under its control by four times.

29  Questionnaire of the Institute of Communication in the Hebrew University. Published in *Yedioth Aharonot* in October 24, 1973.

30  Motti Ashkenazi (together with Baruch Nevo and Nurit Ashkenazi), *Tonight at Six a War will Break Out* (Tel Aviv: Hakibbutz Hameuhad, 2003) (in Hebrew).

31 Abraham Rabinovich, *The Yom Kippur War – The Epic Encounter that Transformed the Middle East* (New York: Shocken Books, 2004), pp. 497–98.
32 On the various effects of the war on Israeli society see Hattis Rolef, 'The Domestic Fallout of the Yom Kippur War'.

# 4

# The Pathologies of Protracted and Displaced Collective Violence in Lebanon

*Samir Khalaf*

For almost two decades (1975–92), Lebanon was entrapped in recurrent cycles of collective strife and civil violence. Indeed, it was besieged and beleaguered by virtually every possible form of brutality and collective terror known throughout human history. From the cruelties of factional and religious bigotry to the massive devastations wrought by private militias and state-sponsored armies, Lebanon witnessed a near endless carnage of innocent victims and an immeasurable toll in human suffering. Even by the most moderate of estimates, the magnitude of damage to human life and property was staggering. About 170,000 people perished, and twice as many were wounded or disabled; close to two thirds of the population experienced some form of dislocation or uprootedness from their homes and communities. By the fall of 1982, UN experts estimated that the country had sustained US$12 to 15 billion in damages, that is, US$2 billion per year. Today, more than one third of the population is considered to be below the poverty line as a result of war and displacement.[1]

For a small, dense, closely-knit society of about 3.5 million, such devastations are, understandably, very menacing. More damaging, perhaps, are some of the socio-psychological and moral concomitants of protracted hostility. The scars and scares of war have left a heavy psychological toll which displays itself in pervasive post-stress symptoms and nagging feelings of despair and hopelessness. In a culture generally averse to psychoanalytic counselling and therapy, these and other psychological disorders and fears are even more debilitating. They are bound to remain masked and unrecognized and, hence, unattended to.

The demoralizing consequences of the war are also visible in symptoms of vulgarization and impoverishment of public life and an erosion of civility. The routinization of violence, chaos and fear only compounded the frayed fabrics of the social order. It drew seemingly pacific and non-violent groups into the vortex of bellicose conflict and sowed a legacy of hate and bitterness. It is in this fundamental sense that Lebanon's pluralism, radicalization of its communities, and consequent collective violence have become pathological and uncivil. Rather than being a source of enrichment, variety and cultural diversity, the modicum of pluralism the country once enjoyed is now generating large residues of paranoia, hostility and differential bonding.

It is also in this sense that, although the outward manifestations of violence have ceased, enmity today is deeper, assumes different forms and is more pervasive than it used to be at the initial stages of hostility. This is why the almost myopic concern with exploring the etiology of violence is not just short-sighted but has become counter-productive.

Unfortunately, much of the literature on civil strife, as I have suggested elsewhere,[2] both in Lebanon and beyond, continues to be concerned with its inception or origins. Consistent with the overwhelming bias inherent in most of the leading perspectives on collective violence, explorations of episodes of political unrest in Lebanon, as elsewhere, have also been skewed in that direction. Hence we know too much already about the preconditions, changing political settings (both regional and global), economic disparities, and cultural and psychological circumstances which motivated and predisposed groups to resort to collective protest.

Instructive as such analyses have been, they tell us little however about the forces which sustained violence and escalated its pugnacious brutalities. Nor do they disclose the changing forms of violence. More strikingly, perhaps, they do not help in understanding how seemingly ordinary citizens get entrapped in it and how traumatized groups come to cope with chronic hostility and fear. Likewise, this obsession with the origin of violence tells us comparatively little about the impact of the war on collective memory, on changes in group loyalties, collective psychology, perceptions and changing attitudes towards the 'other'.

At least in the case of Lebanon this obdurate exercise has become rather futile; at best a laborious elaboration of the obvious. For example, it is not very uncommon that a fragile, pluralistic society, caught up in regional and super-power rivalries, should display a high propensity for violence. The lack of political integration in such fragmented political cultures has been cited over and over again as a major cause, indeed a prerequisite, for political unrest. One could, likewise, write volumes about the destabilizing impact of internal socio-economic disparities, the presence of Syrians, Palestinians, Israelis, or the unresolved regional and global rivalries without adding much to what we know already.

What is, however, in need of elucidation is the persistence, growing intensity, shifting targets of hostility and the way violence acquired a momentum and a life of its own unrelated to the initial sources of conflict. Most atrocious in the case of Lebanon was the way violence splintered further as inter-communal rivalries degenerated into fratricidal bloodletting. The ecology of violence, reinforced by the demonization of the 'other', provided the sources for heightened vengeance and entrapment into relentless cycles of retributive in-fighting. Hence, much of the conventional characterization of the initial stages of civil unrest (that is, 'Christian versus Muslim', 'right versus left'), became readily outmoded as internecine violence and factional turf wars became bloodier and more rampant.

In an effort to redress this gap in the literature, an attempt is made here to elucidate some striking manifestations of collective violence which, in my view, are more instructive in helping us understand why the character of such strife has been both protracted and displaced and, consequently, more difficult to quell and mitigate. Four such attributes stand out.

First, and perhaps most compelling, there is a need to elucidate how some of the menacing cruelties of the war were normalized and domesticated. I will here argue that by 'sanitizing' the war and transforming it into an ordinary routine, terrorized groups were able to survive its ravages. By doing so, however, they also allowed it to become more protracted and diffused.

Second, I will argue that, unlike other comparable instances of collective violence, the nature of hostility was much more diffuse and fragmented into a plurality of warring groups and shifting targets of enmity.

Third, it is equally interesting to show how the war managed to reshuffle the country's social geography and impose its grotesque and ferocious logic on private and public space. Here again, by seeking shelter in communal solidarities, traumatized groups were able to find temporary relief from the atrocities of war. What enabled them, however, to survive its immediate horrors, rendered them more vulnerable to other more menacing long-term consequences. By distancing themselves from the demonized 'other', they could of course release their guilt-free aggression with impunity, but they also made themselves easier and more accessible targets to focused and directed acts of hostility. Casualties on both sides mounted. More damagingly, the obstacles to reconciliation and peaceful co-existence became more formidable, making them more unlikely.

Finally, and equally poignantly, I will highlight the psychological predispositions of traumatized and dislocated groups which enabled them to cope with the pervasive geography of fear, and provided them with the urge to reassemble damaged communal identities and broken history.

## The Sanitization of Violence

In some remarkable respects one might well argue that wars in Lebanon, despite some of their appalling manifestations, displayed comparatively little of the bizarre and grotesque cruelties associated with so-called 'primitive' and/or 'modern' forms of extreme violence; namely, the systematic rape of women by militias, the ritual torture and mutilation of victims, the practice of forcing family members of a family group at knife- or gunpoint to kill each other.[3] Other than episodic massacres and vengeful acts of collective retribution (Sabra and Chatila, Tal-el-Za'atar, Damour, etc.), there was little to compare to such planned and organized cruelty on a mass scale as extermination campaigns or pogroms, for example.

The incivility of collective violence in Lebanon was, nonetheless, visible in some equally grotesque pathologies, particularly those which domesticated killing by rendering it a normal, everyday routine – sanitized *ahdath* (events) bereft of any remorse or moral calculation. A few of these pathologies merit highlighting here.

Collective violence assumed all the aberrant manifestations and cruelties of relentless hostility. Unlike other comparable encounters with civil strife, which are often swift, decisive and localized, and where a sizeable part of the population can remain sheltered from its traumatizing impact, the Lebanese experience has been much more protracted and diffuse. The savagery of violence was also compounded by its randomness. In this sense, there is hardly a Lebanese today who was exempt from these atrocities either directly or vicariously as a mediated experience. Violence and terror touched virtually everyone.

Fear, the compulsion for survival and efforts to ward off and protect oneself against random violence had a levelling, almost homogenizing, impact throughout the social fabric. Status, class differences and all other manifestations of privilege, prestige and social distinctions, which once stratified and differentiated groups and hierarchies in society, somehow melted away. At least momentarily, as people fell hostage to the same contingent but enveloping forces of terror and cruelty, they were made oblivious of all distinctions, class or otherwise. Other than those who had access to instruments of violence, no one could claim any special privilege or regard. As Mai Ghoussoub poignantly put it, when people are suddenly thrown together into "anguished corridors and damp cellars", their statuses as well as their bodies are squeezed:

> The Civil war that sprang upon the country very soon engulfed the neighborhood in which Farid's second home was located. The stagnant, cozy routines of its inhabitants were so abruptly disrupted, and their streets turned so easily into an apocalyptic battlefield, that it was as if it had all happened under the spell of some magician's wand. The settled little hierarchies of these petty bourgeois clerks, these shopkeepers and their families, were suddenly huddled into anguished corridors and damp cellars, in which their status was squeezed as well as their bodies. The powerful and the less powerful, the compassionate and the unfeeling, the arrogant and the timid were brought to one same, common level in their struggle for survival. Nothing of what had once been mattered any longer, in the apocalyptic fires that governed their fate at this moment. They all feared the streets, and submitted willingly to the chaos of control by trigger-happy fighters.[4]

Equally unsettling, the war had no predictable or coherent logic to it. It was everywhere and nowhere. It was everywhere because it could not be confined to one specific area or a few combatants. It was nowhere because it was unidentified, not linked to any one concrete cause. Recurring cycles or episodes of violence erupted, faded and resurfaced for no recognized or coherent reason.

The warring communities had also locked themselves into a dependent relationship with violence and chronic conflict. It was in this sense that violence became both protracted and insoluble. It was a form of self-entrapment that blocked all avenues of creative peaceful change. It was also sustained by a pervasive feeling of helplessness, demoralization and an obsessive dependency on external patrons and foreign brokers. It was then that violence started to assume a 'tunnel vision' effect; that is, a tendency to focus, almost obsessively, on one's involvement in the conflict to the exclusion of any other relevant course of action. In acute cases, every action, every statement and every institution acquired value and meaning in relation to the conflict itself. So much so, in fact, that some observers at the time went as far as to suggest that in Lebanon violence and chronic fear had become an intrinsic part of society's ethos and mythology. It became an absorbing and full-time concern overshadowing, therefore, many other societal, communal and individual interests.[5] It might sound like a cliché, but violence became a way of life; the only way the Lebanese could make a statement, assert their beings or damaged identities. Without access to instruments of violence, one ran the risk of being voiceless and powerless. Literally, the meek inherited nothing. This is perhaps one of the most anguishing legacies of the arrogance and incivility of violence.

Abhorrent as it was, the fighting went on largely because it was, in a sense, normalized and routinized. In the words of Judith Shklar, it was transformed into an "ordinary vice"; something that, although horrible, was expectable.[6] The grotesque became mundane, a recurrent every-day routine. The dreadful and outrageous were no longer dreaded. Ordinary and otherwise God-fearing citizens could easily find themselves engaged in events or condoning acts which once provoked their scorn and disgust. In effect, an atrocious raging war became, innocuously, *ahdath* (literally events). This 'sanitized' label was used casually and with cold indifference; a true wimp of a word to describe such a dreadful and menacing pathology. But then it also permitted its hapless victims to 'survive' its ravages.

This is precisely what had transpired in Lebanon: a gradual pernicious process whereby some of the appalling features of protracted violence were normalized and domesticated. In a word, killing became inconsequential. Indeed, groups engaged in such cruelties felt that they had received permission, some kind of cultural sanction or moral legitimization for their grotesque deeds. Those witnessing these horrors were also able, by distancing themselves from their gruesome manifestations, to immunize themselves against the pervasive barbarism. Witnessing and coping with the dreaded daily routines of war also became remorseless and guilt-free.

The manifestations of such normalization are legion. In the early stages of the war, when bearing arms and combat assumed redemptive and purgative features, any identification with the garb, demeanour, or lifestyle of fighters and militia groups became almost chic; a fashionable mode of empowerment and enhancing one's machismo. Belligerency, in fact, was so stylized that groups literally disfigured themselves to ape such identities. Bit by bit, even the most grotesque attributes of the war became accepted as normal appendages to rampant chaos and fear. Literary accounts and personal diaries, often in highly evocative tones, recorded such pathologies with abandon. The daily body count was greeted with the same matter-of-factness, almost the equivalent of a weather forecast. Fallen bodies, kidnapped victims and other casualties of indiscriminate violence became, as it were, the barometer by which a besieged society measured its temporal daily cycles.

The biggest cause for dismay, however, was when these grotesque features of war began to envelop the lives of innocent children. All their daily routines and conventional modes of behavior – their schooling, eating and sleeping habits, playgrounds, encounters with others, perceptions, daydreams and nightmares, their heroes and role models – were inexorably wrapped up in the omnipresence of death, terror and trauma. Even their games, their language, their cognitive and playful interests became all warlike in tone and substance. Their makeshift toys, much like their fairly tales and legends, mimicked the cruelties of war. They collected cartridges, empty shells and bullets. They played war by simulating their own gang fights. They acquired sophisticated knowledge of the artefacts of destruction just as earlier generations took delight in identifying wild flowers, birds and butterflies.

There is hardly an aspect of Lebanese children's lives, and this is even more the case for adolescents who were involuntarily drawn into the fray of battle, that is exempt from such harrowing encounters. They have all been homogenized by the menacing cruelties of indiscriminate killing and perpetual anxieties over the loss of parents and family members. These and other such threats, deprivations and indignities continue to consume their psychological energies and traumatize their daily life. Successive generations of adolescents have, in fact, known little else.

Norbert Elias's notion of the 'sanitization of violence' could be of relevance here. It will most certainly help us in understanding not only how violence is camouflaged, even stylized so that it no longer seemed offensive, but how in the process it becomes protracted and insoluble.[7] During certain interludes, these same horrors were not only bereft of any moral outrage, they managed to become sources of fascination and venues for public amusement and entertainment. The war, in other words, began to acquire some of the trappings of a spectacle, not unlike the morbid fascination frenzied spectators encounter in the stylized rituals of a Spanish bullfight![8] In his recent book *On Killing*, Dave Grossman argues that a continuous presence of images of violence threatens to blur the line between entertainment and the conditioning of fighters and soldiers. He refers to a "stage of desensitization at which the infliction of pain and suffering has become a source of entertainment . . . we are learning to kill and we are learning to like it."[9]

Mai Ghoussoub recounts the transformation of Said, a cheerful, gentle and spirited grocer's son, the neighbourhood's most beloved boy, who was metamorphosed overnight into a callous and heartless killer. Said, the pride of his doting parents, was slated to fulfil his father's ambitions by pursuing his studies at the Ecole Hôtelière. Instead, he became so enamoured, almost entranced and bewitched, by the machismo and charisma of the militiamen, that he could not resist the temptations of becoming one himself, to the chagrin of his dismayed parents. This is how Ghoussoub depicts the episode signalling this anguishing transformation:

> . . . despite his mother's warnings and lamentations, he watches the groups of militiamen who have settled in at the entrance of the building facing his. They have all that he does not. And they are free of all that he has. The sad, heavy, constant presence of his parents worrying about him. Asking him to hide and keep a low profile, to smile, like his father, at every potential customer on the street. The militiamen are dressed in a relaxed but manly way. They sit on their chairs with their heads slightly tilted back, their feet stretched way in front; cigarettes hanging constantly from the corners of their mouths, they smoke and laugh and play cards just there on the pavement, next to the door of the building. When a jeep stops with a great sudden screech of its brakes, two lithe and powerful young men jump out of it, adjust the position of their Kalashnikovs on their shoulder and give big, generous handshakes to each one of the militiamen that Said sees from his balcony. To Said these men are beautiful. The glamour that emanates from them fills his heart with dreams. He would like to belong to these men, to be as attractive as they are, to feel as young and powerful as they feel, instead of totting in his miserable little apartment.[10]

This facile, almost effortless and light-hearted socialization of innocent adolescents into militancy is another disheartening legacy of the arrogance and incivility of collective violence. Said's case is far from anomalous. Legions of such recruits, often from privileged families, stable and entrenched middle-class groups, became willing volunteers to join the ranks of militias as regular fighters or subsidiary recruits. If one were to believe autobiographical accounts and obituaries of fallen fighters (often doctored to heighten notions of self-sacrifice, daring and fearless courage) they were all lionized into exemplary and mythical heroes. On the whole though, particularly during the early rounds of fighting, one saw evidence of over-zealous fighters buoyed by the bravado of their savagery and warmongering. This is again a reminder that killing is not a byproduct of some crazed deranged monster-like creatures driven by the frenzy of atavistic and irresistible compulsion for aggression. Rather, it is more often the outcome of ordinary people being induced by like-minded peers or the aura of bearing arms in defence of threatened values.

This is precisely what Primo Levi had in mind when he cautioned: "Monsters exist, but there are very few of them to present any real danger. Those who are dangerous are the ordinary men." More anguishing is to bear witness to how ties of trust, intimacy, benevolence and caring among neighbours were readily deflected and deformed into enmity. Once embroiled in such structured and heightened enmity one is compelled to take revenge for his group even though he might bear no particular grudge against those he is driven to kill. Here, as well, entrapped combatants flung themselves, often irrationally, into a relentless war of gang fights linked to one concrete cause. Recurring cycles or episodes of violence erupted, faded and resurfaced for no recognized or coherent reason.

## Multiple and Shifting Targets of Hostility

Unlike other comparable experiences with protracted collective violence, hostility was not confined to a limited and well-defined number of combatants and adversaries. By spring 1984, it had already involved no less than 186 warring factions, splinter groups with different backgrounds, ideologies, sponsors, grievances, visions and justifications as to why they had resorted to armed struggle.

It was this bewildering plurality of adversaries and shifting targets of hostility which rendered the Lebanese experience all the more gripping and pathological. For example, from 1978–82, the interlude falling between the two Israeli invasions, the country was besieged and beleaguered by every conceivable form of collective violence and terror. The sheer volume and magnitude of such incidents peaked in comparison to all other 'rounds' or phases of the war. Keeping track of who was fighting whom, the swift oscillation in proxies and sponsors, the targets of hostility and the motives propelling and sustaining the violence, is a dizzying and perplexing task.

Virtually no area in the country was spared the ravages of war. All traditional battlegrounds were ablaze. East Beirut was still under siege from relentless Syrian bombardments. Many residents had no choice but to seek shelter, much as they resented it, in West Beirut. Even though at the time the neighbourhoods of West Beirut were still riven with turf battles between the Mourabitoun and other Sunni Muslim rivals, the area was still considerably safer than Achrafieh, which repeatedly came under heavy and devastating artillery fire from the Syrian army. Both suburbs of Beirut were embroiled in intra-communal turf wars. After Bashir Gemayel (the future President of Lebanon) gained effective control of the Lebanese Forces (a coalition of all Maronite militias comprising the Phalange, Tanzim, Tigers and Guardian of the Cedars) in spring 1977, he proceeded to consolidate his powers by subduing his potential rivals. Hence there were repeated incursions into the strategic coastal enclaves of Dany Chamoun's Tigers, particularly the military installations at Safra and Amsheit. These were finally overrun (on July 7, 1980), after bloody and fierce assaults which wiped out over 150 innocent civilians. Christian militias were also engaged in intermittent clashes with Armenian leftists and the Syrian National Party (PPS).

On the southern fringe, confrontations between Amal and the Communist Action group were already disintegrating into open shoot-outs, a preamble to the more contentious struggles between Amal (a Syrian proxy) and Hezbollah (an Iran proxy). Further north, Franjieh militias were still trying to thwart the encroachment of Gemayel's Lebanese Forces into their traditional fiefdom. In June 1978 Bashir's commandos made a fateful crossover which ended in the tragic massacre at Ihden where over 40 members of the Franjieh clan were murdered including Tony (the heir apparent to the clan's leadership), his wife and child.

In Tripoli, Sunni centrists and Sunni radicals were engaged in pitched battles. The former were supported by the Syrians, the latter by the PLO and Muslim fundamentalists. In the Beqá, particularly Zahlé, Ba'albek and Chtoura, Bashir Gemayel had hoped to link up with Zahlé, the largest Christian enclave in the central Beqá. Being armed and assisted openly by the Israelis, he was over-zealous in his foray. The Syrians, of course, were not likely to accept such an affront on their hegemony in so strategic a region. They besieged the town for three months and drove Bashir out of the Beqá.

The Palestinians and Shiites were also embroiled in their own pernicious strife between and among their various factions. In addition to the on-going rivalry between pro-Syrian Amal and pro-Iranian Hezbollah, the latter were split further between those loyal to indigenous leaders like Sheikh Fadlallah and those affiliated to Iranian clerics in the Beqá. The in-fighting within the various Palestinian factions was also unabated. Pro-Iraqi and pro-Syrian groups sought to resolve their regional and ideological rivalries in Lebanon. So did Arafat loyalists and those opposed to him.

This became much more pronounced in the wake of mounting public discontent with the PLO's disgraceful conduct during the Israeli invasion of 1982. Syria deployed several of its local proxies to undermine Arafat. It bolstered the 'Palestine Salvation Front' with the military units of Abu Musa, the dissident Fatah rebel. Along with Syria's Sa'iqa and the Yarmouk brigade, they battled Arafat's forces from mid-1983 onwards. In Tripoli they were joined by the local 'Alawi militias and other Syrian client groups such as the Ba'ath and the Syrian Nationalists (SSNP).

Marginal ethnic groups like Armenians and Kurds, as if drawn into the vortex of belligerency by contagion, also found alibis to redress their differences by resorting to arms.

The most beleaguered region was, of course, the South. Added to the inveterate splits between the traditional Zuáma and scions of feudal and neo-feudal families, the South was splintered further by the volatile and vacillating hostility between and among the various Shiite and Palestinian factions, exacerbated by the presence of the Israeli-backed Saad Haddad's South Lebanese Army (SLA). The major breach between

Amal and Hezbollah, fuelled by their Syrian/Iranian patronage, was also compounded by the emergent hostility between Palestinians and Shiite villagers. Embittered by the havoc and terror Palestinians were spawning in the South, some of the Shiites of Jabal Amil were drawn into the SLA.

So multiple, so various and explosive are the sources of belligerency, South Lebanon is doubtless today one of the world's most perennial war zones and killing fields; a peerless example of 'low intensity conflict' that never goes away. Given the mounting casualties, the prefix 'low' does not do justice to the magnitude of cruelties the southerners are subjected to. Its hapless victims live in constant fear of being killed or displaced without anticipating or recognizing the identity of their victimizers. Villagers are not only terrorized by the turf wars of warring factions, they are also the surrogate victims of state-sponsored armies. Indeed, villagers in the south could well be bombarded by at least six different sources: Israelis, Syrians, Palestinians, the so-called Republic of Free Lebanon (SLA), UNIFIL and the Lebanese Army, if and when it ventured south.

Is this not the ultimate in incivility, a feature which compounds the futility and impunity of violence? Innocent citizens are victimized without being cognizant of the source or identity of their victimizers. In this regard it might be argued that Palestinians, Jews, Armenians, Kurds, Corsicans, Ulster Catholics, Basques, Bosnians, Serbs, Croats, and other victims of collective suffering are, perhaps, more privileged. They can, at least, identify and mobilize their outrage against those who might be held accountable for their suffering. The Lebanese are still unable, as a result, to vindicate their collective grievance. They have been homogenized by fear, terror and grief, but remain divided and powerless in identifying and coping with the sources of their anguish. Hence, they are gripped by a crushing sense of impotence and entropy. They are bitter but cannot direct or mobilize their fury and rage towards recognized targets.

## The Geography of Fear

Another striking and unsettling feature of protracted and displaced hostility is the way the Lebanese were caught up, after the outbreak of fighting in 1975, in an unrelenting process of redefining their territorial identities. Indeed, as the fighting blanketed virtually all regions in the country, few were spared the anguish of uprootedness from their spatial moorings. The magnitude of such displacement is greater than commonly recognized. Recent estimates suggest that more than half, possibly two-thirds, of the population has been subjected to some transient or permanent form of uprootedness from their homes and communities.[11]

Throughout the war, in other words, the majority of the Lebanese were entrapped in a curious predicament: that painful task of negotiating, constructing and reconfirming a fluid and unsettled pattern of spatial identities. No sooner had they suffered the travails of dislocation by taking refuge in one community, than they were again uprooted and compelled to negotiate yet another spatial identity or face the added humiliation of re-entry into their profoundly transformed communities. They became homeless, so to speak, in their own homes, or furtive fugitives and outcasts in their own communities.

The socio-psychological consequences of being dislodged from one's familiar and reliable landmarks, those of home and neighbourhood, can be quite shattering. Like other displaced groups, the Lebanese became disoriented and distressed because the terrain had changed and because there was no longer a neighbourhood for them to live in and rely upon. "When the landscape goes," says Erikson "it destroys the past for those who are left: people have no sense of belonging anywhere."[12] They lose the sense of control over their lives, their freedom and independence, their moorings to place and locality and, more damagingly, a sense of who they are.

Bereft of place, they become homeless in at least three existential senses. First, they suffer the angst of being dislodged from their most enduring attachments and familiar places. Second, they also suffer banishment and the stigma of being outcasts in their neighbourhoods and homes. Finally, much like the truly exiled, they are impelled by an urge to reassemble a damaged identity and a broken history. Imagining the old places, with all their nostalgic longings, serves as their only reprieve from the uncertainties and anxieties of the present.

The effusive war literature, particularly the generation of so-called 'decentrist' woman writers and other disinherited liberals, is clearly symptomatic of efforts to grapple with such damaged identities. A growing number of such exiled and uprooted writers felt homeless in their own homes. Much like the earlier generation of exiled Lebanese and Syrian poets (that is, Gibran and Rihani), who had transformed the anguish of their uprootedness into inventive literary movements (the Pen Bond and the Andalousian Group), they too found shelter in a "poetics of disaster".[13] But this brief, blissful interlude turned much too afflictive as the tensions between the vibrant Beirut of old and its foreboding dissent into anomie became more flagrant. Khalil Hawi's suicide on the eve of the Israeli invasion is seen now as a grim icon, a requiem for that dark abyss in Arab cultural history.[14]

Curiously, 'Beirut Decentrist' women found some redemption in the war. The chaos, anarchy, meaninglessness and the ultimate collapse of society gave women, paradoxically, a liberating place and a new voice.[15] Oddly, as society was unravelling itself and the country was being stripped of its identity, women were discovering venues for validating and asserting their own identities. Incidentally, this transformative, redemptive role did not mean that women were in effect challenging patriarchy or that they were partaking in efforts to restore civility in society. The war, as Miriam Cooke put it, gave them merely an occasion to register a voice:

> Their concern was not to gain acceptance into a predominantly male preserve but rather to register a voice. These voices were rarely heard in what has been termed the public domain. Their content was deemed irrelevant. How could the expression of private experience become acceptable outside its immediate confines? How could the apparently mutually exclusive domains of private and public, of self and other, be reconciled? Boundaries had to be challenged and shown to be fluid, elusive. Such a radical reassessment and construction of social and literary order could not be achieved spontaneously . . .
>
> The Lebanese war provided the context. Violence in this case represented universal loss of power, but it also undermined the private/public dichotomy, revealing the private to be public, and the personal to be universal. Private space became everyone's space and it was appropriated literarily in a collective endeavor to express and thereby understand the reign of unreason.[16]

But even as 'voice' or mere writing, the works of women remained marginal and frivolous. The writers themselves harbour few illusions in this regard other than seeing their personal struggles to forge new identities or reconstruct more coherent selves being closely tied to the enveloping malaise surrounding them. Cooke again provides evidence from the works of Ghada Al-Samman, Etél Adnan, Claire Gebeyli, Hoda el-Námani and Hanan al-Shaykh in support of this:

> By the late 1970s, the Beirut Decentrists were using language to create a new reality. Their writings were becoming transformative, even

prescriptive. As self-censorship gave way to uninhibited expressions of self-assertion, the hold of the oppressive male critic was shaken. It was only with the breakdown of Lebanon's identity as an independent patriarchal polity that women began to assert their female identity publicly . . . As the violence persisted and men fought senseless battles or fled, women came to realize that the society of which they were also members was collapsing; unraveling seams revealed the need for collective responsibility, but also for responsibility for the self. The individual had to become aware to survive. The time that was right for assertion of female identity coincided with the disintegration of the country's identity.[17]

This poignant predicament, that is, where the horrors of war are transformed into redemptive features, is most eloquently expressed in Hanan al-Shaykh's novel, *The Story of Zahra*. The torrents of war do not only render all conventions irrelevant and sweep away the hollowness of daily routine and restore normality. They accomplish much more: they became sources of illumination and self-discovery. Indeed, given the catalogue of horrors Zahra was subjected to in her 'normal' life (that is, intimate violence, incest, rape, arranged marriage and divorce), the war seemed more than just a blissful antidote and return to normality. In her own words, it made her "more alive and more tranquil":

> This war has made beauty, money, terror and convention all equally irrelevant. It begins to occur to me that the war, with its miseries and destructiveness, has been necessary for me to start to return to being normal and human.
> The war, which makes one expect the worst at any moment, has led me into accepting this new element in my life. Let it happen, let us witness it, let us open ourselves to accept the unknown, no matter what it may bring, disasters or surprises. The war has been essential. It has swept away the hollowness concealed by routines. It has made me ever more alive, ever more tranquil.[18]

Equally devastating has been the gradual destruction of Beirut's and, to a large extent, the country's common spaces. The first to go was Beirut's Central Business District which had served historically as the undisputed focal meeting place. Beirut without its 'Burj,' as the city centre is popularly labelled, was unimaginable. Virtually all the vital public functions were centralized there: the parliament, municipal headquarters, financial and banking institutions, religious edifices, transportation terminals, traditional souks, shopping malls, entertainment, etc., kept the pre-war 'Burj' in a sustained state of day- and night-time animation. There, people of every walk of life and social standing came together.

With decentralization, other urban districts and regions in the country served as supplementary meeting grounds for common activities. They, too, drew together, albeit on seasonal and interim bases, groups from a wide cross-section of society, thereby nurturing outlets germane for coexistence and plural lifestyles. Altogether, there were very few exclusive spaces beyond the reach of others. The social tissue, like all seemingly localized spaces, was fluid and permeable.

Alas, the war destroyed virtually all such common and porous spaces, just as it dismantled many of the intermediary and peripheral heterogeneous neighbourhoods which had mushroomed with increasing urbanization in cities like Tripoli, Sidon and Zahleh. The war did not only destroy common spaces. It also encouraged the formation of separate, exclusive and self-sufficient spaces. Hence, the Christians of East Beirut had no compelling urge to cross over to West Beirut for its cultural and popular entertainment. Likewise, one can understand the reluctance of Muslims and other residents of West Beirut to visit resorts and similarly alluring spots of the Christian suburbs. With internecine conflict, quarters within urban districts, just like towns and villages, were often splintered into smaller and more compact enclosures. Spaces within which people circulated and interacted shrank still further. The socio-psychological predispositions underlying this urge to huddle in insulated spaces is not too difficult to trace or account for.

This compulsion to huddle in compact, homogeneous enclosures further 'balkanized' Lebanon's social geography. There is a curious and painful irony here. Despite the many differences which divide the Lebanese, they are all in a sense homogenized by fear, grief and trauma. Fear, as it were, is the tie that binds and holds them together – three primal fears, in fact: the fear of being marginalized, assimilated, or exiled. But it is also those fears which keep the Lebanese apart. This 'geography of fear' is not sustained by walls or artificial barriers as one observes in other comparable instances of ghettoization of minorities and ethnic groups. Rather, it is sustained by the psychology of dread, hostile bonding and ideologies of enmity. Massive population shifts, particularly since they are accompanied by the reintegration of displaced groups into more homogeneous, self-contained and exclusive spaces, have also reinforced communal solidarity. Consequently, territorial and confessional identities, more so perhaps than at any other time, are beginning to converge. For example, 44 per cent of all villages and towns before the outbreak of hostilities included inhabitants of more than one sect. The sharp sectarian redistribution, as Salim Nasr has shown, has reshuffled this mixed composition. While the proportion of Christians living in the southern regions of Mount Lebanon (that is, Shouf, Aley and Upper Metn) was 55 per cent in 1975, it had shrunk to about 5 per cent by the late 1980s. The same is true of West Beirut and its suburbs. Likewise, the proportion of Muslims living in the eastern suburbs of Beirut has also been reduced from 40 per cent to about 5 per cent over the same period.[19]

Within urban areas, such territorial solidarities assume all the trappings and mythology of aggressive and defensive 'urban *'asabiyyas'*, which exist, Seurat tells us, only through their opposition to other quarters.[20] In this sense, the stronger the identification with one's quarter, the deeper the enmity and rejection of the other. Seurat's study also suggests that, once such a process is under way, a mythology of the quarter can develop. In it, the quarter is seen not only as the location where a beleaguered community fights for its survival, but also as a territorial base from which the community might set out to create a utopia, a world where one might live a 'pure' and 'authentic' life, in conformity with the community's traditions and values. The neighbour-hood community might even be invested with a redemptive role and mission (such as the defence of Sunni Islam in the case of Bab Tebbane in Tripoli, which Seurat was studying). Hence, the dialectics between identity and politics might be better appreciated. Politics implies negotiation, compromise and living side by side with 'the other'. Heightened feelings of identity, however, might lead one to a refusal to compromise, if negotiation comes to be perceived as containing the seeds of treachery that might undermine the traditions, values and 'honour' of one's community. In such a context, violence and polarization become inevitable: precisely the phenomena that have plagued Lebanon for so long.

A parting inference is in order. The resilience the Lebanese displayed in coping with and adapting to some of the treacherous and threatening manifestations of collective strife should not be viewed, as has been the case in a score of studies, as an enabling and redemptive feature. Yes, of course, the virtuosity of the Lebanese to transform the abhorrent cruelties of internecine and communal violence into a rather normal and ordinary routine allowed them to live with it. Yet, it was precisely those enabling features which allowed the war to persist and assume its most grotesque dimensions.

This is, incidentally, the anomalous context which has beleaguered Lebanon throughout its chequered political history. The more adept they became at adjusting to, or coping with, the barbarous pathologies of collective strife, the more opportunities the wars had to reproduce and sustain themselves. Again and again, in other words, the enabling and disabling features became inexorably locked together. The prospects for breaking such intermittent cycles of violence become all the more improbable.

## NOTES

1  For these and other related estimates, see Theodor Hanf, *Coexistence in Wartime Lebanon: Decline of a State and Rise of a Nation* (London: I.B. Tauris, 1993), pp. 339–57; Boutros Labaki and Khalil Abu Rjeily, *Bilans Des Guerres Du Liban, 1975–1990* (Paris: Editions L'Harmattan, 1993).

2  Samir Khalaf, *Civil and Uncivil Violence in Lebanon* (New York: Columbia University Press, 2002).

3  For further such details, see K. B. Wilson, 'Cults of Violence and Counter-Violence in Mozambique', *Journal of South African Studies*, Vol. 18, No. 3 (September 1992), pp. 527–82.

4  Mai Ghoussoub, *Leaving Beirut: Women and The Wars Within* (London: Saqi Books, 1998).

5  Edward Azar, *The Emergence of New Lebanon: Fantasy or Reality* (New York: Praeger Publishers, 1984), p. 4.

6  J. Shklar, *Ordinary Vice* (Cambridge, Mass.: Harvard University Press, 1982).

7  Norbert Elias, 'Violence and Civilization: The State Monopoly of Physical Violence and its Infringement', in John Keane (ed.), *Civil Society and the State* (London and New York: Verso, 1988).

8  Garry Marvin, 'Honour, Integrity and the Problem of Violence in the Spanish Bullfight', in David Riches (ed.), *The Anthropology of Violence* (Oxford: Blackwell, 1986), pp. 133–35.

9  Dave Grossman, *On Killing* (New York: Diane Publishing Co., 1998).

10  Mai Ghoussoub, *Leaving Beirut*, p. 81.

11  See Boutros Labaki and Khalil Abu Rjeily, *Bilans des guerres du Liban, 1975–1990*.

12  K. Erikson, *Everything in its Path: Destruction of the Community in the Buffalo Creek Flood* (New York: Simon and Schuster, 1976).

13  Ammiel Alcalay, *After Jews and Arabs: Remaking Levantine Culture* (Minneapolis: University of Minnesota Press, 1993), p. 99.

14  See Fuad Ajami, *Dream Palaces of the Arabs* (New York: Pantheon Books, 1998); Ammiel Alcalay, *After Jews and Arabs: Remaking Levantine Culture*.

15  For an elaboration of these, see Miriam Cooke, *War's Other Voices: Women Writers on the Lebanese War* (Cambridge and New York: Cambridge University Press, 1998); Ammiel Alcalay, *After Jews and Arabs: Remaking Levantine Culture*; E. S. Manganaro, *Bearing Witness: Recent Literature from Lebanon* (Madison, New Jersey: Fairleigh Dickinson University, 1994).

16  Miriam Cooke, *War's Other Voices: Women Writers on the Lebanese War*, p. 87.

17  Miriam Cooke, *War's Other Voices: Women Writers on the Lebanese War*, pp. 11–12.

18  Hanan Al-Shaykh, *The Story of Zahra* (London: Pan Books, 1986), p. 138.

19  Salim Nasr, 'New Social Realities and Postwar Lebanon', in S. Khalaf and P. Khoury (eds.), *Recovering Beirut* (Leiden: E.J. Brill, 1993).

20  Michel Seurat, 'Le Quartier de Bab Tebbané à Tripoli (Liban): étude d'une "asabiyya urbaine"', in CERMOC, *Mouvements communautaires et espaces urbains au Machreq* (Beirut: CERMOC, 1985), pp. 45–86.

# 5

# Revolution in Iran, 1979 – The Establishment of an Islamic State

*Stuti Bhatnagar*

On January 16, 1979, literally under the cover of darkness, Mohammad Reza Pahlavi, the emperor of Iran, accompanied by his wife, children and close personal aides, left Iran just days before the Islamic Revolution began. The person who called himself an heir to Cyrus the Great could not find a country that would be hospitable to the *Shahenshah* – the King of Kings. Suffering from non-Hodgkin's lymphoma the fragile Shah briefly went to the United States for treatment, then moved to Isla Contadora in Panama before settling down in Egypt. President Anwar Sadat, who was facing isolation in the Middle East for making peace with Israel through the Camp David Accords, was the only person willing to host the exiled Iranian ruler.

A few weeks later, Ayatollah Ruhollah Khomeini descended from the Air France plane that had brought him from Paris, where he had been living for the previous few years. That flight to Tehran on February 1, 1979, was a personal triumph for the ayatollah. Not only was he returning to Iran after being in exile since 1964, his arrival was marked by the departure of the brutal 'Satanic' Shah. Several million Iranians were on hand to receive the ayatollah in 1979, heralding the dawn of a new era in Iran.

Khomeini's arrival marked the end of monarchy in Iran and heralded a government aspired to by Muslims for centuries, that is a government led by the clergy. While many modern states had taken steps towards Islamic rule, Iran was the first one to give concrete shape to that idea. The prolonged struggle against the monarchy and apt mixing of religion and politics, something shunned by other renowned ayatollahs of his time, made Khomeini the spiritual head of the Revolution. The popular outpouring of protest against the Shah during the final days of the monarchy, spearheaded by the religious cleric, soon transformed into

[95]

massive support in favour of a revolutionary order. Though anti-monarchy sentiments ran deep among different segments of the population, not everyone was in favour of a new Islamic order. However, the clergy had organizational support and social-welfare networks across Iran. This provided them with formidable organizational ability to carry forward the protests into a triumphant revolution.

## Universal Endorsement

Unlike other similar upheavals in the Middle East and elsewhere, the Islamic Revolution enjoyed widespread social and political support and was enjoined by different segments of the population. From the *Tudeh* party on the Left, to the *bazaari* (merchant) elements in the middle, to the largely apolitical clergy, all had strong political grievances against the Shah and his policies. A large segment of Iranians disapproved of the Shah's pro-Western policies and his increasing dependency upon Washington for his survival. Instead of using the United States for his foreign policy designs, the Shah increasingly relied upon Washington to strengthen his domestic support. The oil boom of the 1970s did not help matters. His grandiose plans to build large palaces and resurrect the past glory of Persia angered his subjects. His well-attended celebrations in October 1971, marking the 2,500th anniversary of the founding of the Iranian monarchy by Cyrus the Great, was internationally acclaimed but ignored domestically.

His belated land reforms, commonly referred to as the 'White Revolution', antagonized the landed gentry whose lands were confiscated and re-distributed among the poor. It also alienated the clergy who held large tracts of land. Unlike their Sunni counterparts, the clergy in Shia Islam do not depend upon the rulers for their survival. Their ability to remain the champions of the downtrodden was dependent upon their willingness to stay away from official patronage. Social order is cardinal to Sunni Islam and hence, a bad Muslim ruler is considered better than anarchy or non-Islamic rule. This resulted in Sunni Islam being closely identified with the state and its rulers. Shi'ism, on the contrary, thrives on the notion of justice and rights and hence the clergy could not identify with rulers who were either unjust or un-Islamic.

The Shia ulema in Iran became more institutionalized under the Qajar dynasty. Sometimes supported by the Qajar shahs, the clergy greatly extended their spheres of influence and range of administrative powers.

They reestablished control over the courts, vaqf lands and innumerable other social and political functions.[1] They also developed financial resources that were independent of the state. The largest source of income for the religious establishment came in the form of religious taxes, namely *khums* and *zakat* (the paying of alms). Unlike the state, the ulema in Iran managed to develop one of the most efficient revenue collection schemes. In the absence of the power to enforce these taxes, the clergy made excellent use of moral and societal pressures to ensure the effective levying of the religious taxes on all segments of Iranian society. Apart from these mandatory contributions, the Shia clergy also benefited from the voluntary contributions of the wealthy landlords and middle-class merchants, in the form of charitable donations, wills, trust funds and testaments.[2] The money thus collected was supposed to be used for the maintenance and construction of religious sites, providing services to pilgrims, education and training of the ulema.

The financial autonomy of the ulema was seriously threatened by the establishment of the Office of the Endowments by the Pahlavi ruler, Reza Shah, in 1934. Created by the government to reduce the influence of the clergy, a series of laws were enacted between 1934–68 which enabled the Shah to appoint the caretaker (*mutawalli*) of the religious funds.[3] These laws further alienated the Shah from the people as they stopped making endowments and preferred to give funds directly to the clergy. Thus the trinity of religious scholarship, simple living and ownership of vast landed property, made the clergy not only a powerful institution but also capable of challenging the authority of the Shah, if and when needed. The clergy became the first victim of the land-reform introduced by the Shah. Large quantities of confiscated lands were re-distributed among the poor and through such measures the Shah was not only trying to shore up support from the poor but also trying to undermine the support of the clergy that thrived on landed property. In so doing, the Shah alienated himself from the clergy and also from those wealthy families who had donated such lands for charitable purposes.

The Shah's desire to seek closer ties with Israel and the visible presence of the Baha'i, despised by the conservatives, were fully exploited by the clergy. The monarch was accused of taking lands from the Islamic charity to hand them over to the Jews and 'heretics'. For the clergy, the land reform mainly sought to transfer Islamic lands to non-Muslim control and welfare.

Thus the largest group in opposition to the Shah was the Shi'a clergy. The Shi'a groups were represented by the Islamic Republican Party (IRP), established by Ayatollah Khomeini. The IRP was designed to form a bridge between the intellectuals and the ulema, and to build an Islamic society in Iran. The symbol of Shi'i fundamentalism, it advocated a return to the golden years of early Islam, strict implementation of Sharia and a moral purification of society. It was a coalition of various groups, including the *Hojatiye*, recognized for its fervent anti-Baha'ism, a faction of the *Fada'iyun Islam*, the *Mojahedin-e-Islam*, *Hezbollah*, and other groups. Although it represented irreconcilable interests of both the merchants and the lower classes, Khomeini's charismatic leadership and the recognition by all factions that they could not defeat their opponents on their own, kept the party relatively cohesive. The IRP's membership grew astronomically in the pre-revolutionary phase. It opened branches in major cities, organized political seminars and published a daily newsletter, the *Jomhuri-ye-Islami*.[4] Other groups that rose against Reza Shah Pahlavi were the *bazaaris* and the merchants of Iran, a vast majority of Iranian women and, surprisingly, the Iranian leftist parties.

Social reforms concerning women also boomeranged on the king. Following in the footsteps of his father he sought to improve the status of Iranian women. His reforms declared the wearing of *chador* or the traditional veil worn by Muslim women as illegal. He opened up the educational system to girls at the primary, secondary and post-secondary level and also provided employment access to women. As part of his modernization drive, in 1975 the Shah promulgated the Family Protection Act which considerably increased the rights of women. Diminishing the powers of *Sharia* (Islamic jurisprudence), it increased women's rights in family matters, especially regarding marriage, divorce and child custody. It also made a man's right to have a second wife conditional upon the explicit permission of the first wife. The civil courts began strictly interpreting 'equality' within the broader context of marriage, especially with regard to economic clauses. As a result, it was impossible to sustain polygamy. The Family Protection Act also curtailed the powers of husbands to practise unilateral divorce. It also gave the family courts the powers to decide the child custody of divorced couples. Under the traditional practice, it was the father or the nearest male relative who had custody of children of divorced parents.[5]

These far reaching reforms, however, did not go down well within society. The clergy were angered at their marginalization even in the realm of personal laws and ironically many Iranian women were appalled at social transformations sought by the Shah. The attempts to bring women to the forefront of national politics and their appointment to government positions were resented by conservative society. The modernization drive of the king also came with the mixing of sexes both at educational institutions and in the workplace. They were also accompanied by western cultural motifs like discotheques and public consumption of alcohol, prohibited under Islam.

Some may now be puzzled by the fact that women, who gained so much under the Shah, ended up opposing him so bitterly. But the Shah's reforms did not reach all the women of Iran; rather the beneficiaries were mainly from the privileged classes. The right to vote, for example, was not very meaningful since there was only one political party to vote for. For the majority of women who lived in rural areas, and for the working class and poor urban dwellers, the gains for women that resulted from the Shah's reforms were marginal. While upper- and middle-class women became ministers, attended the Olympics, and even served as delegates to various international conferences, the lives of most Iranian women remained unchanged. The labour force participation rate of women increased slowly during the late 1950s, 1960s and 1970s, but the new jobs were mainly for the members of the privileged class.

Furthermore, the Shah's liberation of women accompanied overall political repression and exacerbated income disparity. Even to many educated middle-class women, the trade-off was not always worthwhile, and many middle-class women – especially students – were highly critical of the regime. With the exception of the elite, the majority of Iranians became increasingly critical of the secret police and the lack of opportunity for any political expression.[6] Large-scale imitation of the West and its culture was used by the clergy as signs of the Shah's un-Islamic lifestyle and anti-Islamic policies. Wearing traditional dress, especially the veil, became a form of protest. During the weeks running up to Shah's departure, scores of protests were held by women in black *chador* in Tehran and other parts of the country. For them, it symbolized not only their commitment to an Islamic lifestyle but also became a powerful protest against the Shah and his policies.

Political participation was not alien to Iranian women. A small number of educated upper middle-class women took an active part in the earlier social movements. The Constitutional Revolution (1906–11) and the movement for the nationalization of the Iranian oil company (1951–53) witnessed some female participation.[7] But the Islamic Revolution was entirely different. While the men were fighting with the security forces and Savak secret service, ordinary women were displaying their power to protest through the black veil. Such a display not only strengthened the Revolution but also sent an unmistakable religious message. In the 1970s, Ali Shariati published a widely circulated book entitled *Fatima is Fatima*, which soon came to embody the aspirations of many women at the time. The image of the daughter of the Prophet Muhammad was portrayed as a woman of strong will who stood beside her husband Ali in the battle for social justice – an image that many Iranian women of the time could relate to.[8] Also, seeing their mothers, wives, sisters and daughters protesting in the *chador* brought many wavering men in line with the Islamic Revolution.

One could attribute different reasons for the large-scale partici-pation of women in the Islamic Revolution. For some, the Revolution symbolized values they stood for, namely, centrality of family, disapproval of individualism and opposition to western socio-cultural influences that had permeated the society under the Shah. The preservation of Islamic values, these women felt, was possible only through maternity and their central role in the family. The Islamic Revolution led by Khomeini provided them with this opportunity.

While some radical women joined hands with the mujahedeen forces and pursued guerrilla activities against the security forces, many opted for a radical form of protest. The *chador* became the simple but powerful instrument of protest for women. On September 8, 1978, a large number of women in black veils held a peaceful protest in Zhaleh Square in the capital. Under the orders of the Shah, the security forces fired upon the peaceful protests and more than 600 women protesters were killed in the violence and scores of others injured.[9] Marked subsequently as Black Friday, this incident shook the foundations of the monarchy. This protest and violence took place months before the arrival of Imam Khomeini and became a powerful reminder of the power of ordinary women to change the course of events in Iran.

The modernization drive of the Shah also did not reach the lower classes, and rural women suffered from their social conditions and poverty. They survived the rural poverty only through the charitable organizations run by or associated with the clergy. The ideas of equality of sexes, popular among urban women, were an anathema to the rural folk ingrained in traditional values and lifestyle. The Islamic Revolution therefore provided them hope for social justice and a chance for removal from their poverty.

Even young and educated urban women who were rebellious about traditional notions of religion and family control were attracted towards the Islamic Revolution. They sought equality with men through their presence and active participation in the unfolding social development. Joining hands with the revolutionaries offered them an opportunity not only to rebel against their urban social environment but also satisfied their desire to achieve equality with men. Radical religious women also found the struggle against the brutal monarchy an attractive proposition. Some even enlisted with the mujahedeen and carried out various guerrilla operations against the security forces. Though their actual number was small, these women represented a radical stream among Iranian women.

In short, women with different social, economic and educational circumstances, from familial, religious, educated and uneducated backgrounds, and those with revolutionary ideas, all joined hands with the revolution that was sweeping the country from late 1978. The degree of their participation, however, differed.[10]

The near universal nature of the Islamic Revolution was made complete by the open participation of the *Tudeh* party and the Iranian left. As with other countries of the Middle East, the communists were a marginal force in Iran. Their brand of non-religious revolutionary ideas borrowed from abroad did not appeal to the Iranian masses. They had small pockets of influence among the educated urban middle class. The leftists were far removed from religious ideals, let alone aspired by the idea of an Islamic revolution. At the same time, however, their shared animosity towards the Shah and his process of westernization brought the communists to the forefront of the Revolution. Though small in number they were organized and this made them an attractive proposition for the clergy. For centuries, the Shia theologians in Iran had been far removed from statecraft but now the clergy found common cause with the radical ideologies of the *Tudeh* party. In turn, the latter was one of the first political forces in the country to herald Khomeini as the leader of the Revolution.

The powerful merchants of Iran, the *bazaaris*, also found common cause with the ayatollahs. Their close proximity to the clergy establishment and their opposition to reforms brought them closer to the idea that the Shah had to be replaced. Even if they could not be termed conservative, they were not opposed to religion and many were deeply religious in their private lives. In short, unlike other political changes in the Middle East, the Revolution in Iran was popular, widespread and indeed total. Except for those immediately surrounding the Shah and benefiting from his weakening rule, the vast majority of Iranians had abandoned the monarch. By late 1978, the Shah was unable even to find people who would join his cabinet and had great difficulty in persuading Shapour Bakhtiar to take over the reins as Prime Minister and facilitate his exile.

## Consolidation of the Islamic Republic

In less than four years, between 1979 and 1983, the revolutionaries had seized power from the Shah and had moved towards the consolidation of the Islamic Republic. Undermining the authority of the Provisional Revolutionary Government (PRG) created immediately after the takeover, the Islamic groups moved towards the creation of a state within a state and laid the constitutional foundation of a theocracy. Taking advantage of the hostage crisis, they passed the new constitution and defeated the secular nationalists and the orthodox ulema. Soon afterwards the Cultural Revolution was launched, seeking to transform the societal structures of Iran in compatibility with Islamic principles of governance, the ultimate aim being the consolidation of power and the Islamization of society in Iran.[11]

Imam Khomeini was quick to recognize the need to consolidate the fruits of his revolution. The overthrow of the Shah and removal of his pro-western policies and modernization were his primary goal. This was not difficult, given the popular disapproval of the monarchy. Khomeini however had a larger agenda, the establishment of an Islamic Republic in Iran – a government based on Islamic principles, particularly the Shia concept of social justice, presided over by the clergy. While the population was still reeling under the euphoria of overthrowing a tyrant, he organized a popular referendum in April 1979, within two months of his arrival from Paris. Over 98 per cent of those participating in the referendum voted in favor of removing the monarchy and establishing an Islamic republic. A broad spectrum of divergent ideologies that were united under the umbrella of opposition to Shah drafted a 175-article constitution.

The Islamic republic in Iran would have to be Islamic in terms of ideology, direction and execution. Islamic laws of social justice were to be interpreted and implemented through Islamic jurists trained in the Sharia. Under the constitution adopted in December 1979, Iran was not only declared to be an Islamic republic, it also emerged as a theocracy, ruled by theologians. To institutionalize clerical rule at the highest level, the office of *Wilayat e-Faqih* (normally translated as Supreme Leader) was established. This office, held by Khomeini until his death in 1989, was intended to perpetuate the rule of theologians. The Faqih has no fixed term but enjoys unlimited and unchecked powers. According to the Constitution

> During the Occultation of the Wali al-Asr (may God hasten his reappearance), the wilayah and leadership of the Ummah devolve upon the just ['adil] and pious [muttaqi] faqih, who is fully aware of the circumstances of his age; courageous, resourceful, and possessed of administrative ability, will assume the responsibilities of this office.[12]

Enjoying divine authority to rule, the Faqih is accountable only to God. Besides being the supreme commander of all the three branches of the armed forces, he has the power to declare war and peace.[13]

Initially Khomeini anointed Hossain Montazeri as his chosen successor. However, following differences between the two over the direction of the Revolution the Supreme Leader named Ali Khamenei as his successor.[14] Shortly before Khomeini's death the Assembly of Experts amended the constitution and dropped the *marja-e-taqlid* (source of emulation) requirement so that Khomeini's position could be inherited by Ali Khamenei, a middle-ranking cleric who was neither a senior religious jurist nor a *marja-e-taqlid*.[15]

To consolidate the rule of the clergy, the Constitution established a 12-member Council of Guardians which includes five clerical authorities as its members. It was bestowed with the responsibility to ensure that all legislation passed by the *majlis* (parliament) was in conformity with

Islam. The constitution declared Shia Islam, particularly the 'Twelver Ja'fari' school, as the official religion of the country while recognizing other Sunni Islamic jurisprudence.[16]

Contrary to the expectations of various groups, including the left-wing forces and *Tudeh* party, Khomeini was quick to dispel any hopes of an egalitarian inclusive post-monarchical order in Iran. A number of domestic developments and external factors also closed the window of opportunity. His reliance on 'ungodly' communists was tactical and temporary and was quickly revoked when the clergy consolidated their power within the country. While they were prepared to share the struggle with others, the fruits of the Revolution could not be shared without the clergy having to abandon their Islamic goals and principles. Khomeini was disturbed by the class character that his revolution was taking due to the influence of the leftist elements. For him the Revolution had mainly cultural aims. He wanted to eliminate the Shah and his close supporters because they were 'evil' and 'satanic'. He also wanted to end foreign, non-Muslim influence in Iran so as to foil what he considered to be a 'Jewish plot to destroy Islam'. He further wanted to eliminate the Baha'i 'heretics'. He believed that the clergy should have the final say in the affairs of the state and that the rules of Islam should be strictly applied.

Hence, removal of dissidents and potential opponents became the primary objective of the revolutionaries. The military, which was closely identified with the Shah and his repressive policies, could not be counted upon to rally around the Revolution or implement its policies. The revolutionaries responded with a twin strategy. At one level, a large-scale purge was carried out within the military establishment and scores of senior officers were summarily executed. In order to consolidate the new regime, the new state created several paralegal institutions whose main aim was to safeguard the interests of the Revolution and to rid it of all opposition and criticism. First among such institutions were the *Komites* (Islamic Revolution Committees). Harking back to Pahlavi rule, they coordinated strikes and street demonstrations. Armed with weapons confiscated from the Shah's army, these 'vigilante' entities maintained order, protected the revolutionaries, and neutralized the menace of counterrevolution through a combination of harassment, imprisonment and on-the-spot executions of the abhorred officials of the former regime.

In addition to the *Komites*, the fundamentalists monopolized the judicial branch in order to reintroduce the *Sharia*. The Revolutionary Courts served this purpose. From their inception, the revolutionary courts were staffed mostly by the trusted lieutenants of Ayatollah Khomeini. They adroitly imposed themselves as the paragons of revolutionary morality and Islamic justice. The revolutionary courts' secret trials of enemies, without the presence of a defence lawyer and with summary executions of the convicted based on charges such as 'corruption on earth' or 'furthering the influence of the foreigners', turned them into the most powerful and feared judicial body.[17]

Khomeini ordered a large-scale purge of high-ranking officials of the Shah's government. A token trial mechanism was set up under Imam Khalkhali (later referred to as 'Judge Blood' due to his ruthless judgments). The execution of the top generals shattered the atmosphere of fear that still prevailed among those revolutionaries who could not believe that the Shah's regime had finally been dismantled. The fear that the army would be reconstituted and used for a coup d'état was thus allayed. Some of these executions were preceded by televised confessions of conspiracy against the Revolution and were carried out by firing squad. The vitriolic atmosphere against the security establishment, especially the notorious secret service Savak, led to large-scale defections into the ranks of the revolutionaries. In a number of cases, such high-profile defections did not reprieve the individuals from the death squads. Thus, during the first six months of the Revolution, the Revolutionary Courts executed 248 officers, 77 from the regular army, 61 from Savak, 86 from the police and 24 from the gendarmerie. In addition, hundreds were imprisoned or internally exiled, while thousands fled Iran.[18]

Secondly, the revolutionaries established a parallel security structure to help implement the policies of the Islamic Revolution. Days after Khomeini's return to Tehran, the interim administration headed by Prime Minister Mehdi Bazargan established the Pasdaran (*Pasdarn-e enghelab e-Islamic*, 'Islamic Revolutionary Guards' or 'Revolutionary Guards') under a decree issued by Khomeini on May 5, 1979.[19] The Pasdaran was intended to protect the Revolution and to assist the ruling clerics in the day-to-day enforcement of the new government's Islamic codes and morality. There were other, perhaps more important, reasons for establishing the Pasdaran. The Revolution needed to rely on a force of its own rather than borrowing the previous regime's tainted units. As one of the first revolutionary institutions, the Pasdaran helped legitimize the Revolution and gave the new regime an armed basis of support. Moreover, its establishment served notice to both the population and the regular armed forces that the Khomeini regime was quickly developing its own enforcement body. Thus, the Pasdaran, along with its political counterpart, Crusade for Reconstruction, brought a new order to Iran. In time, the Pasdaran would rival the police and the judiciary in terms of its functions. It would even challenge the performance of the regular armed forces on the battlefield.[20]

Comprising of young revolutionaries, many of whom were trained in Lebanon while Khomeini was in exile, the Revolutionary Guards were used effectively against left-wing guerrilla organizations that were acting against the interests of the Revolution. Occasionally they were used against ethnic minorities in the northeast who were fighting the Islamization policies of the revolutionaries. The revolutionaries carried out large-scale purges against different segments of the population. Scores of officials who served the previous regime were held responsible for the tyrannical policies of the Shah and were summarily executed.

In pursuance of the Shia notion of social justice, Khomeini also acted against the economic resources of those identified with the Shah. In May 1979 he formed the Foundation for the Disinherited (*Bonyad-e Mostazafan va Janbazan*), which took over all the assets of the Pahlavi Foundation. Mandated to assist low-income groups, the Islamic foundation soon became one of the largest conglomerates in Iran, controlling hundreds of expropriated and nationalized factories, trading firms, farms, apartment and office buildings as well as two large newspaper chains. The Foundation soon emerged as the biggest Holding Company in the Middle East with a workforce exceeding 200,000 employees and an annual budget amounting to more than 10 per cent of the budget of the Iranian government.[21] In 1989, responsibility for the management of the welfare of persons who had been disabled during the war with Iraq was entrusted to this foundation.

In July 1979, six months after the victory of the Revolution, 28 private banks that held in their possession 43.9 per cent of the total assets of all the Iranian banks were nationalized. Major manufacturing industries such as automobile, copper, steel and aluminium as well as the assets of 51 capitalists and major industrialists and their next of kin were taken over by the government. It also took possession of properties it had nationalized whereas those confiscated by the revolutionary courts were put at the disposal of the *Mostazafan va Janbazan* (deprived and war-wounded) Foundation to be spent in upgrading the living standard of the people who had contributed to the downfall of the Shah through their uprising. The foundation was later exempted from rules and regulations of general auditing. In 1982, the foundation possessed 203 manufacturing and industrial factories, 472 big agricultural fields, 101 major construction firms, 238 trade and services companies and 2,786 big plots of real estate.[22]

The Crusade for Reconstruction (*Jihad-e-Sazandegi*) established in June 1979 recruited young people for the reconstruction of clinics, local roads, schools and similar social infrastructure facilities in villages and rural areas. It soon grew rapidly assuming functions in rural areas that were previously managed by the Planning and Budget Organization and the Ministry of Agriculture.

Apart from the political and economic takeover, the Revolution also continued to transform the social structures of Iranian society. Women who were at the forefront of the Revolution soon found themselves on the receiving end of the rule of the clergy. In March 1979, within a month of his return, Khomeini sacked all female judges, and the wearing of *chador*, which had been a form of protest earlier, now became compulsory for all women in Iran. In May, co-education in schools was banned and the following month married women were barred from attending schools. The government also closed down nurseries at work places used by employed married women.

A nationwide code for morality was announced and a vigilante moral police called the Office of the Propagation of Virtues and Prevention of Sins began operating throughout Iran. It was responsible for the enforcement of the dress code and other social restrictions such as social mixing of the sexes. Women were executed by revolutionary guards on charges of prostitution and moral degradation.[23] In October 1979, the regime moved closer to restoring the status quo ante regarding women's rights. It revised the personal laws and bestowed polygamous rights upon men. Repealing the progress made by women under the 1975 law, the regime gave men rights to unilaterally divorce their wives and the right to prevent their wives from taking up any paid employment without permission. It also reduced the official marriage age for women from 18 to 13 and men also regained automatic custody of their children after divorce. In July 1981 the majlis ratified the Islamic *Qassas* laws (laws of retribution) which rested on the 'eye for an eye and a life for a life' principle. Under new laws, adultery was made punishable by stoning.

The Islamic laws of retribution (*Qassas* laws) severely eroded women's legal rights. Not only was the evidence of two women equated with that of one man, as required by the Koran (2:82), but women's evidence, if uncorroborated by men, was no longer accepted by the courts. Women who insisted on giving uncorroborated evidence were judged to be lying and subjected to punishment for slander (article 92 of the laws). Murder was now punished by retribution; but the murderer could opt for the payment of *daheh*, blood money, to the descendants of the murdered, in lieu of punishment (Article 1 of the *Qassas* laws). Whereas killing a man is a capital offence, murdering a women was a lesser crime. Men were also entitled to kill anyone who "violated their harem", while men who murdered their wives, sisters or mothers on the charge of adultery were not subject to any punishment. But women did not have such rights.[24]

The return of the veil and draconian *Qassas* laws angered many women supporters of the Revolution. As early as March 1979 women held a series of protests against the regime and its programs. Such demonstrations were repeated in October and later that year when over 20,000 women took to the streets in protest at the new dress code.[25] By then, however, the regime was firmly in control and the erosion of women's rights was codified by the majlis and enforced by the moral police.

However, in spite of the repression, the Revolution has also enhanced the social, political, cultural and economic activities of women and has radically changed the self-perception of women, who now reject traditionalist values and divine justifications for segregation policies. Through their mobilization against the Islamization of laws and institutions, women attempted to establish their authority in the family, as well as in political, religious, judiciary and other institutions. The result was the emergence of a women's movement in Iran whose demands have included the secularization of laws and institutions, which would entail a separation between religion and state, reconciling Islam with modernity, codifying the equality of rights between men and women, limiting the state's intervention in the private sphere, tolerating political pluralism, etc.[26]

Iranian women have gained greater influence and power to the extent that religious leaders have been persuaded to legitimize female participation in social and political processes. Yet because of the attitude that dominates the legislative circles and preserves the laws based on gender discrimination, women have continued to be treated as second-class citizens. The current economic, social and political conditions of Iranian society have called upon women to play new roles that are essentially different from what their status in a traditional and underdeveloped social system would warrant. Yet what has created a crisis in the area of women's legal rights is the imbalance that exists in the process of development and certain approaches to the question of development. In other words, while the legal system has its roots in the period of traditionalism, the economic, social and cultural attributes of society are undergoing a process of transformation. As a result, the legal system is no longer capable of responding to the needs of this transitional period of political, economic, social and cultural reality.[27]

Education was another area which underwent a massive transition. Within a year after the revolutionaries took control, the High Council of the Cultural Revolution was established with the explicit purpose of revising the entire educational system in tune with the new reality. All textbooks were examined for un-Islamic content, opinions and illustrations. This in practical terms meant the covering up of all female photographs and the removal of non-Islamic illustrations. The rewriting of Iranian history included glorification of the Islamic rather than Persian rule and the marginalization of pre-Islamic Persian history. While the nation was going through tumultuous times, educational institutions became prime casualties. The need to revolutionize young minds through Islamic education delayed things considerably. Schools were reopened after a couple of years, but the universities remained closed for over four years.

Khomeini was wary of the non-Islamic university system and denounced it as a hotbed of western-oriented left-wing activities, which had corruptive influence upon the youth. In April 1980 he publicly called for 'purification' of the Iranian universities. To purge any unwanted 'contamination' among the youth, in June 1980 the High Council of Cultural Revolution set up a *Jahadeh Daneshgahi* (Universities' Holy War) aimed at purifying the system. In a decree on June 12, 1980, Ayatollah Khomeini outlined the objectives of the organization. Officials were "authorized to set up a headquarters and invite the devoted scholars among the Muslim professors and committed and faithful employees and other educated individuals who are committed and loyal to the Islamic Republic of Iran so that a council can be established for planning various courses and future cultural policy of universities in accordance with Islamic culture and selection and training of capable, knowledgeable and devoted professors and take care of other affairs relevant to the Islamic education revolution."[28] The Headquarters of the Cultural Revolution was obliged to ensure "Islamization of the environment of universities" and the changing of "the educational programs of universities aimed at rendering services to the nation". For these reasons a special body named the 'Committee for Islamization of Universities' was formed in the Cultural Headquarters.[29]

The result of this cultural policing was effective. In 1978 on the eve of the Revolution there were about 17,000 university students, about 40 per cent of whom were female students.[30] By 1983 when they slowly reopened, only 4,500 students were registered at university and only 10 per cent of these were women. By the late 1980s the number of students had reached 270,000, partly because more universities were reopened and partly because new universities were founded. The rapid increase in the number of universities and students should not be confused with the relaxation of the educational norms or liberalization of academia. They were allowed to flourish only as long as they remained in tune with the goals and objectives of the Islamic Revolution.

The same rigidity was applied in the socio-cultural sphere. All forms of creative arts, music and other forms of cultural activities not in sync with the Revolution were banned. They were described as un-Islamic imitations of the West and hence were to be banished. In two seminal pre-revolutionary works, Ayatollah Khomeini wrote that expressions of Westernization, such as theatre and dancing, "rape the youth of our country and stifle in them the spirit of virtue and bravery".[31] Such pre-revolutionary declarations, which Ayatollah Khomeini sought to implement upon the commencement of the Islamic Republic, led to the elimination of dance as an art form altogether, while others such as music, theatre, cinema and literature were in June 1980 all required to submit to the watchful eyes and firm hand of censorship of the Supreme Cultural Revolution Council (SCRC). Although not enshrined within the Constitution, as all other major state institutions are, Ayatollah Khomeini decreed the SCRC to be the highest body for producing guidelines and making decisions in relation to all cultural, educational and research activities. Its members are appointed by the Supreme Leader.[32] Within the SCRC is the Ministry of Culture and Information Guidance (MCIG), an elaborate system of councils that regulate and monitor every sphere of artistic expression. In order to exhibit art or photographic work, take photographs in the public domain for journalistic or artistic purposes, shoot a film, publish literature, produce a play, release an album or hold a concert, permission must first be obtained from the MCIG. Authorization can take weeks, months, years, or it can be denied altogether.[33]

While the Constitution of the Islamic Republic accepts the freedom of the press as one of the 'basic freedoms', this is on the condition that it does not contradict the 'the principles of Islam' which are defined by the ruling elite. The media thus also came under the tight control of the regime, which did not tolerate any adverse criticism of the Revolution or its leaders. Radio and television stations were put under the control of the new state immediately after the Islamic Revolution in 1979. But it took until the summer of 1981 before the last opposition newspaper ceased publication. Directly after the Revolution there were 444 different newspapers and magazines being published. By 1988, the number had gone down to 121, and they were without exception fully supportive of the regime.[34]

In the early stages of the Revolution, social violence also increased. The official purges carried out by the Revolutionary Guards were accompanied by organized and unorganized violence carried out by various militant vigilante groups. As mentioned earlier, the moral police carried out a large number of violent attacks against women whom it suspected of indulging in amoral and un-Islamic activities. Such violence was also used to settle personal scores.

The hostage-taking drama was part of this uncontrolled societal violence that plagued Iran in the early days of the Revolution. On November 4, 1979, less than 10 months after the Revolution, a group of students forcibly entered the American embassy and soon took control of the building. The students demanded the Shah to be returned to Iran for trial and execution. This soon became official when the Iranian government and the clergy endorsed both the actions and demands of the students. Until the crisis was eventually resolved in January 1981, Iran's relations with the outside world were dominated by the hostage crisis.

There was also anti-regime violence carried out by loyalists of the monarchy as well as by members of the *Tudeh* party and the *Mujahedeen-e-Khalq* (MEK). The latter favoured the creation of an egalitarian system based on the 'true teachings of Islam', one in which the peasants and the workers, and not the ulema, would rule, the industries would be nationalized, all 'imperialistic treaties' would be annulled, and Iran would have close relations with the Third World and East European nations. The Mujahedeen were mistrusted by Ayatollah Khomeini and were excluded from the PRG and the CIR.[35]

Though active participants in the revolutionary struggle against the Shah, these groups soon fell out with the ruling Islamic government after 1979. The MEK, which shifted its base to Paris in 1981, has been actively targeting Iranian government officials and facilities. On June 28, 1980, the top leadership of the Islamic Republic Party (IRP) held a conference at their headquarters in Tehran. A powerful bomb demolished the party's conference room, killing more than seventy persons, including Ayatollah Hossein Beheshti, the IRP's chairman and the president of the Supreme Court, four cabinet ministers and 25 Majlis deputies.[36] Again on August 30, 1981, during a meeting of Iran's Supreme Defence Council between President Rajai and Prime Minister Mohammad Javad Bahonar at the office of the IRP, a bomb explosion was triggered by the MEK. The explosion killed both the President and the Prime Minister along with three others present. Rajai was the President of Iran for just 14 days.

The apprehensions of the clergy regarding the loyalty of the military was also shared by Iraq and its Ba'athist leadership, which was hoping for large-scale defections from the Iranian military. President Saddam Hussein saw an opportunity in the internal divisions within Iran and growing tension between Iran and the outside world. Revoking the 1975 agreement on the Shatt-al-Arab waterway, on September 22, 1980 he launched a war against Iran. Aggression from an external enemy led by an atheist Sunni ruler galvanized the Iranians, who rallied behind their Supreme Leader.

The war, which lasted for eight years, had severe ramifications for Iran, politically, economically and socially. While it provided an opportunity for political consolidation, the war inflicted significant damage on the civilian population. Despite the predictable casualties of war[37] and the effects on the economy of Iran, the war with Iraq hit the

Iranians much closer to home. The war also resulted in numerous civilian casualties. From February to April 1988, in what came to be known as the 'War of the Cities', both Iran and Iraq began to target civilian population centres with ballistic missile attacks.

A notable feature of the war was the involvement of child soldiers. A few years into the fighting, in 1984, Iranian President Ali-Akbar Rafsanjani declared that "all Iranians from 12 to 72 should volunteer for the Holy War". Thousands of children were pulled from schools, indoctrinated in the glory of martyrdom, and sent to the front lines only lightly armed with one or two grenades or a gun with one magazine of ammunition. Wearing keys around their necks (to signify their pending entrance into heaven), they were sent forward in the first waves of attacks to help clear paths through minefields with their bodies and overwhelm Iraqi defences. Ayatollah Khomeini delighted in the children's sacrifice and extolled that they were helping Iran to achieve "a situation which we cannot describe in any way except to say that it is a divine country".[38]

The war also witnessed the use of chemical weapons by Iraq. The single most publicized incident of the conflict occurred in March 1988, when Iraqi forces bombarded the town of Halabja (then under Iranian occupation) with various chemical agents over the course of three days. The psychological impact of the use of chemical weapons by Iraq and the targeting of civilian population centres is often cited as one of the reasons for Iran's acceptance of the ceasefire agreement in 1988.[39]

## Minorities in an Islamic Republic

Like other Iranians, the minorities also had their share of problems after the Revolution. At one level, the regime acknowledged Christians, Jews and Zoroastrians as 'recognized religious minorities' and in the 270-member Iranian parliament these minorities have four seats. Given the small size of these religious groups, this degree of representation is significant. Despite the existence of a specific status in the Constitution, however, these three recognized religious minorities have faced severe discrimination. First of all, they are discriminated against by a number of legal provisions, which discriminate *per se* against all non-Muslims. Moreover, all three minorities complain of discrimination in the field of employment, report clear limitations imposed upon their upward mobility and complain of being treated like 'second-class citizens'.[40]

Among the recognized minorities, the Jewish community in particular came under severe pressures. Even during his days in exile, anti-Zionism and anti-Israeli sentiments were a critical component of Khomeini's worldview. He and his followers demonized Israel as 'Little Satan' and anti-Zionist rhetoric formed a constant theme in the Friday prayers and mass rallies addressed by Imam Khomeini. Anti-Jewish sentiments abounded among segments of the population and occasionally found expression in official statements. To begin with, the distinction between Jews, Israel and Zionism was often blurred, much as it is in the Arab world. There were numerous references to Israel as a 'bunch of Jews'. Khomeini himself – often careful not to incite against the Jews – made a revealing slip. In 1982, he began one of his speeches by saying that those who followed in the path of Jesus Christ were even worse than the Jews, although it was perhaps "impossible to say that there is anything worse than the Jews". He then retracted: "I mean the Jews of Israel."[41]

Anti-Israeli rhetoric in the official media brought the Iranian Jewish community under pressure. Within a few months after Khomeini's return, Habih Elghanian, a businessman and influential figure in the Jewish community, was executed. Besides 'corruption on earth' and 'warring with God and his emissaries', he was accused of 'friendship with the enemies of God and being an enemy of the friends of God'.[42] The regime also imprisoned a number of Jewish citizens and also executed a few more. Such developments sent a strong signal to the Jews of Iran, leading to slow emigration. From around 80,000 in 1979, the number of Jews had dwindled to around 30,000 by the time Khomeini passed away.

However, the Revolution reserved far worse treatment for the Baha'i community. With an estimated population of 300,000 in 1979, the Baha'is represent the largest religious minority in Iran. Nevertheless they have been deliberately omitted from the list of recognized religious minorities in the Islamic constitution. The Islamic Revolution introduced a policy of institutionalized discrimination and oppression against its largest religious minority. From the very beginning the clerical authority targeted the Baha'is, and the House of Bab, one of the holiest Baha'i shrines in Shiraz, was destroyed within months of the Islamic Revolution. The limited protection available to Christians, Jews and Zoroastrians was not available to the Baha'is, whose faith was not recognized and who were considered apostates and infidels. The Baha'is were systematically denied rights to education, jobs, social welfare and also faced severe restrictions in their personal lives. Attacks on their physical integrity involved mass imprisonment and torture throughout the 1980s, resulting in over 200 Baha'is being killed[43] purely for their religious beliefs, as well as many public attempts to force Baha'is to become Muslims.

Attacks on Baha'i community structures began with a concerted wave of killings and the disappearance of elected national and local Baha'i leaders throughout Iran in the early 1980s. This culminated in the Baha'i Administration being declared illegal by government authorities in 1983, hence it was disbanded. Since the Baha'i community does not have a religious hierarchy, the banning of the administrative structure dismembered the community in terms of its internal organization – its religious and social activities, religious educational classes within the community, and its organization of matters of personal status such as the registration of marriage, divorce, burials and births.

The Baha'is in Iran are totally excluded from all forms of representation. They constitute legal and political non-persons, suffering total civil non-existence since 1979. The exclusion of the Baha'is from the Constitution means their population has been eliminated from the Iranian political scene. They cannot vote, they are not conceded any level of internal community organization, tens of thousands of Baha'is were eliminated from the Iranian civil service in the early 1980s, their pensions have not been honoured, many community and individual properties have been confiscated over the decades, and no political or legal recourse exists for them. There have even been government campaigns to oust Baha'is from private businesses, and cemeteries have been raided, assets confiscated and all passports and exit permits denied to all Baha'is until very recently. No single Baha'i has been permitted to study or teach in tertiary education since the onset of the Revolution.[44]

## Conclusion

Spending his last months in a military hospital outside Cairo, the Shah passed away on July 27, 1980. The funeral was attended by Sadat and a very few international personalities. There was no visible display of public mourning for the man who until recently had reigned over a foreign country. Iranians, however, still under the euphoria of the Islamic Revolution, were dancing in the streets of Iran as well as in other parts of the world.

On June 3, 1989, the death of Khomeini was received with public outpourings of grief, disbelief and grave personal loss. Many resorted to self-flagellation, a Shia custom during the Ashura festivals where the believers mourn for the death of Ali, the Prophet Mohammed's grandson and the fourth Caliph. Millions thronged to the place where the ayatollah's body was to be buried. The public rush to touch the coffin carrying the body of the 'Supreme Leader' made the funeral arrangements unworkable and at one point even forced the helicopter carrying the coffin to take off briefly.

The difference between the funerals of these two leaders is indicative of the large-scale changes that had occurred in Iranian society since 1979. Within a decade of its establishment, the Islamic Revolution had succeeded in transforming the political and social structures in Iran and came to be defined on the basis of Islamic principles. While there was disappointment among the people regarding the nature and policies of the new government, at the time of Khomeini's death in 1989 and after the end of the Iran–Iraq war, there still existed considerable hope among the people of Iran for further reformation and positive changes in the country.

## NOTES

1 Azar Tabari, 'The Role of the Clergy in Modern Iranian Politics', in Nikki R. Keddie (ed.), *Religion and Politics in Iran – Shi'ism from Quietism to Revolution* (London: Yale University Press, 1983), p. 49.

2 Sana Jaffery, 'Development of State-Clergy Relations in Iran and Turkey: A Structural Explanation', http://sitemaker.umich.edu/comparative.speaker.series/files/sana_jaffrey.pdf

3 Ibid.

4 Mohsen Milani, *The Making of Iran's Islamic Revolution: From Monarchy to Islamic Republic* (Boulder, Colorado: Westview Press, 1988), p. 244.

5 Kourosh Eshghipour, 'The Islamic Revolution's Impact on the Legal and Social Status of Iranian Women', *New England International and Comparative Law Annual*, Vol. 3 (1997), available at http://www.nesl.edu/intljournal/vol3/iran.htm.

6 Roksana Bahramitash, "Revolution, Islamization, and Women's Employment in Iran", *The Brown Journal of World Affairs*, Vol. IX, Issue 2 (Winter/Spring 2003), p. 231.

7 Azadeh Kian-Thiebaut, 'Women's Movement in Post-Revolutionary Iran', in M. Hamid Ansari (ed.), *Iran Today: Twenty Five Years after the Islamic Revolution* (New Delhi: Rupa & Co., 2005), p. 316.

8  Roksana Bahramitash, 'Revolution. Islamization, and Women's Employment in Iran', *The Brown Journal of World Affairs*, Vol. IX, Issue 2 (Winter/Spring 2003), p. 232.

9  Mohammad Mehdi Khorrami, *The Islamic Revolution*, http://www.internews.org/visavis/BTVPagesInews/Theislamicrevolution.html.

10  Azadeh Kian-Thiebaut, 'Women's Movement in Post-Revolutionary Iran' in M. Hamid Ansari (ed.), *Iran Today: Twenty Five Years after the Islamic Revolution* (New Delhi: Rupa & Co., 2005).

11  Mohsen M. Milani, *The Making of Iran's Islamic Revolution: From Monarchy to Islamic Republic*, p. 240.

12  Article 5 of the Iranian Constitution. Full text available at http://www.iranonline.com/iran/iran-info/Government/constitution-1.html

13  Hamid Algar (trans.), *The Constitution of the Islamic Republic of Iran* (Berkeley, California: Mizan Press, 1980), pp. 67–68.

14  Bahman Baktiari, 'The Governing Institutions of the Islamic Republic of Iran: The Supreme Leader, The Presidency, and the Majlis', in Jamal S. al-Suwaidi (ed.), *Iran and the Gulf: A Search for Stability* (Abu Dhabi: Emirates Center for Strategic Studies and Research, 1996), pp. 52–53

15  Ervand Abrahamian, *Khomeinism: Essays on the Islamic Republic* (Berkeley, California: University of California Press, 1993), p. 34.

16  Article 12 of the Iranian Constitution. Full text available at http://www.iranonline.com/iran/iran-info/Government/constitution-1.html

17  Mohsen M. Milani, *The Making of Iran's Islamic Revolution: From Monarchy to Islamic Republic*, p. 256

18  Ibid.

19  Jehan Lazrak, 'The Pasdaran's Private Empires', *Le monde diplomatique*, 2006, available at: http://mondediplo.com/2006/12/05empires.

20  http://www.globalsecurity.org/military/world/iran/pasdaran.htm

21  'Bonyad-e-Mostazafan va Janbazan: Oppressed and Disabled Veterans Foundation', available at: http://www.globalsecurity.org/military/world/iran/mjf.htm.

22  Ibid.

23  Homa Omid, *Islam and the Post-Revolutionary State in Iran* (London: St. Martin's Press, 1994), pp. 182–83.

24  Haleh Afshar, 'Women and the Politics of Fundamentalism in Iran', *Women Against Fundamentalisms*, Journal No. 5, 1994, pp. 15–20, available at http://waf.gn.apc.org/j5p15.htm.

25  Homa Omid, *Islam and the Post-Revolutionary State in Iran*, pp. 182–83.

26  Azadeh Kian-Thiebaut, 'Women's Movement in Post-Revolutionary Iran' in M. Hamid Ansari (ed.), *Iran Today: Twenty Five Years after the Islamic Revolution*.

27  Mehrangiz Kar, 'Second Class: The Status of Iranian Women', *The Iranian*, April 18, 2000, http://www.iranian.com/Opinion/2000/April/Women/.

28  *Secretariat of Supreme Council of Cultural Revolution*, available at http://www.iranculture.org/en/about/tarikh.php.

29  Ibid.

30  Homa Omid, *Islam and the Post-Revolutionary State in Iran*, pp. 182–83

31  *Unveiled: Art and Censorship in Iran*, September 2006, http://www.article19.org/pdfs/publications/iran-art-censorship.pdf, p. 7.

32  Ibid.

33 Ibid.

34 Asghar Schirazi, *Media in the Islamic Republic of Iran: Between Self Censorship and Repression,* available at http://www.qantara.de/webcom/show_article.php/_c-478/_nr-635/i.html?PHPSESSID=5.

35 Mohsen Milani, *The Making of Iran's Islamic Revolution: From Monarchy to Islamic Republic,* p. 296.

36 Ibid.

37 One source indicated that during the war Iran suffered between 400,000 to 600,000 dead while Iraq suffered 150,000 dead, 500,000 wounded and 70,000 prisoners. See Javed Ali, 'Chemical Weapons and the Iran–Iraq War: A Case Study in Non-Compliance', *The Nonproliferation Review,* Spring 2001, p. 43.

38 P.W. Singer, *Child Soldiers – The New Faces of War,* http://www.brookings.edu/views/articles/fellows/singer20051215.pdf.

39 Javed Ali, "Chemical Weapons and the Iran-Iraq War: A Case Study in Non-Compliance," *The Nonproliferation Review,* Spring 2001, p. 52.

40 *Discrimination against Religious Minorities in Iran,* Report presented by the International Federation of Human Rights to the 63rd Session of the Committee on the Elimination of Racial Discrimination, August 2003, p. 6.

41 David Menashri, *Iran, the Jews and the Holocaust,* The Stephen Roth Institute for the Study of Contemporary Anti-Semitism and Racism, Tel Aviv University, http://www.tau.ac.il/Anti-Semitism/asw2005/menashri.html

42 Eliz Sanasarian, *Religious Minorities in Iran* (London: Cambridge University Press, 2000), p. 112.

43 UN Commission on Human Rights, 52nd Session, February 29, 1996, UN Doc. E/CN.4/1996/95/Add.29.

44 Nazila Ghanea-Hercock, 'Ethnic and Religious Groups in the Islamic Republic of Iran', *United Nations Office of the High Commissioner of Human Rights,* October 2004.

# 6

# The Al-Aqsa Intifada: Snapshots from the Field*

*Amira Hass*

## Introduction

First-hand experience offers a better insight about the impact of war upon civilian lives. Devoid of abstract arguments, these human interest stories depict a more accurate picture of the impact of conflicts. By capturing small and individual incidents, they help us understand how individual lives are lost, dreams shattered and hopes buried on the battlefield. Such an approach becomes even more relevant when the distinction between home and war fronts becomes blurred, as in the case of the Palestinian Intifadas. During the two uprisings, both Israeli and Palestinian civilians suffered directly but the latter are the prime victims of the violence. For the Palestinians, trying to lead a normal life became an enduring daily experience.

Using her prolonged personal experience of living with the Palestinians in the occupied territories, Amira Hass paints for us here a poignant picture of how the al-Aqsa Intifada has irreparably affected and in some cases altered their lives. By sharing these moments captured in time, she helps us appreciate the true magnitude of the conflict and its adverse effects. Unlike in the other contributions in this volume, here the human suffering does not just comprise numbers, ideas or political rhetoric, but the individuals have names, identities and above all human feelings.

**Editor**

\* \* \*

---

\* The dispatches in this chapter were first published as columns in the Italian weekly *Internazionale*.

**[Gaza, March 5, 2001]**

The A'idy family lives in the middle of a typical Gazan orchard. It is a lush scene of evergreen leaves, thick stems, heavy oranges and lemons and the constant singing of birds, so unexpected in this, the world's most densely populated region. Now, the Israeli army has uprooted the greater part of its trees, as it has done to other orchards, vines and fields all over the Gaza Strip.

The 'crime' of the A'idy family: their proximity to a road which leads to an Israeli settlement. There are some 7,000 Israeli-Jewish settlers in the Gaza Strip, living in two separate privileged enclaves and in three isolated settlements. In total, 20 per cent of the Gaza Strip's 360 square kilometres remains under direct Israeli military and civilian control, where these settlers live. In the remaining 80 per cent live some 1.3 million Palestinians.

The orchard was uprooted in order to guarantee maximum range of vision for the Israeli military unit which has occupied the roof of the A'idy's house, turning it into a little military base, observatory and shooting ground.

The unit has ordered that at least four of the ten family members must remain inside the house at all times, thus protecting the soldiers. Anybody who needs to leave the house and go into the yard must have the permission of the soldiers, and wait until a soldier opens the front door. Visitors are not allowed. If members of the family wish to leave for Gaza town, the soldiers must be notified – so that they can pass on the information to the other soldiers, positioned around the house. Likewise, any family member returning from town must notify the soldiers. Leaving by car is not allowed and neither is donkey riding, a common phenomenon among poor Palestinians. They can leave only on foot. Sometimes the soldiers in one position fail to inform the others, and they shoot towards the 'suspicious trespasser'.

And when the soldiers on the roof shoot at night, towards distant, suspicious targets, the entire house quakes.

\* \* \*

**[Ramallah, May 1, 2001]**

In an interval of five to six hours, on April 30, two powerful explosions killed six Palestinians in the residential areas of two different cities: the first in Gaza and the second in Ramallah. In the first explosion, the victims were two cousins, aged 16 and 21, who were loosely associated with the militant Islamic group Hamas. Early investigations reveal that an anonymous person brought his car for repair in the family's garage.

In the second explosion, two kids – a brother and a sister – and two adults were killed and buried beneath the collapsed walls of a two-storey building. The first rumour said the house belonged to a Hamas supporter. According to another rumour, one of those killed was a Fatah activist who was suspected of being involved in the murder of an Israeli high school student.

Palestinian political activists, excluding the probability of such a coincidence – two similar accidents around the same time – blame Israel for carrying out two assassination missions, aided and assisted by Palestinian collaborators. An Israeli military spokesperson denied any connection to the two blasts. During the last seven months of the al-Aqsa Intifada, Israel has not bothered to deny outright its involvement in assassinating Palestinians who were portrayed as 'chief terrorists'.

Is this the beginning of a new Israeli tactic? Hitting at Palestinian human targets, disclaiming responsibility and thereby sowing more confusion, suspicion and fear? No one is safe in their own home. No noise is innocent. No blast is accidental. And the worst thing: no passenger or unknown visitor is to be trusted. Anyone might carry a suitcase full of explosives, and plant it under your building. A legitimate reprisal, Israel would say, even if the authorities did not acknowledge that it was a state action.

And the next morning, a Palestinian gunman killed an Israeli settler near Ramallah.

✳  ✳  ✳

**[May 15, 2001]**

Two scenes of mass gatherings were screened on local televisions on May 14. The Israeli screens showed tens of thousands of Israelis celebrating the victory of an Israeli basketball team in a European match. The Palestinian stations transmitted the scene of tens of thousands of Palestinians mourning the death of five members of the Palestinian National Security Forces, killed by an Israeli military unit.

The five policemen and one of their colleagues who escaped the bullets were in their position at the western road which connects

Ramallah to Jerusalem. This road, however, has been completely blocked to Palestinian movement and vehicles for the past six months. The Palestinian police post marks the seam-line between one of the Israeli security-controlled areas (which in total comprise 88 per cent of the West Bank) and a Palestinian 'security-controlled' area – where, according to the Oslo Accords, Palestinian security forces were allowed to carry arms. Half a kilometre away, Israel has a huge military base and a military detention camp, one of the many where Palestinians are detained or imprisoned. And another kilometre south lies the huge settlement of Givet Ze'ev.

All six are Gazans, as West Bankers have fewer economic motivations to join this thankless police force. The improvised-looking military position has a tin shack, some beds, another cabin for the kitchen and bathroom, a few rocks to mark the end of the road and some sand-filled sacks. Four were sleeping and two were on their guard shift when an Israeli unit opened fire from a temporary position on a half-constructed Palestinian building nearby, which the army 'occupied' some months ago. Later, soldiers approached and shot inside the building. Or rather, it was not a building but a tin shack. One of the Palestinians managed to crawl and roll into a ditch. He heard the footsteps of the soldiers, and then the shots.

Later the Israel Defence Forces (IDF) admitted that this shooting and killing was 'an error'.

## [July 9, 2001]

Jammal decided to leave the country. Five years are enough, he said. A 38-year-old musician and craftsman who was born in Jordan to Palestinian parents, Jammal had been active in the *Fatah* movement in some other Arab countries, including Lebanon during Israel's war against the Palestinians in that country, until he finally came to Palestine; that is, to Ramallah, the uncrowned capital of the West Bank. It was 1995. His imagination was captivated by the promises of the Oslo process, or rather, by the inspirations it ignited among some Palestinians. He returned to the beloved, unknown homeland, looking forward to experiencing the prosperity of a modern society coupled with the warmth of his own ethnic, family-based welcoming group. This is something you don't experience abroad, where people point at you as 'Palestinian' because of your different accent and history.

He came as a tourist. Israel gave him a tourist visa for some months, then renewed it once again and no more. He should leave and ask for a new visa, he was told. Yet he had come to settle down, was tired of the life of a vagabond. But without Israeli consent and approval, no Palestinian could become a resident of the Palestinian Territories. So stipulate the Oslo accords. And Israel, since 1967, has done its best not to allow the naturalization of Palestinians who were born abroad.

For years Jammal moved around without legal documentation, risking arrest or deportation. He had his artful ways at military checkpoints. Once, a soldier wanted to see his papers. "I am Jordanian," he said and showed an ageing Jordanian insignificant document with an ancient photo of his. This is my Jordanian identity card, he claimed, I am sorry, I left my passport at home. "But it's all written in Arabic," said the soldier, and Jammal replied: "But of course, in what other language should it be?"

But when he had a golden opportunity to teach music to children in a Palestinian village within Israel proper, he declined. Too dangerous. You can do the trip and take the risk once a month, not four times a week.

So, no work, no real ability to move beyond the boundaries of Ramallah – a situation which got worse during the al-Aqsa Intifada, where every two kilometres you would bump into an Israeli roadblock and a searching soldier.

Last week Jammal bid farewell to his friends, gave presents to each of them, packed a few clothes, polished his saxophone, and made a phone call to the Jordanian embassy, which promised there would be no problem, even though his tourist visa had expired five years ago. "The Israelis would be happy to let you go."

"I am not going just because of the bombing and the mobility restrictions," he told his friends. "I am also going because of what is happening inside the society." He was reminded of Lebanon and the PLO rule over the Palestinian society in Lebanon. Armed men spreading fear and extorting comforts and benefits from the unarmed. One group of armed men, controlled by a war lord, competing and clashing with the other. No, he admitted, it hasn't yet reached these levels of chaos in Ramallah, but he is certain it eventually will. "The 'big shots' here – that is, the Palestinian leadership – just don't give a damn about us, the people. Their policies aren't clear, their tactics towards Israel do not bear fruit. So why should I pay the price?"

* * *

**[July 24, 2001]**
Of the three and a half million Palestinians who live in the Gaza Strip and the West Bank, more than 2 million, or more than two-thirds, are now living below the poverty line. This is what the Palestinian Central Bureau of Statistics is estimating, based upon a survey it conducted in May–July 2001 among some 3,000 households. Its findings were released early this week and can be seen in almost every grocery in every community, with their empty shelves and counters (no need to order what one cannot sell anyway). The findings can also be seen at street junctions, where more and more kids are trying to sell packs of chewing gum or coffee to pedestrians and drivers who stop at the traffic lights.

Before the outbreak of the al-Aqsa Intifada almost 30 per cent of Palestinians, mostly in Gaza, lived below the poverty line. The intense and rapid growth of this ominous figure is directly related to Israel's main strategy in repressing the uprising: the massive restrictions on movement, otherwise known as 'closure'. Tens of thousands of workers are prevented from reaching their jobs within Israel proper, villages and cities are disconnected from each other by a primitive and very efficient set of earth mounds, blocks of concrete and ugly ditches along and in the middle of paved roads. Construction and development projects within the Palestinian areas have been stopped. Indeed, 14.2 per cent of the households (with an average of two adults and four children in each) reported that they have lost all sources of income since the outbreak of the Intifada.

More than fifty per cent of the families reported that they have had to reduce the quality of their nutrition. Thirty-five per cent reported that they have reduced the quantity of their food consumption. Some 65 per cent have reduced the consumption of meat and fruits; 71.7 per cent of the families in Gaza and 48.9 per cent of the families in the West Bank needed humanitarian aid during May and June. But in most cases this was below 25 dollars per month.

**[September 4, 2001]**

The shopping centre of the West part of Jerusalem is almost deserted. It is the fresh memory of the horrific sights of blown-up, scattered, bleeding bodies that is keeping people away. It is the thought of another human bomb which may once more reach a busy, popular gathering site: a mall, a pizzeria or a bar.

The empty streets scream of fear. So do the busy streets. Parents fear when they send children to school, people look around suspiciously wherever they sit, others are menaced by the very sight of a car with Arab-looking passengers.

Just 15 or 20 minutes drive away, the horror may fall from heaven: helicopters constantly hover above the Palestinian towns. Will this one launch another deadly missile? Or should one fear the sudden silence: some of the assassinating missiles were fired from unheard and unseen aircraft. Or the planes that cut through the air? Is this another bombarding warplane, F-16 or F-15, a roaming earthquake just rolling down from the sky? And shouldn't one fear the countless rings of visible and invisible Israeli military posts and tanks and watch towers with sophisticated cameras and guns? Haven't dozens been killed by the anonymous soldiers in these posts? Shouldn't one fear the soldiers with deadly weapons who guard the entrances of practically every Palestinian village and town, and at times shoot and kill a person who simply tries to reach home? Thousands of Palestinians have seen how Israeli military attacks result in spilled brains, mutilated bodies, bleeding necks.

Fear, this unquantifiable sentiment, reigns now over our country.

* * *

**[October 2, 2001]**

Time: Tuesday, October 2, 2001, at 10.30 hrs

Place: Surda checkpoint north of Ramallah, on the road to the Palestinian Bir Zeit University.

Background: An army position which controls the whole valley prevents Palestinian cars from crossing. Only pedestrians are allowed through.

People walk at least one kilometre from one taxi to another, or from their own car, parked on the packed fringes, to the car which takes them to Bir Zeit University or some 30 villages to the north of Ramallah. Delay is the name of the game. Mass robbery of time.

Who: Two armies. The few: Some 20–30 Israeli soldiers. The many: Some hundreds of Bir Zeit students, teachers and Palestinian grass-roots activists.

What: Four to eight Israeli armoured vehicles, guns, stun grenades, tear gas grenades, gas masks, dozens of boxes of ammunition.

Versus: One loudspeaker, some English written placards. Leaflets. A lot of stones along the road fringes.

Why: The students demand the removal of this military post, stationed right in the midst of Palestinian populated communities. It delays thousands of people on their way to work, studies, family, doctor, etc. "Even as soldiers", was written in English, Arabic and Hebrew, in leaflets which were handed over to the soldiers, "you should search your conscience and your hearts, and ask fundamental questions about what you are doing."

How: The 'army' of several hundreds marched towards the military post. An armoured vehicle rolled down from the hill above the checkpoint, also occupied by the Army. As a symbolic act, some tens of people started to remove the mound of sand and dirt, which the army had placed in the middle of the road. The others marched on, towards the checkpoint itself where soldiers check the IDs. They sat down some 15 metres away. The soldiers put on their gas masks. The students chanted some slogans. The soldiers took off their masks. The students went on chanting. Some rose and sat at a distance of half a metre away from the jeeps and the soldiers. The rest followed suit. One soldier in one jeep started the car. Its engine roared. The others put on their gas masks again. A university professor tried to explain to the officer why such a roadblock only engineers suicide bombers.

Some students stood in front of the soldiers, their hands lifted, not signalling surrender but nonviolent resistance. The chanting grew louder. Another jeep, and another one, rolled down from another path. Reinforcement for the soldiers who, within seconds, stormed the students with tear gas and stun grenades and then sprayed shots of rubber-coated metal bullets. The ambulances were whining back and forth. Students threw back stones and some tear gas grenades, which they grabbed from the ground. The pedestrians bypassed the belligerent road block, went down into the valley, among the olive trees. They carried bags full of groceries, or construction materials, or babies, or computers wrapped in new boxes. They climbed down and up. And the stun grenades echoed behind them.

* * *

[October 24, 2001]

Our neighbourhood in Northern Ramallah was the first one to be occupied by the Israeli army, on Thursday, October 18. It was one day after the Popular Front for the Liberation of Palestine (PFLP) acknowledged that its members had assassinated Rehavam Zeevi. Zeevi, an ex-general who had entered politics. Until he became the Israeli Minister of Tourism, for years he had been advocating a 'solution' to the conflict: the expulsion of Palestinians to other states or 'transfer by consent', he and his followers claimed.

An eye for an eye, a life for a life, said the ex-Marxist, secular, nationalist PFLP. Their Secretary General, Abu Ali Mustafa, had been assassinated by Israel on August 27.

Zeevi was not targeted because of his views, but rather it was his refusal to be body-guarded or to watch his steps that made him an easy target.

The tanks roamed into the relatively new neighbourhood, where some Palestinian ministers and high officials live. That made our neighbourhood the first of Ramallah (and its twin-town, El Bireh) to be occupied. A curfew was imposed right from the start, with only one recess of two hours after five days. The army claimed this operation was meant to protect nearby Israeli communities, that is, Jewish settlements.

With the blockade of most of the main entrances to the town, during the past year this north-eastern neighbourhood has turned into a main link for people who live in the villages and a refugee camp north of the town. They cross by foot a hill and a valley. Parking taxis are waiting for them on the other side, always risking confrontation with armed Israeli soldiers.

The curfew disconnected them from the rest of the town, which is not under curfew, and where they work, study, go shopping or go to give birth and get medical treatment. These villagers, then, are the only ones to seriously defy the curfew order. By the hundreds, they keep crossing the occupied neighbourhood. Tanks and APCs chase after them, soldiers confiscate the cars' keys. The drivers find a solution: they always have a set of spare keys.

Unlike Bethlehem, which was occupied the following day, there is no Palestinian attempt here to fight the invading army, or to pretend that an armed resistance is an option. Except for occasional stun grenades and shouts, it is quiet. In Bethlehem there is fierce fighting: exposed and poorly trained youngsters, armed with guns, revolvers and home-made explosives, play hide and seek with the metal monsters which bloat the narrow streets, and their invisible crews fire back. In the houses, people hide in back rooms, under staircases or in the bathrooms. A week later, the army occupied other populated parts in other towns in the West Bank. And this is the balance of fighting: in six days, seven Israeli soldiers have been injured, one severely and the rest lightly. Twenty-eight Palestinians have been killed in the West Bank: of whom nine were armed and in battle, four others, armed as well, were assassinated ex-judicially, with no battle. And fifteen civilians: among whom four women, two boys and one girl.

\* \* \*

[October 30, 2001]

Searching for the suspected assassins of Israeli Minister Rehavam Zeevi and the suspected perpetrators of a recent ferocious suicide attack in Jerusalem, which killed 15 Israelis, the Israeli army entered the small village of Beit Reema, north-west of Ramallah. Before dawn, on October 24, a train of armoured vehicles of all sorts penetrated into the sleeping village. Two or three helicopters above spat out fire. Omar, 4 years old, all shaking, asked his mother: "Has America invaded our village?"

Five Palestinian security people were killed. Some, at least, were sleeping when the onslaught began. Even if they intended to, they had no time (or skill, if you ask me) to fight back. Three houses of suspected terrorists, where some 35 people live, were blown up. Sentenced without trial. Another house was set on fire because its inhabitants were absent, and the army suspected it sheltered wanted people. Eleven people were arrested.

All this might and fright, says the army, is necessary to prevent future terrorist attacks.

But this is not what the villagers conclude. One old man said after the attack: "I hope now that those who Israel defines as terrorists will multiply." And little Omar asked his mother: "When we die and go to Paradise, will we have a rest from it all?"

**[November 7, 2001]**
Blessed silence. It is almost six o'clock in the morning, Wednesday, November 7, and the tanks are no longer penetrating one's sleep with their imposing motor roar and the clatter of their caterpillars. They left after midnight, three weeks after they first entered and paralysed life.

Gradually, many of the residents of this middle-class neighbourhood had left their homes, to stay with family or friends in those parts of the town which were not occupied. With growing rudeness, the soldiers in their tanks succeeded in steadily reducing the number of people who 'trespassed' and defied the curfew order – to reach downtown Ramallah. After the confiscation of car keys proved insufficient a deterrent, the soldiers blocked roads, threw more and more stun grenades and tear gas bombs at the people who insisted on trying to reach work, clinics, market, family, etc. When it was still possible to cross the neighbourhood by foot, people did it, even old women and men, who lost their breath climbing up the steep hill.

After three weeks the tanks returned to their base, just across the road, in a huge military camp and military headquarters adjacent to a settlement. No Palestinian is allowed to use that road, which existed before the camp and the settlements were built, and connected Ramallah to Nablus. In spite of the three weeks of curfew, an Israeli soldier was killed in an ambush, just outside the town. And the unarmed civilians, who had been chased by tanks daily, were heard murmuring sentences in favour of a painful Palestinian retaliation.

\* \* \*

**[January 16, 2002]**

On Sunday, January 12, Raed al Karmi, a Palestinian local leader of a paramilitary group, was killed by a mysterious explosion. Israel didn't claim responsibility, but Palestinians and Israelis alike assumed it was yet another Israeli assassination, enabled by the effective work of Israeli intelligence and its collaborators. Karmi's group – 'The Martyrs of Al Aqsa', linked to Arafat's Fatah movement – immediately declared that they would not be bound any more by their previous promise to observe a ceasefire.

On the next day, an Israeli soldier was killed by armed Palestinians, two days later a woman settler was also killed and so was an old Jewish man, an invalid, who was visiting the area of Bethlehem. If killing settlers and soldiers is generally seen by the Palestinians as a justified means of fighting occupation, the murder of the old man was met by general indignation, contempt and anger.

Still, it is Palestinians, probably close to the Fatah movement, who felt free to murder an old man who had been well known in Bethlehem area. He even used to live in a Palestinian hotel, knew the local gossip, had friends all over. It seems some criminal elements took a ride on the national cause.

\* \* \*

**[Ramallah, March 14, 2002]**

The shootings and sound of explosions around the normally quiet stone-house neighbourhood in Ramallah seemed to get nearer and nearer. The sirens of ambulances cut through the air. The electricity was cut. This is when one is supposed to be afraid. Less of the shooting, more of the ignorance, of the failure to know what is really happening in the next block and intersection of roads. The family members were preparing their bunkers: mattresses on the floor, away from glass windows, behind heavy desks.

This place is privileged: the 80-year-old house is built of one metre-thick stones and normal bullets seem not to be able to penetrate. Maybe even a missile will be less destructive here than in a refugee camp – whose houses are built of thin concrete, tin roof and asbestos. A tank turning around is enough to tear down a house. Just as did one tank in the near-by tiny refugee camp, Kadura. Five minutes walk from this well-to-do quarter, there the invading force manifests a completely different attitude. The four refugee camps nearby were all severely affected by shelling.

Is it just because they assume that in refugee camps there are more 'terrorists' and people ready to die, or is it because the soldiers and their commanders show more respect to the property of the better-off?

Class differences persist in warfare, and how. In the refugee camps and poorer towns which experienced earlier incursions of the Israeli army, electricity was cut by the army for the entire period of the 'operation'. Here, in wealthier Ramallah, it was cut off only for a couple of hours, and even then not in all neighbourhoods. Incursions into Gazan cities and camps and to West Bank refugee camps are always accompanied by immediate heavy shelling from tanks and helicopters, anticipating armed resistance even when this is unlikely.

The result? Poorer areas pay an unbearably heavy toll of dead in a matter of a few hours, even minutes. Last Monday night – 17 people were killed, some tens wounded, in an attack which lasted some five hours in the biggest refugee camp, Jabalia, in the Gaza Strip.

Some of those killed were indeed trying to combat the massive force which broke into the eastern side of the camp. Combating it with home-made explosives and simple guns. Many others were civilians who were at home or in the streets. At least three were to bleed to death, as the Israeli army prevented rescue teams from reaching them. Two brothers (who, so it seems, were in a combative cell trying to plant anti-tank explosives) were among the dead. Two others: a father who was hit and injured while he was on his roof watching the incursion, and his son, who came to his rescue. Just four days before, another incursion into Gaza killed 16 people in a matter of one hour or so, with no serious counter battle.

Anticipating an Israeli incursion into Ramallah, last Monday, I moved to my friends' place in the middle of town, to be close to the events. So, in the middle of this shooting, which engulfed us, and the tanks whose engines shook the glass windows, the eldest daughter aged 19 said: "And why don't we organize a mass demonstration of civilians, to protest the invasion?" She even took her phone-book and looked up numbers. So logical, so sober, yet so impossible at this stage of the conflict.

Her father goes to sleep with his shoes and clothes on. Just in case. If soldiers knock at the door, he should be dressed. If one has to flee, it would save time. The mother is just the opposite: extremely calm, joking a lot. She had been organizing a meeting of a new Palestinian group – feminist women-activists for democracy – which had been supposed to take place in Ramallah on the day of the incursion. She is now busy cancelling the meeting by e-mail.

In between, I receive phone calls from Gaza: two of the dead, the two brothers, are my friend's relatives. An extended family of refugees, from the destroyed village of Burayr. It is a blow not only to the family but to the many descendants of the village of origin, which was destroyed in 1948 and whose people were expelled. They are dispersed all over: Gaza refugee camps, Jordan refugee camps, Europe and Ramallah.

Palestinian refugees have maintained and nurtured throughout their years of exile the typical Palestinian local-patriotism: a conscious act and a symbol of stability in circumstances of severe and ongoing temporariness.

With time, this local patriotism has extended not only to the descendants of the same village, but to all refugees: a refugee killed in his camp, let alone when the whole refugee camp is attacked, arouses special sentiments of revenge and anger among other refugees, from distant camps. It is no surprise then, that it was a refugee from Deheishe camp south Bethlehem who went to retaliate for the attacks and killings of some 25 refugees in two other camps – Balata, in Nablus, and Jenin. He blew himself to death and thus killed ten Israelis, who had just left a Jewish orthodox guest house in west Jerusalem. Among the dead were one whole family. Kids and parents. Just celebrating the birthday of one relative.

Another refugee, from Jabalia, retaliated by going to the centre of Tel Aviv and shooting at the customers of a popular restaurant, at two o'clock in the morning. One policeman and four civilians were killed. These are just two samples of the chain of retaliations that has taken place in response to Israeli raids in refugee camps.

In Israel, the raids are seen as a necessary step to locate and destroy 'nests of terror'. They are launched to arrest gunmen and planners of armed attacks, to expose laboratories of explosives and home-made missiles and rockets. Such laboratories, it is said, have been found in Balata, Tulkarem and Jabalia refugee camps. The exposure of this requires so much killing and destruction that a new generation of youngsters vows to take revenge.

Israelis count their dead with fear and wrath. So do Palestinians. Ask an Israeli how many Palestinians were killed, he wouldn't know. He'd guess, and then assume they were all 'wanted' and 'terrorists'. He wouldn't bother to find out that mothers and children and elderly people were among the casualties, and were very often shot dead from helicopters. Israeli TV does not show scenes of Palestinian death and mourning and open heads and spilled brains by Israeli bullets.

Palestinians do count the number of Israeli dead. Do they count. For them, it is proof that Prime Minister Ariel Sharon's promise of security, and his policy to regain this, have failed. They also closely watch Israeli TV when it shows horror scenes from blown-up cafés and dismembered corpses. "If Israel does not respect the life of our civilians, if Israelis do not care for our civilians, why should we respect and care for theirs," they say. And they also say: "If we had war jets and tanks and helicopters, we would have had no need of human bombs."

One such café in Jerusalem was the target of the latest suicide bombing, perpetrated by another refugee from Al-Aroub camp, north of Hebron. His family is originally from a village called Masmiye. This café is a childhood milestone for me. I would go there to fetch my mother, who sat with her friends, some decades ago. In her last years, we again frequented the place: it has no stairs, so she could easily get in.

This café, *Moment*, is located just next to the Prime Minister's residence. But more importantly, it is close to 'Paris Square', where for the last 15 years the Women in Black movement protest every Friday against the Israeli occupation. Some of them, after the protest is over, go for a chat and coffee at this very *Moment* . . .

## [Jenin Refugee Camp, April 17, 2002]

Darkness wrapped the refugee camp of Jenin, last Monday. Um Mohammed lit some candles. It was a hot day, but some breeze did penetrate through the windows which just 10 days previously had all been hit and broken by the heavy shelling. Ziad, a grey bearded man, was calling his family on his host's mobile phone (recharged by a car battery, as the electricity supply is still cut). Ziad had made them leave the camp on the eve of the army's attack. He now told his children, who were begging to come home: "But there is no home now, everything is gone, no schoolbooks, no radio. No video cassettes. The house was hit and burnt by some missiles." So were the houses nearby, all built by Ziad, a construction worker.

It was the 12th day in a row that this hilly, steep camp, of 13,000 people in one square kilometre of dense houses, had been without electricity, running water or direct quick medical assistance. It was the first day that journalists managed to sneak into the camp in any numbers, since it had been declared a closed military zone by the Israeli army. A few had managed to get in on previous days, and had been documenting the destruction caused by the bulldozers, helicopters, tanks and searching soldiers. But last Monday their and our shock at what our eyes saw somewhat lifted up the people's spirits, until then sealed in a cage of endless shooting, devastating destruction and complete isolation from the outside world, even from the hospitals only a distance of 200 metres from the entrance to the camp, to which the wounded could not be transferred in time because the army would not allow ambulance teams to enter the camp without coordination, and coordination took several days.

People were going up and down the rubble, mountains of smashed concrete, crooked iron bars and broken glass, puddles of water, sewage and mud, torn mattresses and leftovers of the last suppers. Some people were pointing to the heaps of rubble and murmuring: My father is buried under it, or my son, or no one knows if the neighbours, two elderly sisters, had fled or not. In a matter of a few days hundreds of houses of civilians were totally demolished or rendered uninhabitable. People now search in the rubble and try to rescue a torn shirt, a shoe, a sack of rice. People share the little water they have saved, waiting for rescue teams to be allowed entry and bring some fresh water and food.

One does not know yet how many people were killed in the endless shooting. Ziad estimates that around 50 people have been killed. How many of them were Palestinian militia, determined to fight back the Israeli army, which was determined to eradicate all 'pockets of terror', said to be concentrated in this refugee camp, out of which some dozen suicide bombers and gunmen had sprung out during the last year? How many were civilians, hit, injured and killed by indiscriminate shooting from tanks and then helicopters? How many were wounded and bled to death, how many were killed when bulldozers dug in and around and made the houses collapse on them, and how many fled in time?

Two of Ziad's nephews had died, both of them armed, killed while fighting the invading Israeli army. They are termed terrorists in Israel, as their groups were engaged in attacks against Israeli soldiers and civilians. One was a leading member of Fatah, an ex-prisoner from the first Intifada and the other a young member of the Islamic Jihad. Both were disappointed by the Oslo process, when in spite of all promises they discovered there was no decent future awaiting them and their children. At least nine of Ziad's neighbours, all civilians, were also killed. Now, their relatives swear that this attack on Jenin refugee camp has only given birth to more people who are willing to kill and be killed.

\* \* \*

**[April 24, 2002]**

First, it's the shock. Shock at seeing one's office totally damaged. The computers gone, broken or thrown in a heap. The servers gone, the printers gone or dirtied. The copy machine smashed. Walls and doors and windows broken in and smashed. Then, it's even more shocking, when one learns it's not only one's office but the office next door, and one's friend's clinic, and the Ministry of Education, and Ministry of Higher Education, and Ministry of Finance, and other ministries and research centres and two banks, and an internet café and another one, and some schools. Hundreds of civilian offices were mutilated in a similar way by the Israeli army, in its three-week operation against the 'infrastructure of terror'.

Then, it's rage. What the hell did they think they were achieving, if not the opposite. So many of Palestine's yuppies ('Pup'ies', in Ramallah's slang) were saying the same: Now, after all our efforts to build up a normal civil society have been smashed by some groups of soldiers on a vendetta campaign, we believe there is no other way but suicide bombings.

Then, it's energy. From the first hours after the army left some parts of Ramallah and other towns, everybody was engaged in cleaning up, sweeping floors, removing the rubble, estimating the damage, ordering new shelves, new chairs, checking what database could be saved and how, sending children and teachers to schools, calling technicians to repair safes and elevators.

Until the next Israeli operation against terror.

**[April 30, 2002]**

One of the senior employees of the Palestinian Ministry of Planning just got back from 18 days in Israeli detention camp. He was apprehended at home, in one of the many raids that the Israeli army was conducting in Ramallah and elsewhere. Many thousands – accurate numbers are still not available – have been arrested. Many thousands have already been released.

Luckily, the Ministry of Planning was not invaded and mutilated like so many of the other ministries. So the employees didn't have to clean up the mess and had time to sit with this newly released 18-days-suspected terrorist, and hear him talking about his experience.

He also told them about his son, who had seen him arrested. Your role, the mother told the little boy, is to go to school, to study well, to grow up, then to study engineering and build houses. The kid clung to his mother. I don't want to go to school, he said. Because then when I grow and build homes, the Jews will destroy them.

This reminded one of the attendants in the room the joke about the fisherman who was approached by a grand businessman who tried to talk him into starting a business. What for, asked the fisherman. So you can get rich, and richer, and get so rich that you can give up work and go fishing . But that is just what I am doing now, came the reply.

**[Gaza, June 26, 2002]**

People here in Gaza no longer want to see those juicy, fleshy and colourful summer fruits, plums, grapes, nectarines, apricots and peaches, which come from Israel and are exhibited at every corner. Some asked the merchants to stop selling them. Not because people boycott Israeli products: You can't, after all, boycott 90 per cent of your imported goods. But because they cannot afford to buy them for their children. Fathers ask the local vendor of watermelons not to come to their street.

Some people stop buying fruits to support their unemployed relatives instead. Fresh fruits have become then a symbol of life beyond reach for most Palestinians. That's what one learns here these days in some protest tents, which unemployed Palestinian workers erected some five months ago.

Most of them used to work in Israel. They protest against Israel's order to seal up Gaza's gates, but they also protest at what they regard as the indifference and negligence of the Palestinian National Authority. It has failed to establish a special fund, to which their social-security taxes were supposed to be transferred from Israel to the Palestinian Authority's treasury, in order to guarantee their unemployment benefits. They protest the unequal distribution of incomes: "This big shot's son studies abroad, while my son, who got A's only, can't even attend the Open University," some say. Others mention another Palestinian official who recently bought a piece of land.

Under the pressures of unemployment, poverty and hermetic closure, internal Palestinian class tensions are being accentuated.

## [Ramallah, September 17, 2002]

A musical interlude. The *oud* [a basic string instrument of Arab music] concert was scheduled for last Tuesday, 4 o'clock in the afternoon. Night curfew is at 7 o'clock, and that is why most cultural activities take place in the afternoon.

Some tens of people started gathering in the yard of the cultural centre in Ramallah. Many women came, some writers, some couples, some mothers with their infants, some hippie-like youngsters. All yearning for an outbreak of normality. The artist is a Palestinian from Israel, Khaled Jubran. Performing with him are another *oud* player and a cellist.

The programme had to be short, because of the curfew, etc. He played his own music. Emotional but not sentimental, insisting but not obstinate, at times harsh, at times soft. People drank the music, adored the flirting between the cello and the *oud*. Then, when he wished to depart – because of the curfew, etc – they protested. They suggested he play some melodies of known songs, so that they could join in. He hesitated. Someone suggested a song; he said "No political songs" – obviously fed up by empty verbiage. He ended up with three love songs, and the audience – mostly some women – joined in. Some had tears in their eyes.

On the way back home I was startled by an Israeli armoured car and a mobile fence of barbed wire, which was blocking the main road. I noticed two anonymous youngsters, seated on the sidewalk next to the military car, hands cuffed, eyes covered. They are wanted, the soldiers told me. An hour earlier, the army had been firing back at youngsters who had thrown Molotov cocktails at them.

* * *

**[Gaza, June 25, 2003]**
Bassam was sitting, smiling, on his hospital bed. It was his sixth day in the Gazan hospital. I am already used to it, he joked – like Gazans often do, even during the worst situations. He could smile now, after the pain in his thighs and hands – which had been hit and penetrated and cut deeply by missile shrapnel – has somewhat receded. He is finishing his PhD in education and works at the Palestinian Centre for Human Rights in Gaza. That's how I know him. He was driving in a taxi to work, June 10, when Israeli missiles tried to assassinate the Hamas leader, Abd al-Aziz al-Rantisi. After the first boom, Rantisi's car got nearer to them, moving at high speed. The taxi passengers managed to jump out, but then came more missiles. Bassam crawled, wounded, until he lost consciousness. The driver died of his wounds a few days later.

June 1. Bus no. 14, Jerusalem. One of the passengers on the back seat is Yonatan, the son of Ayala. She is an architect, a member of *Bimkom* (In place), a group of planners and architects who fight against discrimination in urban planning. That's how I know her, especially thanks to her work with Palestinian residents of Jerusalem, where the municipal laws clearly violate their housing rights. She was in Tel Aviv when the news broke that a suicide bomber had exploded in a bus. She knew her son was due on that bus. "Should I drive to Jerusalem, to look for him in the hospitals, or should I go straight to the official pathological institute in Tel Aviv, where they identify the bodies?", she asked herself, in her typical, calm cynicism. Only after half an hour of anguish was her son able to use his mobile to let her know he was okay. Only some scratches on his shoulder.

**[November 19, 2003]**

Maher came all the way from Tulkarem, sealed off like all other Palestinian cities, to see his brother Khalil. In the midst of the casual talk, something reminded Maher to tell us: When an Israeli undercover unit killed Sirhan Sirhan in full daylight some six weeks ago, his son Jaber, aged 12, saw it all. For more than a week afterwards he couldn't sleep, hardly talked, jumped in fright at every sound. And this is in a town which has witnessed endless lethal military incursions.

Sirhan Sirhan was suspected of attacking and murdering five Israeli civilians, including a mother and her two sleeping children, in a Kibbutz within Israel proper. It was a joint Fatah–Islamic Jihad 'operation'. Coincidentally, this Kibbutz had publicly protested against the Separation Fence because it destroyed Palestinians' land.

Sirhan Sirhan had been hiding in the refugee camp of Tulkarem for more than a year, until an Israeli undercover unit, disguised as arms dealers, traced and reached him. In the process of killing him, the soldiers also killed a Palestinian child, in a passing car. Jaber had just had his haircut at a nearby barber shop. Everything happened in front of his eyes.

Khalil was surprised that his brother hadn't mentioned this before. Maher – himself a political prisoner in the past, an ex-member of the Popular Front – shrugged his shoulders, cursed Sirhan Sirhan ("No hero, no freedom fighter"). His eyes – always so expressive, more than his meagre sentences – told us how painful it was.

**[April 7, 2004]**

Y sighed with relief. His nephew, S, had finally been arrested by the Israeli army. It was a double sigh of relief, actually. The nephew had been 'wanted' for almost a year and the family had feared he might be killed in one of the frequent military ambushes and searches for wanted armed activists. His arrest guaranteed he would remain alive. And the second reason for the sigh of relief? He had been caught on his way to conduct some 'armed operation'. The family does not know exactly what. Shooting at Israeli vehicles, planting a bomb in a settlement, directing a suicide bomber? "How lucky we are that he was arrested before the 'operation'," his uncle told me. "We are saved the agony of having one of us be a killer of a human being."

S had already been involved in directing suicide bombers to an Israeli settlement in the West Bank. Even though no Israeli had been killed, he may still be charged with the killing of the two suicide bombers. At times, his uncle considered extraditing him: life, even in prison, is worth more than any heroic, senseless death.

The family has lost by now most of its land because of the 'separation fence'. Losing it equals losing life, the family said at first. Y and his brother feared for their old parents' health and will to live. S's involvement in the failed suicide attack and his subsequent underground life as a wanted man have not brought the land back. And the family has discovered that life – and the future of the children – are the most sacred asset it has.

* * *

[May 5, 2004]

Yasser Abu Laymoun, 32 years old, was a teacher of hospital administration at Jenin's American Arabic University. Israeli soldiers killed him on a Friday, April 23, in his village Taluza, north-west of Nablus. Military sources admitted he was not armed, but claimed he had had contacts with Hamas people. This deadly 'fact' was printed and published by military correspondents, who cited the soldiers' initial version. Two wanted, armed men fled away from a military force which entered the village and had shot towards them. It was a hilly, bushy area, out of the village. The force unleashed a dog trained to attack, which after a few seconds caught a running man. Assuming this was one of the wanted men, they shot and killed him.

Two days after the killing I spoke with the widow, Dallal, 21 years old, pregnant and mother of a 10-month-old baby. She, her husband and his sister had gone out for a short walk, to the family's piece of land where he had planted some fruit trees, two years ago, at a distance of 200 metres from their home. Bushy, but an open area. No big trees, but one oak tree, from behind which came the shots. She heard her husband saying "ay", and saw him falling down. The hidden soldiers kept on shooting "like pouring rain", as she described it to me, then showed themselves, aiming their guns towards the two women. The soldiers had a dog with them. It hadn't attacked her husband. Confronted by this information, a military spokesperson had to admit: the man had not been armed, had not been wanted, and had not been attacked by a dog; but the woman had exaggerated: there are many trees at the site.

\* \* \*

## [Rafah, May 19, 2004]

"But aren't you afraid of this endless shooting", I asked Ahmed, 12 years old, who lives with his family in one of the refugee neighbourhoods adjacent to the border. Last Monday I stayed there overnight, awaiting a new military incursion into the town of Rafah.

Israeli military patrols control this border area and the road along the Egyptian–Gazan border. Patrols mean constant shooting. Night and day. This is where the Israeli army has demolished hundreds of houses during the last three and a half years, in the same manner. Shortly after midnight, some metal monsters called tanks accompanying two or three giant bulldozers position themselves in front of the houses, a helicopter hovers above and vomits fire at anybody seen outside the houses, presumably armed men of the Palestinian resistance. Then some houses are razed to the ground. In the beginning, people remained indoors, finding it hard to believe that the army would dare demolish while they were inside. Now they know better. Last week the army demolished some 100 houses and made some 1,000 people homeless, overnight. "Operational reasons", the army said. Military convenience, that is. "The houses were empty" or hosted "terrorists", was their alternative version.

But not only Palestinians, also Israelis sensed there was much more beyond it, or much less: REVENGE. Palestinian guerrilla fighters – poorly equipped, poorly trained, unskilled and unorganized as they are – had killed seven Israeli troopers. The mass demolition was the answer. Prime

Minister Ariel Sharon said he would "widen" the border zone. Meaning: more demolitions.

And then came the exodus. Hundreds of families have been leaving their houses. During the past week, they have been taking everything possible out of the houses: water tanks, mattresses, pots, doors, windows, TV dishes, ceiling fans, iron bars, taps, pipes, all loaded in carts led by horses, donkeys or tractors, or in vans and taxis or even two-wheeled small carts. Fleeing northward, away from the threatened, targeted, zone. There are no flats left for rent now in Rafah, or their rent is too high for most of the new refugees. They stay with relatives, store the furniture in some asbestos makeshift shacks or even outside, in courtyards. These carts and vans keep rolling in the streets of Rafah, behind them the family members walk or drive, with faces ashen, glances fixed, old men holding their sticks, old women limp from side to side, eyes dry of tears. They gave up hope that world opinion or the Israeli high court or the Arab states might intervene.

Everybody then expected an incursion into this border zone. That is why I moved into one of the houses there, a solid one though, I wouldn't have dared to stay in an exposed tin construction, flimsy as air. But the army tricked the Palestinian resistance: its first shots and launched missiles were indeed directed, from the air, towards armed men in the refugee camp Yibneh. But two hours later, the army took over a northern refugee neighbourhood, far from the border. 25,000 people live there. The streets are broad – unfit for guerrilla warfare – people said, explaining the non-existent resistance. In less than 20 hours, during last Tuesday, 19 people were killed, 11 of whom were civilians. Now this neighbourhood is disconnected from the rest of Rafah, placed under curfew, heavily invaded by soldiers – in tanks or in houses that they occupied, forcing their tenants to stay in one room.

Ahmed's family lives near the occupied neighbourhood. "So, aren't you afraid of the shootings?" I asked him. He shrugged his shoulders and smiled. "We got used to it," he said. "Even the birds did." And how would you know? "In the beginning," the experienced 12-year-old child told me, "with every shot, they immediately flew up, now, even when there is heavy shooting, they remain where they are."

\* \* \*

**[September 29, 2004]**

Before dawn, on Wednesday, September 29, the fourth anniversary of the al-Aqsa Intifada, heavily armed Israeli military troops ordered the Zbeidi family out of the house: take your money, valuables, documents, and leave, as we are going to detonate the house of Zakaria Zbeidi (which stands empty). Some hundreds of the neighbourhood's inhabitants, children, old men and women, left in a hurry. Dusk and fear enveloped them all.

At 04:30 there was a huge explosion. And people discovered that not only Zakaria's house had turned into rubble, but all the adjacent buildings had been severely damaged. "We always start from zero", the uncle told me, Jammal, a 55-year-old activist and ex-political prisoner, whose house has been destroyed twice already; once, as punishment for his cousin's activities during the first Intifada. The second time, by a missile, during the April 2002 invasion. And now a third time.

Zakaria Zbeidi, in his 30s, is considered to be the head of the Fatah military wing in the Jenin refugee camp. He is a typical, tragic representative of a lost generation of young refugees, adherents of Arafat's organization, Fatah. The first Intifada severed their school studies; the Palestinian Authority, instead of encouraging them to complete their studies, recruited many as poorly paid policemen and armed guards. They have been watching with growing anger how the golden Oslo 'promises' have been transformed into benefits and privileges for a narrow stratum, while occupation has continued to dictate their lives.

When the al-Aqsa Intifada broke out, Zakaria and his like joined in and encouraged its militarization, after many of their pals were killed by Israeli soldiers while demonstrating and throwing stones. No real training, no real political strategy and vision. Only the philosophy: *Je suis armé, donc je suis* [I am armed, hence I exist].

His uncle, brother and mother were all killed in spring 2002; the first two in real battles, his mother in her home.

Zakaria has been active in marketing himself as a hero (waving a gun and shooting into the sky in front of TV cameras) and threatening Palestinian officials, more than in challenging Israeli occupation. Some shootings at Israeli settlers and vehicles – and recently, an explosion which caused the death of two Palestinians – are attributed to his group.

Yes, his is the conduct of a petty hooligan, an amateur. But what his neighbours and family see is the vengeful crusade of Israel – a military superpower – and the drive for on-going collective punishment.

* * *

**[October 6, 2004]**

The Gaza Strip has been sealed off for journalists for the last two weeks. So we have not been able to cover from close quarters the latest Israeli assault on the northern parts of the Strip, which started on September 28. The assault's aim was, once again, to deter and kill Palestinian launchers of home-made, primitive rockets.

So I depend on my friends' accurate testimonies, to counter the standard military jargon of "fighting against terrorists", and "all Palestinian casualties are terrorists".

It was easy to get exact information about the explosion of an Israeli tank mortar, and the killing of 10 people thereby, among them eight children. It was easy to find out that these were civilians, and that no 'fighting' took place. It happened just 20 metres away from my friends' home in the refugee camp of Jabalia. This mortar finally convinced them to flee, leave home and stay in Gaza, until the tanks leave the area. They now live in fear that they will return to a demolished home.

But the accurate information about the killing of two other civilians, both farmers, came from a surprising source: a soldier. He contacted me to inform me about the unjustified killing. I sent my Palestinian friends to double check the circumstances. Now they faced a problem: one family insisted that their son was 'a fighter', who died in battle. Many families, I have discovered, are giving false, glorified versions of what happened, for reasons of honour and social acceptability, thus giving the Israeli army another reason to claim it is targeting armed people, 'terrorists' only.

**[December 1, 2004]**

The casualties ratio of this current bloody round of the Israeli–Palestinian conflict is about 1:3, one Israeli to every three Palestinians; during the first Intifada it was 1:7 or 1:10. Doesn't it indicate that this Intifada is more 'successful' than the former?

This was the logic expressed in a private talk by an American woman, who runs a news website that covers the Israeli occupation of the Palestinian territories. It is indeed common to find this logic among

Palestinians, when they are asked to assess the last four years of oppression, occupation, resistance and terror.

But measuring 'success' or 'failure' by the ratio of corpses has nothing to do with a real, emancipating idea of resistance. Apart from the moral flaw, it indicates a lack of political understanding of Israel's long-term policies; that is, rapid colonization, carving the Palestinian territories into enclaves and fragmenting Palestinian society into disconnected, dispersed communities.

The current uprising, clumsy as it is, broke out because of the insulting gap between the sweet promises of the Oslo years, and the dire reality of siege, confiscation of land and a basically indifferent Palestinian Authority. Unfortunately, the message has been blurred by Arafat's obsessive reference to holy sites instead of settlements in general, and by the quick, chaotic militarization of the uprising. The embryonic guerrilla strikes turned into terrorist attacks against civilians, which overshadowed Israel's acts of state terrorism.

Has the 'good' ratio of corpses done anything to stop the process of colonization? On the contrary: the construction in and for the settlements is frighteningly rapid. More and more Israelis seem to have a vested interest in keeping this process going.

\* \* \*

### [Ramallah, June 29, 2005]

This has already become a weekly, if not a daily, scene, often in Gaza, far too often in Nablus and Ramallah. A group of armed men spray the air – or worse, a restaurant or a bar, a police station or the house of one of the Palestinian ministers – with their bullets. In one such incident last week in Jenin a Palestinian policeman was killed.

Last week it was also the turn of a Ramallah bar, at 2 after midnight. Luckily only the guards were around, to witness how the glass and windows broke into pieces. The next morning a leaflet was said to have been distributed, calling on people to stop frequenting the bars and restaurants.

The signature contained the word "Islamic", but it should not mislead anyone. These are not Hamas activists, as the only gunmen who dare to terrorize their fellow residents belong to Fatah, the backbone of the Palestinian Authority. In general, it is believed, they hope to intimidate and force the Palestinian Authority security officials into recruiting them into one of the security organs. As if the mere knowledge of how to shoot qualifies them for the job!

At the same time, targeting Ramallah restaurants represents a genuine, not unjustified anger. A stratum of officials, NGO employees, businessmen, foreign-press journalists and permanent or visiting diplomats fill such places every night, and are a testimony to the incredible economic and social gaps in a society still fighting for liberation. It speaks volumes about how internal social solidarity is falling apart, of a nomenclature which benefits from international donations, of money in abundance which does not reach the majority of the population. The problem, of course, is that the anger is spoken with guns, and not channelled into political-social action.

* * *

**[October 26, 2005]**

Shuruq is a 19-year-old student at the veterinary faculty of An-Najah University, in Nablus. She is one of only two female students, among 70, in this new faculty, which opened in 2000, the first veterinary faculty for Palestinians. During the first year, lessons are given in Nablus. The other five years they are given in Tulkarem, southwest of Nablus.

Shuruq has a brother, who studies computer engineering in China. It is his second year, too. Both were home during the summer vacation. Now the father is planning to visit his son. But as much as he would like to, he is not planning to visit his daughter, in Tulkarem, only one hour's drive away.

Shuruq's family are Jerusalemites. That is, they live in the only refugee camp which is within the boundaries of Jerusalem – Shuafat. In 1967, some 70 square kilometres of Arab East Jerusalem and the villages surrounding it were annexed to Israel and included within the municipal boundaries of Israeli Jerusalem. Shuruq's family holds Jerusalemite identity cards, being Israeli residents (not citizens, they don't have the right to vote).

With the outbreak of the al-Aqsa Intifada, the military central commander issued an order, prohibiting Israelis from entering Palestinian Authority-held towns. The order included East Jerusalem Palestinians.

People have found ways to sneak into these cities, especially Bethlehem and Hebron, where they have relatives and long-standing economic and social ties. The army did not impose this order on people who enter Ramallah, as thousands of Jerusalemites do every day. Probably, this is because many international agencies and diplomatic representatives employ East Jerusalemites. But, with the advance of the separation wall and the sealing off of cities with tight gates, such as Tulkarem and Nablus, Jerusalemites realized they could not get into these cities.

Therefore Shuruq is 'illegal' in Tulkarem. She doesn't dare to go home more than once every two or three months. If caught leaving, she might have to pay a fine. If caught entering, she might be detained, sent back and prevented from attending classes. Her family cannot visit her. Just one hour's drive away.

**[Nablus, November 23, 2005]**
A huge Hamas poster is hanging on the wall of a living room, with the imposing portrait of one of its life prisoners, with the expected emblems and praises to Allah. The parents, wife, children, brothers and cousins of this prisoner fill the well-attended living room, and chat with their three guests. About their land which has been taken for the sake of nearby settlements, about a niece who was killed by an Israeli soldier when she tried to return to the besieged village some five years ago, about the frequent military raids.

Then they insist that their guests have dinner, and apologize for not having prepared more as they hadn't known they would come. One youngster has just finished music school, but intends to join the Palestinian police. He is the only Fatah supporter "and do we quarrel", they all laugh. The rest of the family supports Hamas.

All this is told in utter confidence and with ease to the three guests – three Israeli women; two are activists of a relatively newly formed group, *Yesh din* ('There is a Law'), which monitors the ever-increasing cases of Palestinians harassed by Israeli settlers. The third guest is myself, and I have just accompanied the two women and the 70-year-old father to an Israeli police station, in a distant settlement, where he testified about severe harassment at the hands of anonymous settlers.

Palestinians are not allowed entry to settlements, so the group's earlier coordination with the police is vital. The man had been beaten up by masked settlers only six months ago, in a similar attack. This time he spent one week in hospital. With a fatherly smile he told me: "It's only because of you three that I complained to the police. Experience tells us that the Israeli authorities do not bother to investigate complaints and suspicions against settlers." Off the record, the policeman confided to us a similar conclusion.

*  *  *

**[March 1, 2006]**
Twelve-year-old Ayoub from Nablus has spent almost half his life in curfews, military invasions, incessant shelling, long 'town arrests'. He has witnessed people being killed, his school mates wounded, tanks 'parked' for days at a time under his window. For some months he was so traumatized that his parents considered sending him abroad. If they had the money.

Last week Ayoub was seen throwing stones at an Israeli jeep. The army conducted a several-day-long attack against the refugee camp of Balata. The school is close by, many of his school mates are residents of the camp. "I cannot tell him not to throw stones, it's his right as a child under occupation," says the father. "But here is another reason to remain sleepless at night." So many youngsters and children who threw stones have been killed and wounded by Israeli soldiers, including two last week.

Fourteen-year-old Yoav lives in London, with his Israeli parents. Angry and desperate at the invincible occupation, they emigrated. Whenever they return for a visit, Yoav joins all sorts of anti-occupation activities. Yoav spent almost half of his life travelling, absorbing new cultures, meeting people from all over the world. They will visit Israel next month, and he already plans to demonstrate with his anarchist friends against the Separation Fence/Wall, along the construction sites. "I cannot tell him not to demonstrate, it's his duty as an Israeli, and I am proud of him," wrote his mother. "But here is another reason to worry." Every such demonstration – of Palestinians, Israelis and 'internationals' – is dispersed violently by the Israeli army. Last week a rubber-coated bullet hit the eye of a 17-year-old Israeli protestor.

* * *

**[February 19, 2003]**

Catastrophe: sudden or widespread or noteworthy disaster; event that subverts the system of things; disastrous end, ruin.

Routine: regular course of procedure, unvarying performance of certain acts.

But there is no definition for a routine catastrophe, or for a routine of catastrophes. At first glance, it is an oxymoron. But this is exactly what befalls the Palestinians, in their cities and villages occupied and controlled by Israel and its mighty army. There is a daily routine of unarmed and armed individuals being killed by Israeli ammunition; a routine of youngsters attempting to reach and attack an Israeli target and who get killed; a routine mourning, wake houses, funerals, a routine of arrests; a routine of alerts about planned Palestinian infiltrations into Israel; a routine of military attacks within Palestinian residential neighbourhoods; a routine of home demolitions by explosives or bull-dozers, homes of families whose son is suspected of and wanted for military engagement against Israeli civilians and soldiers; a routine of demolishing small metal workshops, allegedly producing mortars; a routine destruction of agricultural land, fields and orchards; a routine of tear gas being thrown at the throngs crossing roadblocks; a routine of delays at checkpoints and abusive behaviour of soldiers positioned there; a routine of being denied visits to prison, when one's son or husband or brother is jailed; a routine of losing a job due to new Israeli measures.

Each individual and family lives daily through several sorts of catastrophic routines. Life is turned upside down every single day. Routinely. And it is an ever-escalating routine. Being a routine, it totally escapes the world's attention. Being a routine, it is not news.

# 7

# Kuwait: Never Before, Never Again

---

*N. Janardhan*

Like all weekday mornings, Camillo D'Souza, an Indian employed in an advertising agency in Kuwait, set out from his house for work in a friend's car. Minutes into the drive, he turned on the radio, only to be greeted by silence. His friend immediately blamed the mechanic for tampering with the radio while fixing the music system the previous day. On reaching the office, Camillo was surprised to see a skeletal staff and enquired the reason from an Arab colleague, almost in tandem with the reverberating noise of an explosion. "The Iraqi Army invaded Kuwait during the night," his colleague said with a sigh.[1]

Most people in Kuwait awoke to similar experiences on August 2, 1990.[2] Faleh Khalaf – a 17-year-old Kuwaiti – was still in bed when his mother rushed into the room and woke him up in a worried tone. "There are confusing reports on television. Wake up and tell me what's happening," she said. Sleepy-eyed Faleh walked to the front room and increased the volume of the Kuwaiti television channel, which was already fairly loud. "Arabs, help us," was the short message that was repeated by the presenter. Faleh quickly changed channels. "We have won," was the equally short message that the presenter on the Iraqi television channel was repeating. Faleh ran up the stairs to the terrace, which overlooked the sea, and saw army tanks with Iraqi flags on the bridge next to his house. It was then that Faleh put things into perspective.[3]

The media had reported the tension between the Iraqi and Kuwaiti governments for a few days prior to the invasion. While an air of uncertainty prevailed, "there appeared to be no cause for alarm," according to Faleh, especially since Egyptian President Hosni Mubarak had announced during a visit to Kuwait only days earlier that all the 'problems' between Iraq and Kuwait would be solved.

## Causes for Aggression

The immediate provocation for Iraq was the alleged overproduction and siphoning of oil by Kuwait from Iraq's side of the Rumaillah oilfield, which lay across the undemarcated Iraqi–Kuwaiti border. It was also alleged that Kuwait's military was stationed inside Iraqi territory. A large part of Iraq's problems, however, was financial. Despite being one of the world's largest oil producers, Iraq had paid heavily for the eight-year hostilities against Iran and was desperate to get its debts to the Gulf Cooperation Council (GCC) countries waived.[4] In all, the Iraqis were reported to have demanded US$10 billion in aid, debt write-offs of an additional US$10 billion, the relinquishing of Kuwait's section of the Rumaillah oilfield, US$2.4 billion in payment for oil which Kuwait had legitimately extracted from Rumaillah, and finally a long-term lease of the Bubiyan and Warba islands.

Kuwait rejected the demands as unjustified, unreasonable and threatening. The efforts to resolve the flaring tempers failed and less than two days after the Jeddah conference in Saudi Arabia, Iraq invaded and occupied Kuwait. The Iraqis initially declared that it was a visit by Iraqi forces in response to an urgent invitation by internal 'revolutionaries' who were mounting a popular coup against the Kuwaiti government. Having taken control of the broadcasting station a 'Provisional Free Kuwait Government' went live on air and a week after the occupation, Kuwait was unilaterally declared a part of Iraq.[5]

It was not long before the people of Kuwait, both the minority nationals and majority multicultural expatriate community – who formed the backbone of the skilled, semi-skilled and unskilled workforce – realized that the country was under Iraqi occupation.[6] However, most believed that it was only a temporary phase, a belief reinforced by the assertions of the 'provincial' government led by Colonel Alaa Hussein Ali.

## First Tremors

The first few days following the invasion were confusing because nobody could relate to the chaos of a normally quiet Kuwait. With the Amir (head of state) and Crown Prince, along with most other members of the Al-Sabah ruling family, flying to Taif in Saudi Arabia after the invasion, the people were ignorant about what to expect and how to react.

Hardships soon began to mount. Most government and private school buildings were taken over shortly after the invasion and converted into barracks by the Iraqi army. They proceeded to remove equipment in trucks and then to vandalize and destroy as much as they could. Others were transformed by the Iraqi soldiers into detention and torture centres. Apart from those providing essential services, such as water, electricity, hospitals and fire-fighting, all other institutions refused to function.[7]

Most schools and colleges were also closed for the first few weeks. Even if a few remained open, whereas some expatriates sent their children to school, Kuwaitis preferred not to. Though the main electricity station survived the Iraqi onslaught as a building, electricity all over Kuwait gradually shut down as the occupation continued. With no salaries, people sold cars and air conditioners to Iraqis to get money to buy essential commodities from a fast depleting market.

Iraqi civilians crossed over to Kuwait and looted locked houses. In some cases, soldiers entered houses of Kuwaitis too, but left without taking anything or harassing anyone. "Their motive was to ensure that there were no weapons hidden in the house which could be used later for resistance," Faleh said. Still others entered houses, demanded food and water, stole money and jewellery, and even harassed women.

The cooperatives and few supermarkets that remained open were full of people buying supplies in panic. Since the Iraqi army was allowed to raid the central stores, food shortages became apparent as the occupation persisted. Merchants closed their doors, adding to the woes. The prospect of dying of hunger and thirst seemed a grim possibility, which encouraged people to start leaving Kuwait.[8]

Within days, people were seen packing their belongings and leaving for 'don't know where'. Some Kuwaiti families moved away from houses close to the sea, which they feared could become a battleground at some point, to residences that were part of a nearly-complete government housing project for nationals. By August 20, Iraq had ordered all foreign embassies to shut down and relocate to Baghdad. But about 25 of them, including the American and British embassies, refused to close. Their buildings were immediately surrounded by armed soldiers and tanks. Ambassadors and their staff became prisoners in their compounds, cut off from supplies of food, electricity and even water.

American and other Westerner expatriates attempted escape by driving across the desert into Saudi Arabia. Some were lucky to cross over, but in a few cases where they were either caught escaping or found lost in the desert, there were reports of them being killed. Still others suffered dehydration when their cars got stuck in the desert and they waited for help.

Conditions at the border posts – Turkey, Saudi Arabia, Iran and Jordan – where nationals and expatriates were trying to leave Kuwait, were chaotic. Apart from handling the procedures at a lethargic pace, which took its toll on people because of the very high temperatures during that season, many were arbitrarily informed that their papers were not in order, or that no more papers would be processed for the day. As a result, many were forced to return to Kuwait.

Kuwaitis were hard-pressed to decide if they should stay on or leave the country. Many organized pockets of resistance on their own. Irrespective of gender, sectarian or class affiliations, people engaged in acts of defiance until Iraq began to react with violent reprisals in October 1990. The need to maintain essential services and to establish security control over the population of occupied Kuwait led the Iraqis to demand that key workers return to their jobs. While some Palestinians and a few other Arab nationals responded to this demand because Iraq linked its withdrawal from Kuwait to Israel's withdrawal from Palestinian territories, many Kuwaitis refused to work. Those who agreed to work tried to use the opportunity to serve society, by disbursing salaries, maintaining electricity and water, etc.

Such activities gave birth to the 'Free Kuwait Movement', which played an active role in collecting and collating information about the invasion, liaising with the media, coordinating demonstrations and meetings, and cooperating with international agencies concerning relief for Kuwait following its liberation. A few Kuwaitis returned once they discovered that it was possible to manage under occupation. A group even started a weekly bus service between Kuwait and Iraq so that Kuwaitis could visit arrested family members.[9]

**Rampant Looting**

Coming from a society that had been gradually deprived of even bare necessities following the war with Iran, Iraqi soldiers were awed by the array of vehicles in Kuwait – BMWs, Mercedes, and four-wheel drives were major attractions. While some cars were stolen and several others deliberately destroyed, a popular method of removing a car from its owner was to stop it at an inspection point and ask the driver to produce his or her ID and the registration papers. If the name on it did not match the driver's ID, the person would be taken to the police station on theft charges, and the car never returned. Another ploy was to ask the driver to leave the car where it had been halted and fetch the person who owned the car. When the person returned with the rightful owner, invariably a family member, the car would have disappeared. Iraqis stole and destroyed about half-a-million vehicles. Television programmes showed many cars, buses and vans from Kuwait being driven around the streets of Baghdad and other cities; and auctions were announced in various Iraqi towns of cars and buses as well as office machinery stolen from Kuwait.[10]

## Constructive Cooperatives

Among the most important sources and distributors of food during the occupation were the cooperatives. In 1990, Kuwait had 42 cooperative societies, which controlled four-fifths of the market in items that fell under 'basic necessities'. Their widespread presence made them accessible and useful for Iraqis and Kuwaitis alike. While Iraqis looted most other Kuwaiti businesses, the cooperatives, like utility companies, were allowed to continue operations because they provided essential services to Iraqis as well. The cooperative societies in residential neighbourhoods also doubled up as a communication channel because Iraqi officials allowed Kuwaitis working in them to move around without restrictions for business dealings.[11]

Apart from cooperatives, mosques also played a dual role. While prayers were sometimes held under the supervision of Iraqi soldiers, who ensured against anti-Saddam statements, mosques served as a place of comfort, safety, bonding, distribution of food and even pamphlets with suggestions on first-aid measures in case of attacks with chemical weapons.

## Expatriates Experience Extremes

Expatriates underwent diverse experiences depending on their nationality.

Hanan Sayed, a Lebanese oil company executive in Kuwait with an additional Egyptian passport, married her American colleague Steve

Worrell in March 1990 and moved to Kuwait, where she was born and brought up, and where her parents stayed.[12] "My parents and I weren't worried for ourselves, but we were obviously terrified for Steve," Hanan said. Within the first three days of the occupation, her parents persuaded Steve to leave Kuwait at the earliest opportunity and by any means available. Through a network of family and friends, Steve was joined by a Briton who was just as eager to get away from the uncertainty. Taking cue from some well-informed Palestinian friends and BBC News that southern Kuwait was still free from occupation, the two men were handed Hanan's father's off-road vehicle to drive toward the Saudi border. Friends also arranged a map and compass, which Steve was familiar with because of his brief army training in the United States. Loading the vehicle with only the bare essentials, and lots of cigarettes – which they were told would come in handy to 'bribe' Iraqi soldiers if they were caught – the two set out on a desert path following an oil pipeline rather than the highway.

It wasn't too long before the two men realized that they were lost and had no clue about getting back on track to Saudi Arabia. Their hearts sank as a vehicle approached them. One of the men in the vehicle asked what they were doing there and slowly revealed that they were smugglers involved in bootlegging between the Saudi–Kuwaiti borders, and could help them to the Saudi border.

With the tricky task of getting to the border now completed relatively easily, the two began to face difficulties at the border post, which they had assumed would be easy. Many of the Western embassies were clueless about crisis management during the first few days of the occupation and had no contingency plans to deal with such a situation.

On the contrary, Asian embassies responded better because they were not a party to the war. In a society where the Westerners were employed in better jobs, drawing better salaries and enjoying better privileges than their Asian counterparts, the occupation seemed to have turned the tide. Suddenly, the Asian community appeared to be receiving preferential treatment, with Iraqi officials and soldiers being very sympathetic, refraining from harassment and even cooperating with them to ensure safe passage. "It was funny how some Palestinian families with Canadian and British passports were lining up outside the Palestinian Liberation Organization (PLO) office in Kuwait seeking

Palestinian travel documents to escape trouble. It was a completely new world with new priorities," Hanan recounted.

Adding to Steve's woes was the fact that he had forgotten to carry the vehicle registration papers. Through a process of trial and error, Steve tracked a friend at the British embassy in Riyadh, who managed to get them to Riyadh airport. "Steve was so relieved that evening that he simply left his vehicle at the airport with the key inside and took the first flight to New York."

With Steve gone, Hanan wanted to leave too. But her family, especially her father, refused to leave the country. "My father resorted to a form of civil disobedience by not using the Iraqi dinar, which became the only trading currency and not buying anything sold by Iraqis, which was increasingly becoming the norm because Iraqis from towns and villages close to the Kuwaiti border were taking over the local trade by bringing their produce for sale in the Kuwaiti market."

Hanan stayed in Kuwait with her parents till mid-October. With no sign of the occupation ending and the American embassy refusing to help her because she was merely an applicant for a Green Card, Hanan's parents convinced her to leave. "Throughout that period, I never felt threatened as an Arab expatriate. In fact, on a number of occasions, I was told at checkpoints that the Lebanese government was in no position to intervene. Moreover, as a Lebanese who had visited Beirut during the 1975–90 civil war, I felt that the occupation was not as bloody. We faced hardships like driving to either Baghdad or Basra to make an international phone call and the like, but it was manageable."

"But I felt threatened as a woman. When two of my women colleagues and I went to the office one evening to pick up some important documents, we had a close brush with some Iraqi soldiers who pursued us. We were lucky to quickly get out of the gate and melt into the darkness of a nearby residential colony," she added.

With a few other friends, Hanan finally joined a convoy that was headed for Egypt. "The practice was to go in batches by joining the convoy that was headed to the country of which you bore a passport. That made getting across checkpoints easier," she explained. With the cars loaded with personal belongings, there was hardly enough space for the passengers, apart from making them vulnerable to theft and looting, which indirectly threatened their lives too. "For once I wished that I had none of what I was carrying and valued my life more than any material assets," she said in a philosophical tone, adding: "Those few days changed my outlook toward life. I decided to live life for that day and no more."

Rest came in the form of one person guarding and sleeping in the car, while the others slept on sheets spread on the ground. After three days of driving to Jordan through Iraq, she encountered problems at both the Iraqi and Jordanian borders. While Iraqi officials would not allow any vehicle to leave its territory with Kuwaiti number plates because "Kuwait no longer existed," Jordanian officials had turned a sleepy town into a major business hub by demanding hefty bribes to let in vehicles with new number plates. With no other way out but to do what was expected and pay up what was demanded, she took a boat from Aqaba port to Cairo, and then flew to New York to join Steve.

Hanan's adventure and tale didn't end with that journey. Her siblings – who were living in the United States then and who had had no communication with her family since August 1990 – were horrified that she had left her parents behind. Under pressure, she decided to go back to Kuwait by the end of October. She was on the last flight from Amman to Baghdad and then took a taxi to Kuwait City.

Hanan pointed out a major difference in the attitude of the people between the two trips – "while they were confident earlier that the occupation would be temporary, people were now resigned to a life under occupation." Her parents, who had just been relieved to learn about their daughter's reunion with Steve, were angry to see her return. Rather than persuade them to leave Kuwait, she was again convinced to leave. The second trip out of Kuwait seemed easier though the drive – in a Kuwaiti friend's Jaguar car with fake registration papers – through Basra, Baghdad, Amman, and the flight to Cairo was just as arduous.

### Golden Nightmare

Sanya Kapasi, an Indian born and brought up in Kuwait, returned from a holiday in London two days before the invasion.[13] Her toddler daughter was in Delhi with her sister and her infant son with a nanny at her brother's residence in Kuwait. Her husband Feroze – owner of two clothes shops in Souk Maseel in the Mubarakiya area of the city – had left some of their savings, jewellery, important documents such as degree certificates and their son's and nanny's passports in the safes of the two shops when they left on vacation. Unfortunately for them, one of the first Iraqi missiles to hit Kuwait targeted one of their shops, and "there was nothing that we could find in the rubble, especially under those circumstances."

Shattered as they were, Sanya's family resigned themselves to their fate and decided to carry on like many others who had lost their possessions to 'collateral damage'. She hoped that her family would one day be able to claim compensation for their losses. The following weeks were less anxious. "Men ventured out in groups and women hardly went out. If we were identified as Indians with the help of our civil IDs, we were treated in a friendly manner by the Iraqis. In fact, some houses of Indians served as a haven for Kuwaiti families." Even if women stepped out, many did so with children as a ploy to win the sympathy of the Iraqi soldiers. There was no looting reported in her building or vicinity, but many villas deserted by rich Indians were looted.

Interestingly, many people sympathized with the soldiers – not really Stockholm Syndrome, but more in terms of feeling sorry for their economic plight.[14] Most soldiers "begged us to give them watches or gold that we or the children wore," Sanya said, a fact that was reinforced by Hanan too. She regularly saw unkempt soldiers with their toes sticking out of torn shoes and wondered how they could be soldiers. "One of them had a pineapple in hand and asked me what it was, as he did with a shaving cream tube. In another case, a group of soldiers walked into the room of a watchman in a residential building and couldn't believe that it was a watchman's room because it had an air conditioner, television and refrigerator." Faleh too saw some "old soldiers, who were left behind without any information about the retreating Iraqi army, being beaten by Kuwaiti youth after the US-led troops started driving Iraqi soldiers out."

While the first week witnessed panic buying of food products, the first month after the occupation passed without any shortages of food or medicines. But with no immediate respite in sight even after three months and the rumour mill ripe with news of impending US-led attacks, the Kapasi family decided to leave the country. They sold one of their better cars for jewellery and also exchanged plenty of Kuwaiti dinars in return for more gold. "We knew carrying gold was risky, but we decided it was better than driving a new car or carrying Kuwaiti currency, which were being confiscated all around." They joined a convoy of Indian families and reached Baghdad.

After hearing from friends that soldiers were extorting ornaments from those leaving the country, the Kapasis sought the help of an Iraqi business friend in Baghdad and converted all their jewellery into 'raw' gold, which they hid in their video player and some even in their son's toys. Leaving the car behind with the friend, they travelled to Amman enduring several anxious checks by Iraqi soldiers. Accompanying them on the bus was an Indian woman married to a Kuwaiti. Her three-year-old son spoke only Arabic and that in a Kuwaiti accent, which could have proved dangerous for everyone on the bus. As a result, the woman either held her hand against the baby's mouth at every checkpoint or sedated the child for the remaining part of the journey. Relieved to be in Amman, they requested a Sri Lankan family to help their maid – who was left without travel documents – reach Colombo, and happily got on board a flight to Bombay (now Mumbai).

Just when they thought that the worst was over, their real nightmare began. The customs department at the Mumbai airport confiscated all their gold because it was not in the form of ornaments and charged them with smuggling. While the charges were dropped after much pleading, persuasion and repeating their woes, customs refused to return their 'illegal' gold. "Imagine losing nearly $15,000 of gold, which was our only savings, and which we had guarded with our lives. We regretted fleeing. Our experience in India was worse than our plight in Kuwait," Sanya recollected emotionally.

Not having lived in India except for a month every year, Sanya had to stay on with her two children for about six 'unending' months, thankfully supported by some of her relatives. "I regretted not going to one of the European countries like many of my friends and family members did during the crisis in Kuwait. Many of them found refuge with relatives there, applied for asylum and never returned."

Feroze, however, went back to Kuwait in January 1991 and found his second shop untouched. Sanya's brother too returned to find his house, shop and car in good shape to restart life relatively easily. "After more than a year, we received $800 each as compensation from the government. But our business losses were never compensated."

### Political Victims

Like in most wars, there were victims of politics during and after the invasion. Among the worst affected were about half a million expatriates, chiefly Palestinians, hailing from countries whose leaders supported the invasion or remained neutral.

Just days before the US-led coalition attempted to liberate Kuwait, some Iraqi officers entered the Plaza Hotel and ordered Khalid and Ali to hand over the women "you have hidden. We will have a last party. If you do not provide, you will die."

Without worrying much about the consequences, the two men instinctively shifted the women who had taken refuge in the hotel to a mosque. Luckily for them, the Iraqi party ended before it started with several Iraqi soldiers either getting killed or being forced to return home amid the Allied bombing.

The two Palestinian employees, who had spent most of their young lives in Kuwait, had acquired fake Iraqi identity papers for their Kuwaiti employer and kept the hotel open throughout the occupation. Both of them took advantage of the Iraqi soldiers being 'cool' with Palestinians and helped the Kuwaiti resistance by transporting money and weapons around the city in their vehicle.

After the liberation, however, Khalid and Ali were among only a handful of Palestinians to keep their jobs because of the influence their employer wielded. Even with work, Ali said, "daily life is hard. People who talk nicely to me turn harsh when they find out I'm Palestinian. My Kuwaiti friends say I shouldn't visit because they will be branded Palestinian lovers. And God help me if I get into a traffic accident with a Kuwaiti, even if he is at fault. I'm the one the police will blame, and surely I will be beaten before I'm released – if I'm released. You think my work with the resistance will save me? No way."[15]

Most Palestinians were not even as lucky as Khalid and Ali. Influenced by the PLO's political statements supporting Saddam Hussein's proposal to withdraw from Kuwait only if Israeli troops withdrew from the Palestinian territories, the Kuwaiti government was convinced that all Palestinians were conspirators. After the Iraqi soldiers were driven out, the Kuwait government severed ties with the PLO, cut its financial backing and expelled most of the 400,000 Palestinians, who represented about 30 per cent of the country's population. Except for those urgently needed in critical government posts, the work and residency permits of most Palestinians working in the country were either cancelled or not renewed after liberation. While most returned to Jordan, small numbers also went to Iraq, Syria, Lebanon, the West Bank and Gaza, among other destinations. Only about 10 per cent of the original number are said to be currently employed in Kuwait.[16]

Many Palestinians reportedly became victims of private vigilante groups, with some human rights monitoring organizations reporting arrests, imprisonments and even deaths. Due to international criticism, the Kuwaiti government later commuted many death sentences. But the exodus of Palestinians left a vacuum in several key sectors of the economy and society, of which they had been an integral part for decades.

The Palestinians themselves were unable to cope with the sudden loss of a home they had adopted, a means of livelihood and a relatively high standard of living. "It was totally unfair to brand them collaborators because most of them, nearly all of them, were in fact cooperating with Kuwaitis. While they may have been in sync with the political call of some of their leaders, they knew where their real interests were. They were simply victims of political statements made by Palestinian leaders living outside Kuwait."[17]

### Easily at Ease

As soon as Camillo heard about the invasion, he was worried for his wife who was due to deliver their second child in a couple of weeks. "As we got through the first three days, I felt certain that I had nothing to worry about. Neither I nor my family was threatened. I went for regular walks with my son nearly every evening through the period of occupation." He then reflected on an unpleasant relationship between the Kuwaitis and Asian expatriates in several quarters, which was otherwise concealed, but came to the fore because of the occupation. While Kuwaitis called the Indians *Hind maskeen* (poor Indian) or in a tone that implied 'hey man', Iraqis used *rafiq* as a term of endearment or as an alternative to 'friend'. "There was warmth in the way the Iraqis approached Indians. They never demanded anything from us; even if it was water, they requested it. I felt more at home than ever before."

But there were hiccups too. Since the general hospital in Al-Mubarak area was the closest to his house, Camillo took his wife there for regular check-ups and even had their baby delivered there. A few weeks after Kuwait was liberated, he applied for his newborn child's birth certificate at the same hospital, which was refused on the grounds that the hospital never had a maternity section. "Little did the hospital officials know that the Iraqis had offered all services possible in that hospital during occupation, including maternity services." It was several days before he could track two other men whose wives had delivered in the same hospital during that time. "Only after all of us drove home the point together did they respond with birth certificates, which were mandatory for our embassies to issue passports, which in turn facilitated travel."

However, many expatriate workers suffered a great deal. As is the practice in the Gulf countries, most of them had surrendered their passports to their employers as a guarantee against them leaving abruptly or indulging in any fraud. Fearing the worst after the invasion, many Kuwaiti nationals left the country overnight, leaving their employees without valid travel documents. "Many of them were sleeping on the road with their baggage hoping that a way out could come anytime."

## Women Wage War

While women were harassed, the occupiers did not treat them as harshly as they did the men. However, Kuwaitis – who were used to the tradition of women and children not being harmed – were shocked by some of the incidents under the occupation. Furthermore, since Kuwaiti women were relatively better educated than their counterparts in the region and were exposed to political movements, they were well equipped to play a proactive rule during the crisis. Within the first week of the invasion Kuwaiti women decided to demonstrate on the streets against the occupation.

Sena Al-Foudry, one of the leading women activists, was at first reported to have been only injured by a bullet during a demonstration, but when her body was recovered, it was found to be full of bullet holes. After the liberation, she was recognized by the people as one of the first martyrs and the road on which she had lived was named after her.

While some children painted over street signs to confuse Iraqi soldiers, others sprayed graffiti – 'Death to Saddam' – along the walls of houses. There were also slogans such as 'Long Live Kuwait' and 'Long live the Amir'. In some cases, like in Failaka, five young boys caught in the act of pinning up posters were shot.[18]

Sarah Salah (Akbar) was a real heroine. As an employee of the Kuwait Oil Company (KOC), she concealed computer disks containing vital details before joining the resistance. After the liberation, she returned the computer disks to the KOC, which helped restore the country's oil industry much faster. She was also assigned to lead the Kuwaiti firefighting team formed in September.[19]

Reports of atrocities against women began to circulate within the first 10 days of the invasion. Filipina women had been lined up and raped, two young Kuwaiti women trying to run away from some soldiers had been shot down in cold blood, and a German woman had been caught in her flat and assaulted.[20] While reports of some 6,000 rapes during the period are termed as exaggeration, 2,000 Kuwaiti rape victims is a more widely accepted reality. However, this excludes the rape cases of expatriate women. Young Kuwaiti women and Westerners in the accommodation provided by oil companies were also harassed and raped by soldiers from both the regular forces and Saddam's undisciplined 'Popular Army'.[21]

After the war, the Kuwaiti women's movement brought the voting issue to the forefront. The heroic roles of women under Iraqi occupation, sacrifices of female martyrs and wartime hardships were invoked as justification for granting them political rights. Women participating in armed resistance and risking their lives smuggling food, money and medicine through military checkpoints were highlighted, as were instances of many being caught, tortured and killed. These played a significant role in women finally achieving political rights in 2005.[22]

**Media Manipulation**

The surreal experiences of August 2 persisted for about two weeks. Most people were in denial of the occupation. With people cut off from the world in terms of information flow, the Iraqis unleashed a well-planned media campaign to condition the minds of the people. Kuwaiti presenters were forced to appear on television to convey that the situation was the result of an internal coup, which was being stabilized by the Iraqis. Realizing the power of the media, the Iraqis also broadcast the usual soap operas, music shows and films. The news segment was manipulated with assertions from coerced Kuwaitis or Iraqis in Kuwaiti garb that they were happy to be reunited with the 'motherland'. Rallies in Iraq praising Saddam Hussein were superimposed with Kuwaiti surroundings, and placards in Western demonstrations were digitally tampered to reflect international support for the Iraqi presence in Kuwait. The Iraqis also broadcast short film clips with dated pictures of well-stocked supermarkets, which in fact were depleted because of panic buying.

Putting the misinformation campaign into perspective, Hanan revealed that "the ability to brainwash even educated people through such an orchestrated campaign was shockingly true. They showed tinkered images of American troops trying to inject people with the deadly and dreaded HIV virus and most often broadcast dated images of rosy events, which were repeated to drive home the message that all was well."

Another tactic employed by the Iraqi officials in their bid to force Kuwaitis to disassociate themselves from Kuwait was changing the names of public landmarks. As a result, Sabah Hospital became Saddam Hospital, and Sabah Street was renamed Saddam Street. Other signposts were suddenly replaced with Iraqi names, which made people believe that they were in Iraq's '19th province' indeed.

News of how the occupation forces were behaving did not immediately reach the outside world because journalists were not allowed in Kuwait at first. This resulted in people sending out letters and audio tapes informing family members and friends about what was really happening. People fleeing Kuwait were used as secret couriers though it entailed considerable risk, including penalty, imprisonment or death if they were caught. Many took the risk and even returned with reply mails and relief material. When the Iraqis realized the source of information to the outside world, they introduced tough checking measures at the borders, which made messaging difficult, but not impossible.

While the Iraqis were engaged in one form of propaganda, the Kuwaitis were engaged in another. It is estimated that the Kuwaiti government funded as many as 20 public relations (PR), law and lobby firms in its campaign to mobilize US opinion and force against the Iraqis. Nine days after the Iraqi Army marched into Kuwait, the government agreed to fund a contract under which US-based Hill & Knowlton, then the world's largest PR firm, would represent 'Citizens for a Free Kuwait'. Over the next six months, the Kuwaiti government channelled $11.9 million to the group to facilitate payment of fees for the PR firm.[23]

Reports suggest that Hill & Knowlton employed wide-ranging devices to shape public opinion in the United States. These included press conferences showing torture and other abuses by the Iraqis, and distribution of 'Free Kuwait' T-shirts and bumper stickers at college campuses in the United States. In all, 119 Hill & Knowlton executives in 12 offices across the United States were handling the Kuwait campaign.

The firm's activities included arranging media interviews for visiting Kuwaitis, planning events such as National Free Kuwait Day, organizing public rallies, releasing hostage letters to the media, distributing news releases and producing a daily radio show in Arabic from Saudi Arabia.

The Citizens for a Free Kuwait group distributed a 154-page book about Iraqi atrocities titled *The Rape of Kuwait*, which was featured in newspapers and talk shows. The Kuwait embassy bought about 200,000 copies for distribution to American soldiers.

Hill & Knowlton also produced dozens of videos at a cost of over half a million dollars, which provided them tens of millions of dollars worth of 'free' air time. The releases were shown around the world, without identifying the source. After the war ended, the Canadian Broadcasting Corporation produced an Emmy award-winning TV documentary on the PR campaign entitled *To Sell a War*, which featured an interview with those involved in the making of the videos. It demonstrated how audience surveys were even used to physically adapt the clothing and hairstyle of the Kuwaiti ambassador so that he would be liked by the TV audiences. The aim was "to identify the messages that really resonate emotionally with the American people" and condition them to support Washington's role in Kuwait's liberation.

### PR Blunder

On October 10, 1990, the US Congressional Human Rights Caucus held a hearing on Capitol Hill which provided the first opportunity for formal presentations of Iraqi human rights violations. A 15-year-old Kuwaiti girl, Nayirah, sobbed while describing what she had seen with her own eyes in a hospital in Kuwait City. "I volunteered at the Al-Addan hospital," and saw "the Iraqi soldiers come into the hospital with guns, and go into the room where babies were in incubators. They took the babies out of the incubators, took the incubators, and left the babies on the cold floor to die."[24]

Three months after the world consumed that testimony, it was revealed that Nayirah was a member of the Kuwaiti royal family and the daughter of Saud Nasir Al-Sabah, Kuwait's ambassador to the US. Later, even Kuwaitis disbelieved the false testimony. Human rights investigators attempted to confirm the story, but found no witnesses or evidence. Amnesty International was forced to issue an embarrassing retraction.

The overwhelming technological superiority of US forces no doubt won a decisive victory in a brief war. However, the media later admitted that they were manipulated to produce sanitized coverage that almost entirely ignored the war's human costs.

## Economic and Environmental Expenses

People living in Kuwait suffered immense social and psychological damage as a consequence of the occupation and war. According to Amnesty International, the methods used to inflict torture included fracturing limbs and ribs, administration of electric shocks, burning naked body parts, pouring acid into the eyes eventually leading to blindness, subjecting victims to mock trials, etc. The Iraqis even forced Kuwaitis to change nationality to obtain medical facilities. Public places such as hospitals, schools, parks and museums were used as detention and torture centres.

In terms of economic damage, with oil constituting about 90 per cent of Kuwait exports, Iraqis hit the nerve centre. Within a week of the invasion, explosives were wired to all Kuwaiti oil installations, and vital desalination and electricity plants. While preparing for a long occupation, Iraq was also determined to destroy as much as possible if it was forced to withdraw. In the face of imminent defeat at the hands of the Allied forces, the Iraqi troops set ablaze hundreds of oil wells across Kuwait in an act of 'environmental terrorism'. Twenty-five of the 26 oil terminals and six of the 81 petrol stations were extensively damaged, causing major disruptions in the pipeline network.

While there are usually only about 20 blowouts worldwide per year, the oil-well firefighting exercise in Kuwait was extensive, since over 700 wells were set ablaze by the fleeing Iraqis. Almost 8,500 personnel from 35 countries were engaged in fire-fighting operations. The daily burning of three million barrels of crude oil created half a ton of air pollutants that filled the entire atmosphere with heavy smoke, leaving very little to choose between day and night. Temperatures recorded unusual highs and the water cycle was affected by the increased quantities of bacteria at the seashore level, leading to inadequate supplies of potable water. While the desert area was littered with hidden mines, the 'oil lakes' affected vegetation, birds and the marine ecosystem.

The invasion also wreaked havoc on the real estate, civic amenities, communications, and transportation sectors. Iraqis damaged 15 of 23 aircraft belonging to the Kuwait Airways Corporation, which resulted in a loss of about $1.2 billion. The already limited farming business suffered heavily because irrigation works were badly hit. Most fishermen lost their boats resulting in huge losses. Many academic institutions were torched, including the prestigious Kuwaiti Institute for Scientific Research.

With the lifeline of the Kuwaiti economy suffering, the banking, financial services and insurance sectors recorded a drop of 23 per cent after the liberation compared with pre-occupation. As a result, the gross national product dropped more than 70 per cent in just six months.[25]

### Human Costs

Kuwaitis paid the highest human price relative to their population. An estimated number of 439 foreign nationals, 118 Kuwaiti soldiers and 113 Kuwaiti civilians died. Kuwait's human loss was proportionately equivalent to about 400,000 Americans or 100,000 British. The wide-spread landmines, estimated to be two million, left many more dead and physically disabled.[26]

A quantitative risk assessment of mortality due to exposure to smoke from the oil fires suggested about 100 deaths. Kuwait's preliminary analysis of trends in crude mortality rates suggested that after the war, death rates of Kuwaitis were much higher than they had been before the invasion. However, these findings were proved to be untenable after consequent revision of the analysis. Similarly, Kuwait's early studies of cardiovascular and respiratory diseases appeared to show substantial increases in the years following the liberation. However, evaluation of such ailments increasing during 1992–94 could not be definitively proved.[27] About 15,000 people sought psychological counselling from the Kuwaiti Social Development Office. Links between the war and apparent increases in divorce, suicide attempts, juvenile crime and drug use were also established.[28]

### Reconstruction Costs

The government established the Public Authority for Assessment of Compensation to ascertain the damages resulting from Iraqi aggression. Accordingly, several relief measures were undertaken to bail out Kuwaiti people – all government employees were paid salaries for the period of occupation; billions of dollars worth of mortgage, car and consumer loans were waived; government grants and interest-free loans to all Kuwaiti men who marry nationals were increased from $10,500 to $14,000, with only half the amount repayable; monthly child allowance for Kuwaiti parents was raised from $100 to $175 per child; government assistance to all Kuwaiti widows, orphans and the poor was doubled; the base salary for all Kuwaitis in the public sector was increased by 25 per cent; and all electricity and water bills were waived. The only sop that the government rejected, after much consideration, was the bill that would have given every Kuwaiti family $18,000 as compensation for suffering during the Iraqi invasion.[29]

The cost of rebuilding and repairing Kuwaiti facilities reflected the damage caused by Iraq's occupation. It is estimated that Kuwait's share in its liberation, including the expenses of Kuwaitis in exile and under occupation, was more than $22 billion. Final estimates for rebuilding exceeded $40 billion. Another $7 billion was spent towards unpaid salaries.[30]

Since he was outside the clutches of the occupiers, the Amir-in-exile was able to tap Kuwaiti wealth located abroad to finance efforts to limit the damage. It is estimated that almost $25 billion was made available to coalition members to support the rollback of the invasion, sustain exiles and help returnees. Some wealthy and prominent Kuwaitis also distributed money secretly to their fellow citizens. While the real source of that money flow has remained uncertain, it was rumoured that the ruling family channelled the money to retain their influence and showcase their involvement and concern even while they were not in the country.

**Hostages and Human Shields**

As the Iraqis became convinced of the resolve of the international community to end the occupation, Iraq took many Kuwaiti nationals and expatriates – men only – as hostages to serve as 'human shields'. These people were transferred to strategic sites such as air fields, weapons plants, nuclear facilities and oil installations in Iraq.

A technician in the Kuwaiti Air Force, Hussein Khalaf, was forced to change his military ID for a civilian one for fear of being coerced by the Iraqis to report for work.[31] As a result, he remained jobless for a year after the war until he was able to legally verify that he was part of the government service earlier. "Every ministry – health, education, power – was functional within days of the occupation. While Iraqis were also manning many of the ministries, they identified top Kuwaiti officials from various ministries, got the details of the remaining workers and forced them to report to work. They were out to prove that everything was normal. In cases where they faced resistance, soldiers black-marked such houses and harassed the inmates."

Hussein recounted his experience of an attempt to take him hostage to serve as a 'human shield', a desperate practice to 'tilt the balance' that started when Iraqis were in the last throes of the occupation. "After hearing about the impending US attacks, which were rumoured to be launched from the sea, I set out in my car to check on my cousins who lived by the beach." The visibility was getting worse by the day because the Iraqis had set the oil wells on fire. "Headlights of vehicles were turned on even during the day." Hussein was surprised to be stopped and asked to get out of the car at a checkpoint in Al-Rigga, Al-Ahmadi province, because he was usually allowed to proceed after showing his *mulkhiya* (identity card) and was equally surprised to see several cars parked along the road. He was a led to a building nearby, where about 300 men were housed. "From about 3 pm to 7 pm, there was no communication from the Iraqis about why we were in that house." All of them were then packed into three buses and taken to a police station in the vicinity to join several hundred other Kuwaiti men. As he sat in the bus, Hussein saw his car being driven away by an Iraqi officer. "Though they didn't say anything, it was unnerving because rumours ran wild about the Iraqis possibly using us as human shields." After documenting the details of all the 'detained', they were moved to a juvenile home in Al-Fardouz, where a few more hundred people joined them. "Amid all the fear, the only comforting feeling was the warmth on a January winter night because so many people were packed into one room." The room was dark because there was no electricity and soldiers flashed torches randomly to check when needed.

"The next afternoon, we got two dates each. It was our first 'meal' in nearly 24 hours. During this time, several diabetics had collapsed. The soldiers identified cooks among us and a few hours later, we were served only plain (white) rice. Each one of us got a handful, but we were happy. Suddenly, an Iraqi officer physically picked out the old and the sick and asked them to go home." From that point onward, room after room, floor after floor, people were taken by buses, presumably to Iraq. "At no point did the Iraqi soldiers intimidate, shout or beat us . . . in fact, they were polite. If we had questions, we were asked to talk to the 'officer' who rarely visited us."

As the events unfolded, Hussein and two other men who got acquainted during the detention discussed escaping, but couldn't reach a consensus about any plan. "When it was our turn to board the bus, we were taken outside the building. We noticed that there was a long queue ahead of us. A lone soldier ensured that we were all in line and walked to the bus door to instruct people to get in. We realized that the visibility was poorer because it was night . . . we could barely see the soldier as he walked away from us. We decided we would run . . . run for our lives in the opposite direction. With our hands on our ears to avoid the sound of possible gunfire from the soldier, we ran. We heard nothing but silence from behind us. When I stopped and turned back to look, all I could see was darkness. We immediately knew the worst was over. Walking further for about half an hour, we reached a residential colony where a relative lived. We stayed there for three days with no news of our families and very little news about the developments in the country." However, they heard that the Americans were coming and the Gulf joint forces – Al-Jazeera Force or Peninsula Shield – was being deployed.

"When I returned home, the reunion was like a dream to me, my mother, brother, and sisters. A few days later, Kuwait was liberated. I never met any other person from the juvenile home again, and never found my car," Hussein said.

Several other Kuwait nationals were not so lucky. Even when some of them were freed, they were forced to sign documents which promised cooperation with the new government in terms of information flow, and that they would respect the 'revolution' and the Ba'ath Party. They were also ordered to hand over televisions, video tapes, money and cars in return for their freedom – a kind of extortion.[32]

"I didn't see any deaths myself . . . People who resisted were killed . . . If they did what the Iraqis wanted them to do, they were not harassed," Faleh said. But there were reports of violent deaths of civilians. Mubarak Al-Nout, director of the Al-Ardiyah Cooperative Society, was shot in the head in public for stopping Iraqi soldiers from entering the premises without a permit.[33]

Information flow was poor because much of the torture and killing of civilians took place in secret locations. Relatives were afraid to speak about their fears in case they were themselves arrested or their actions brought more suffering or death for their arrested relatives. About half a million people left Kuwait during the occupation. Around 5,000 Western men were detained in the two countries with at least 500 of these deployed as human shields. While many Western captives were released following political negotiations with the Iraqi government, Kuwaitis were not spared.

### Prisoners of War (PoWs)

In March 1992, the Kuwaiti government informed the Red Cross that about 850 persons, two-thirds of them Kuwaiti citizens, had neither been released nor their remains returned during the post-war repatriation programme. But the Iraqi government insisted that all prisoners and remains had been returned. The PoWs issue deeply affected the very fibre of Kuwaiti society as 605 people represented about 0.1 per cent of the Kuwaiti population. The same percentage translated roughly into more than a million people for India, nearly 1.5 million for China and 270,000 for the United States. The National Committee for the Missing and PoW Affairs was assigned the task of working toward the release of the detainees.

Since the 2003 downfall of Saddam Hussein's regime, a Kuwaiti team searched mass graves in Iraq for 605 missing prisoners of war captured during the Kuwait occupation. The last count of the PoWs whose remains were identified by the end of 2004 was 209. The rest still remain unaccounted for.[34]

### Endgame

Between August 2, 1990 and January 15, 1991, the United Nations passed several resolutions (660–670). At an early stage the United Nations Security Council resolutions identified Iraq's actions as illegal and called for its immediate withdrawal. In order to add teeth to its demands the world community first agreed upon a strategy of sanctions which would isolate Iraq and hopefully persuade its leaders to withdraw from Kuwait. Everyone suffered as a result of these sanctions. Vast quantities of food and medical supplies which had been stored in Kuwait were looted ahead of the war and transported to Iraq.

On November 29, UN Resolution 678 set January 15, 1991 as the deadline for Iraqi troop withdrawal, failing which the coalition would launch a military offensive to free Kuwait. Fearing that Iraq would retaliate with chemical weapons, Faleh's family prepared an 'emergency' room that had all its windows sealed, and stocked it with food and water that would last a few days.

The liberation of Kuwait – 'Operation Desert Storm' – began on January 16 with the help of 30 countries led by the United States. Unable to make any meaningful military response to the coalition's aerial bombardment campaign, Iraq launched inaccurate Scud missiles at Israel, Saudi Arabia and Bahrain. The human toll from the missiles during January was five killed and 224 injured. Iraq continued to fire Scuds right up to the end of the war, but for the most part these were successfully destroyed by Patriot missiles. The one major exception occurred on February 25–26 when a Scud landed on a US army reserve barracks in Al Khobar, Saudi Arabia, killing 28 US military personnel and injuring another 100.

On February 22, the United States demanded complete withdrawal in seven days. The final phase of the Coalition forces' joint action to free Kuwait began on February 24. On February 25, the Iraqi army began pulling out of Kuwait in a state of mounting panic and on February 27 came the announcement from Washington – "Kuwait is liberated; Iraq's army is defeated."

## Positive Spin-off

For the people of Kuwait, liberation heralded relief. Though the invasion and occupation left an indelible mark, there were some unexpected dividends too. Having got used to a sedentary lifestyle facilitated by the oil boom and a welfare state, Kuwaitis had lost touch with several existential realities. Since public services ground to a halt during the occupation, day-to-day survival became tough. For example, garbage piled up outside houses and street corners. But unusual circumstances forced people to react unusually. Having got used to migrant workers doing menial jobs in the past, Kuwaitis truly became 'classless' and engaged in garbage disposal. Where they couldn't, people burnt it in open spaces.

A sense of camaraderie that didn't exist before was evident during the time of distress with people caring, sharing and helping each other. Wherever possible, Kuwaitis also volunteered as staff in hospitals and cooperatives.

Steve Worell, Hanan's husband, worked in Africa till January 1991 and returned to Kuwait as an employee of Bechtel, which was engaged in the reconstruction of Kuwait. Hanan returned with a baby in July. "The society was totally different. People appeared to be more in touch with reality, helpful and definitely considerate. But Palestinians were unwelcome; the social structure had changed with expatriate men coming back without their families; schools only half full as a result and business very dull. For about three to four years, people lived in fear of Saddam repeating his adventure."

The negative repercussions of those six months were so clearly etched in the minds of the people that they realized that it was a period like 'never before', and hoped it would happen 'never again'.

## NOTES

1 Sixteen years on, Camillo D'Souza and his family still stay in Kuwait. His experiences were elicited in an interview in Kuwait on March 8, 2006.

2 For more, see Mary Ann Tétreault, 'Kuwait: The Morning After', *Current History*, Vol. 91 (January 1992).

3 Faleh Khalaf works as a data entry analyst in a Dubai firm. He recounted his experiences in an interview on May 15, 2006.

4 The six GCC countries are Bahrain, Kuwait, Oman, Qatar, Saudi Arabia and the United Arab Emirates.

5 For more, see N. Janardhan, *The Al-Sabahs and the Kuwaiti National Assembly – The Legitimacy Factor* (PhD thesis, Jawaharlal Nehru University, New Delhi, 2001). Kuwait's immediate military response after the invasion is well documented in Peter Vine and Paula Casey, *Kuwait: A Nation's Story* (London: IMMEL Publishing, 1992).

6 In the early 1990s, Kuwait had about 800,000 nationals and over 1.3 million foreign workers, mostly Asians.

7 Vine and Casey, *Kuwait: A Nation's Story*.

8 Jehan S. Rajab, *Invasion Kuwait* (London: The Radcliffe Press, 1993).

9 Mary Ann Tétreault, 'Divided Communities of Memory: Diasporas Come Home', in Haideh Moghissi (ed.), *The Muslim Diaspora: Gender, Culture and Identity* (London: Routledge, 2006).

10 Rajab, *Invasion Kuwait*.

11 For more, see Mary Ann Tétreault, *Stories of Democracy: Politics and Society in Contemporary Kuwait* (New York: Columbia University Press, 2000).

12  Hanan Sayed Worrell is currently the Projects Manager of the Supervision Committee for the Expansion of Abu Dhabi International Airport in the United Arab Emirates. She narrated her experiences in an interview on May 17, 2006.

13  At present, Sanya Kapasi works as a human resources executive in a private company in Dubai, UAE. She narrated her experiences in an interview on May 1, 2006.

14  Stockholm Syndrome explains the nature of kidnap victims who become sympathetic to their captors over a period of time. The term evolved from a 1973 hostage episode in the Swedish capital, in which several captives in a six-day bank robbery resisted rescue efforts and later refused to testify against their captors.

15  Michael Kramer, 'Kuwait: Back to the Past', *Time* (United States), August 5, 1991.

16  In 2004, Palestinian leader Mahmoud Abbas apologized for the Palestinians' support of Saddam Hussein during the invasion. Abbas' visit to Kuwait was the first by a senior Palestinian since relations were frozen 14 years earlier. For more, see Shafeeq Ghabra, *Palestinians in Kuwait* (Boulder, Colorado: Westview Press, 1997); Ann M. Lesch, '*Palestinians in Kuwait*', Journal of Palestine Studies, Vol. 20, No. 4 (Summer, 1991); and British Broadcasting Corporation, December 12, 2004.

17  Views gathered from an interview of Dr Sulayman Awad, a Palestinian residing in Dubai, UAE.

18  Rajab, *Invasion Kuwait*.

19  'Job well done', *Technical Review (Middle East)* – http://www.alba.net/content/tech.htm, last accessed on May 15, 2006.

20  Rajab, *Invasion Kuwait*.

21  See Haya Al-Muhgni and Fawzia Al-Turkait, 'Dealing with Trauma: Cultural Barriers to Self-Recovery – The Case of Kuwaiti Women', paper presented at the Seminar on Effective Methods for Encountering the Psychological and Social Effects of the Iraqi Aggression, sponsored by the Social Development Office of the Amiri Diwan, Kuwait, March 1994. Also see Mary Ann Tétreault, 'In Search of Justice: Wartime Rape and Human Rights', in Mary Ann Tétreault and Robin L. Teske (eds.), *Partial Truths and the Politics of Community* (Columbia: University of South Carolina Press, 2003).

22  For more, see Haya Al-Muhgni, *Women in Kuwait: The Politics of Gender* (London: Saqi Books, 2001).

23  Center for Media and Democracy, 'How PR Sold the War in the Persian Gulf', http://www.prwatch.org/books/tsigfy10.html, website last accessed May 15, 2006.

24  John R. MacArthur, *Second Front: Censorship and Propaganda in the Gulf War* (Berkeley, California: University of California Press, 1992).

25  Kuwait Information Office (KIO) website, Embassy of Kuwait New Delhi, http://www.kuwait-info.com/sidepages/gulfwar_impact.asp, last accessed on May 15, 2006.

26  Ibid., a Martyrs' Office was established in the Amiri Diwan but, despite popular demand, it did not publish a list of martyrs.

27  'Public Health Impacts of Iraq's 1990 Invasion and Occupation of Kuwait (Phase I) – Summary of Epidemiology and Risk Assessment', Harvard School of Public Health, June 29, 2005.

28  'Kuwait Seeks Role 10 Years After Invasion', *Washington Post*, July 21, 2000.

29  Abdullah K. Al-Shayeji, 'The Iraqi Invasion of Kuwait: A Small Nation-State's Ceaseless Quest for Survival', *The International Conference on the Effects of the Iraqi Aggression on the State of Kuwait: Political and Economic Implications, Volume I* (Kuwait: The Centre for Gulf and Arabian Peninsula Studies, 1994).

30  Shafeeq Ghabra, 'Kuwait: The Post-Liberation Era', *Journal of the Gulf and Arabian Peninsula Studies*, Vol. XVII (May 1992).

31  Hussein Khalaf, like his brother Faleh, is working in Dubai. He spoke about what he endured in an interview on May 15, 2006.

32  For more, see 'Human Rights in a Crisis Situation: The Case of Kuwait after Occupation', *Human Rights Quarterly*, Vol. 23.

33  Tétreault, *Stories of Democracy: Politics and Society in Contemporary Kuwait*.

34  *Kuwait Times,* December 5, 2004.

# 8

# Iraqi Civilians under the 1990–2003 Sanctions

*William W. Haddad*

Problems for the civilian population of Iraq ironically began on August 2, 1990, when its armed forces invaded and captured Kuwait. Saddam Hussein's military needed only four days to accomplish its goal, and Iraq seemed poised to re-align the strategic forces in the Middle East, now with Baghdad at the centre. The motivations for the invasion were many. There was the Iraqi sentiment that Kuwait was not a legitimate nation-state but more realistically, as has famously been declared, a tribe with a flag. There were also Iraqi nationalists who recalled that Kuwait had been a *qadha*, or district, nominally under the control of the *Vilayet* of Basra, during the Ottoman period.[1]

Further exacerbating relations between the two countries were financial tensions left over from the Iraq–Iran war of the 1980s. During that war, Iraq had received US$14 billion in financial support from Kuwait, and from other Sunni-dominated Arab countries. When the war ended, Kuwait demanded that Baghdad repay the moneys since they were loans. Hussein countered that the money had been an outright grant to support an Arab cause and keep the Shiite Iranians at bay. Oil was also an issue between the two antagonists. Kuwait was accused of slant-drilling into Iraqi oil fields and keeping the price of oil artificially low by pumping more than its production quota set by the Organization of Petroleum Exporting Countries (OPEC), thus hurting the Iraqi economy as it tried to recover from the ravages inflicted by the war with Iran. Secondary goals were increased maritime access to the Persian Gulf and a desire for Baghdad to be recognized as a pan-Arab leader.

Finally, there were perhaps the misinterpretations attached to the statement by the American ambassador in Baghdad, April Glaspie, when she told the Iraqi leader that the United States was not interested in becoming involved in inter-Arab border disputes. As reported in the *New York Times*, Glaspie was quoted saying, "We have no opinion on the Arab–Arab conflicts, like your border disagreement with Kuwait. I was in the American Embassy in Kuwait during the late '60s. The instruction we had during this period was that we should express no opinion on this issue and that the issue is not associated with America."[2] Some have argued that her statement was a signal to the Iraqi president that he could attack if he wished.

Within hours of the invasion, the United Nations Security Council met to condemn the violation of Kuwait's territorial sovereignty and passed Resolution 660 that called on Iraq to immediately and unconditionally withdraw. The invasion was seen almost universally as a threat to the world order based on the inviolability of the nation-state, and as a result, similar calls for withdrawal came from the League of Arab States, the European Community, the Gulf Cooperation Council and many other organizations, not to mention from scores of individual nations. The unanimity of the response came in large part from Iraq's new proximity to Saudi Arabia's Hama oil fields, and from Baghdad's belligerent statements toward the Saudi regime. The West might be able to live with Hussein controlling Kuwait, but Saudi Arabia's oil resources were far more important.

As a follow-up, on August 6, the Security Council passed Resolution 661 which imposed sanctions on Iraq and created a sanctions committee composed of the members of the Security Council, to oversee the resolution's implementation. Sanctioned, or forbidden, were food imports, oil exports, international air travel, arms imports, and any financial transactions between Iraq and other countries.[3] Three weeks later the Security Council called for a sea blockade, and in September 1990, the Council called on member states to stop all aviation contact with Iraq. The sea blockade was implemented largely by the United States and to a lesser extent Great Britain and other states. The Persian Gulf was effectively sealed from any ships attempting to ingress or egress Iraqi waters at the Shatt al-Arab. Ships plying the Red Sea were also subject to search; the United States and its allies worried that the blockade could be breached at the Jordanian port of Aqaba where goods might be taken overland to and from Iraq. The oil blockade was successful when Turkey and Saudi Arabia shut pipelines going from Iraq through their countries.

Taken as part of a larger development, the passage of Resolution 661 marked the movement of the world's nation-states in the 1990s into an era of sanctions. Between its formation in 1945 and the passage of

Resolution 661, the United Nations had imposed sanctions only twice in its history – on the Union of South Africa and Rhodesia (now Zimbabwe). During that same period, the United States used sanctions about twice a year for a total of about one hundred times. But since 2000, the implementation rate has risen 50 per cent to about three per year. The view of sanctions at the beginning of the 1990s was that it was a cheap and effective way to put pressure on any government to change its policies. Certainly, it cost only a fraction of what war would have and so was widely favoured by groups opposed to the violence and death brought about by armed conflict. What was unforeseen was the devastation that could be wrecked upon a nation in a unipolar world. With no counterbalance to US power, the more than 12-year sanctions regime on Iraq wrecked havoc that the sanctions supporters could not have imagined. The devastation was also magnified by the fact that Iraq was an import-dependent country. It produced, besides oil, very little for consumption. Prior to the war, Iraq imported 70 per cent of its food and almost all of its medicines. Thus, any embargo that affected these two commodities could theoretically deal a mortal blow to Iraq.

Between August and November 1990, the struggle around Iraq had several fronts. There was the steady tightening of the sanctions, spearheaded by the United States and the United Kingdom; the transfer of military capital, both men and materiel, to the Middle East in preparation for the possible outbreak of war; the US wooing of potential allies that resulted eventually in a multinational force of 34 countries;[4] and a focus on the United Nations as a locus of pressure that demanded Iraq's withdrawal from Kuwait. In this process, Jordan's position required careful manoeuvring. King Hussein used his considerable diplomatic skill to avoid the wrath of the stronger Iraq, which was also Jordan's primary trading partner and sometime ally, and at the same time sought to reassure his traditional Western allies that he would not be an impediment to moves against the Baghdad regime. The monarch urged Iraq to withdraw from Kuwait and counselled patience from the West. Recognizing the negative economic consequences the sanctions were having on Amman, Jordan was allowed some exemptions from the blockade, for example being allowed to import Iraqi oil by truck.

Unable to effect Baghdad's removal from Kuwait, the Security Council on November 29, 1990 passed a third resolution, Resolution 678, which authorized the use of force. The stick was accompanied by a carrot, 'a pause of goodwill', that gave Iraq until January 15, 1991 to withdraw completely.

At the same time as diplomacy and the sanctions were being given an opportunity to remove Iraq from Kuwait, the United States began to assemble a coalition of nations that ultimately numbered thirty-four. Surprisingly, the coalition included nine Arab countries: Bahrain, Egypt, Kuwait, Morocco, Oman, Qatar, Saudi Arabia, Syria and the United Arab Emirates. Germany and Japan did not contribute troops but gave money and military hardware to the alliance.

A day after the January 15 deadline for Iraqi withdrawal passed without Kuwait being evacuated, the coalition struck in an air campaign named 'Operation Desert Storm'. In an earlier TV and radio broadcast, Saddam Hussein called the impending war *Umm al-Ma'arik*, the Mother of All Battles.[5]

Once coalition air superiority had been established,[6] another phase of the air war began – the attacking of both military and civilian facilities, some of which could have military importance. One economist wrote of the bombing that it was the "most devastating strategic bombing attack since World War II".[7] Before the war began, the United States had identified approximately sixty sites to be attacked by air. However, when the campaign was at full throttle, more than 700 targets were hit. Virtually every structure larger than a house became a target: sewage treatment facilities; water purification and distribution sites; electrical generating, relay and distributing systems and plants;[8] chemical, fertilizer, food, veterinary and medical production facilities; oil refineries and oil-related materiel (pipelines, pumping stations, fuel trucks, gas stations, storage areas, oil wells); and various warehouses. Toward the end of the air campaign, American pilots complained that there was nothing left to attack. A larger tonnage of various kinds of bombs were dropped on Iraq during the air campaign period, January 17–February 24, than had been used against Germany during all of World War II. The bombing was the equivalent of seven atomic weapons like those dropped on Nagasaki or Hiroshima.[9]

Toward the end of February, the land campaign began. Amongst the ordinance used in the ground war were depleted uranium projectiles capable of breaching armour, napalm, cluster bombs, plus the bullets, cannon shells and mortars usually associated with warfare. The American-led alliance attacked first into Kuwait, quickly resulting in the air-warfare-demoralized Iraqi forces' defeat. Choosing to fight from fixed positions that were easily attacked from the air with fuel air explosives designed to create fireballs, the Iraqi military, though larger in size than the coalition forces, proved no match for the technologically superior US-led forces. Within days of the beginning of the coalition's land attack, Iraqi troops began to retreat from Kuwait, setting fire to that country's oil fields as they left. On February 27 a miles-long convoy of Iraqi forces and civilians became trapped in two traffic jams, one along the principal Iraqi–Kuwait highway and the other along a secondary coastal road connecting the two countries. Both were attacked unmercifully from the air, in what British and American pilots later described as shooting fish in a barrel.[10] On February 28, President George H. W. Bush announced that he had no intention of attacking into Iraq proper and declared a ceasefire.

The following day, United Nations Secretary-General Javier Pérez de Cuéllar ordered his under-secretary to go to Iraq and Kuwait to report on the condition of these two countries and to make recommendations on how they could be helped. Martti Ahtisaari, the former President of Finland (1994–2000) and a well-known United Nations diplomat who had considerable diplomatic experience on peace missions, left almost immediately for the Middle East. His report, issued upon his return, was not diplomatic. "The report of the Ahtisaari mission described 'near apocalyptic' destruction and observed that war damage had relegated Iraq to a 'pre-industrial age' in which the means of modern life had been 'destroyed or rendered tenuous'."[11] In Ahtisaari's words prepared for the Secretary-General:

> I and the members of my mission were fully conversant with media reports regarding the situation in Iraq [especially those relating to water, sanitary and health conditions]. It should, however, be said at once that nothing that we had seen or read had quite prepared us for the particular form of devastation which has now befallen the country. The recent conflict has wrought near-apocalyptic results upon the economic infrastructure of what had been, until January 1991, a rather highly urbanized and mechanized society. Now, most means of modern life support have been destroyed or rendered tenuous. Iraq has, for some time to come, been relegated to a pre-industrial age, but with all the disabilities of post-industrial dependency on an intensive use of energy and technology . . . Underlying each analysis is the inexorable reality that, as a result of

war, virtually all previously viable sources of fuel and power (apart from a limited number of mobile generators) and modern means of communication are now, essentially, defunct.[12]

The Report went on to address the near-total destruction of the government's ability to care for its people due to the massive bombing and the obliteration of Iraq's industrial capability – most especially the ending of the ability to pump oil and the destruction of the electrical grid serving the country. The Report ends:

> . . . it will be difficult, if not impossible, to remedy these immediate humanitarian needs without dealing with the underlying need for energy . . . The need for energy means, initially, emergency oil imports and the rapid patching up of a limited refining and electricity production capacity, with essential supplies from other countries. Otherwise, food that is imported cannot be preserved and distributed; water cannot be purified; sewage cannot be pumped away and cleansed; crops cannot be irrigated; medicaments cannot be conveyed where they are required; needs cannot even be effectively assessed. It is unmistakable that the Iraqi people may soon face a further imminent catastrophe, which could include epidemic and famine, if massive life-supporting needs are not rapidly met. The long summer, with its often 45 or even 50 degree temperatures (113–122 degrees Fahrenheit), is only weeks away. Time is short.

The United States lost less than 200 killed in the war. The total number of Iraqis who died is of several magnitudes higher. In fact, one estimate, discredited by the US government at the time in 1992, initially put the number at 158,000 Iraqis killed, including 86,194 men, 39,612 women, and 32,195 children. This estimate, prepared by Beth Osborne Daponte, a doctoral student at the University of Chicago, who was hired to help on a survey by the Department of Commerce's Census Bureau of Foreign Countries, was pulled by supervisors in the US Census Bureau, and the Defense Intelligence Agency eventually estimated that 100,000 Iraqi military were killed in the war, with perhaps another plus or minus 50,000, but they did not give a civilian estimate. Since 1992, she has revised her original estimate to include additional deaths caused by the war but occurring post-war, arriving at a figure of 205,000.[13]

Following President George W. H. Bush's unilateral declaration of a ceasefire, the Security Council passed Resolution 687 on April 3,

1991. When Iraq accepted the provisions of 687 nine days later, the hostilities of the Gulf War over Kuwait formally ended. The Resolution established a ceasefire and set the terms for the continuation of the sanctions – the 'Sanctions Regime' that lasted twelve years. If, as Saddam Hussein described it, the Kuwait War was the 'Mother of All Battles', then Resolution 687 was the Mother of All Resolutions, not only for its length but its complexity. It is perhaps the longest resolution ever passed by the UNSC, containing over 3,500 words and more than three-score paragraphs. More importantly, it listed eight separate items to which Iraq had to agree. Below is a description of the seven demands and the additional paragraph describing the demilitarization and patrolling of the Iraq–Kuwait border, the paragraph(s) where they are found in Resolution 687 and verbiage directly from the Resolution:

1   *Requires Iraq to recognize Kuwait's territorial integrity according to the 1963 agreement between Iraq and Kuwait.* Resolution 687, Paragraph 2. Demands that Iraq and Kuwait respect the inviolability of the international boundary and the allocation of islands set out in the 'Agreed Minutes between the State of Kuwait and the Republic of Iraq regarding the restoration of friendly relations, recognition and related matters', signed by them in the exercise of their sovereignty at Baghdad on October 4, 1963 and registered with the United Nations;

2   *Establishes a UN peacekeeping force to be placed on the Iraq–Kuwait border. The peacekeepers will operate within a demilitarized zone.* Paragraph 5. *Requests* the Secretary-General, after consulting with Iraq and Kuwait, to submit within three days to the Council for its approval a plan for the immediate deployment of a United Nations observer unit to monitor the Khawr 'Abd Allah and a demilitarized zone, which is hereby established, extending ten kilometres into Iraq and five kilometres into Kuwait from the boundary referred to in the 'Agreed Minutes between the State of Kuwait and the Republic of Iraq regarding the restoration of friendly relations, recognition and related matters';

3   *Calls for the destruction of Iraq's missile, chemical, and biological capabilities and their monitoring.* Paragraph 9bi. The forming of a special commission which shall carry out immediate on-site inspection

of Iraq's biological, chemical and missile capabilities . . ., [9bii] and the destruction by Iraq, under the supervision of the Special Commission, of all its missile capabilities, including launchers . . .

4    *Iraq must not develop or acquire nuclear weapons. This is to be monitored by the International Atomic Energy Agency.* Paragraph 12. Decides that Iraq shall unconditionally agree not to acquire or develop nuclear weapons or nuclear-weapon-usable material or any subsystems or components or any research, development, support or manufacturing facilities related to the above and [Paragraph 13] *Requests* the Director General of the International Atomic Energy Agency, through the Secretary-General . . . to carry out immediate on-site inspection of Iraq's nuclear capabilities based on Iraq's declarations and the designation of any additional locations by the Special Commission; to develop a plan for submission to the Council within forty-five days calling for the destruction, removal or rendering harmless as appropriate of all items listed in Paragraph 12.

5    *Requires Iraq to return all stolen Kuwaiti property.* Paragraph 15. *Requests* the Secretary-General to report to the Council on the steps taken to facilitate the return of all Kuwaiti property seized by Iraq, including a list of any property that Kuwait claims has not been returned or which has not been returned intact;

6    *Requires Iraq to pay for war damage, and establishes a commission to administer the fund* [that Iraq will presumably pay into]. Paragraph 16. *Reaffirms* that Iraq . . . is liable under international law for any direct loss, damage – including environmental damage and the depletion of natural resources – or injury to foreign Governments, nationals and corporations as a result of its unlawful invasion and occupation of Kuwait; [and in Paragraph 18] *Decides also* to create a fund to pay compensation for claims that fall within paragraph 16 and to establish a commission that will administer the fund.

7    *Calls on Iraq to repatriate all Kuwaiti and other nationals that it is holding.* Paragraph 30. *Decides* that, in furtherance of its commitment to facilitate the repatriation of all Kuwaiti and third-State nationals, Iraq shall extend all necessary cooperation to the International Committee of the Red Cross by providing lists of such persons,

facilitating the access of the International Committee to all such persons wherever located or detained and facilitating the search by the International Committee for those Kuwaiti and third-state nationals still unaccounted for.

8   *Iraq must 'not commit or support any act of international terrorism'.* Paragraph 32. *Requires* Iraq to inform the Council that it will not commit or support any act of international terrorism or allow any organization directed towards commission of such acts to operate within its territory and to condemn unequivocally and renounce all acts, methods and practices of terrorism.

The passage of Resolution 687 moved the world's nations, and especially Iraq, into a new and far different era. Though according to 687, the sanctions were to be reviewed every sixty days with the aim of alleviating them if their provisions were met by Iraq, this did not happen.[14] Washington made it clear that the sanctions regime would continue until there was regime change in Baghdad. This point-of-view was reiterated numerous times by President George H. W. Bush; his spokesman, Martin Fitzwater; Robert Gates, the newly appointed head of the Central Intelligence Agency; and British Prime Minister John Major. That this viewpoint was not authorized by the United Nations, not part of 687, nor supported by the international community had little impact on the thinking in Washington or London for the next twelve years until President George W. Bush began the Iraqi invasion in 2003. The sanctions were only ended when the United States and the United Kingdom had occupied Iraq and driven Saddam Hussein from Baghdad in 2003.

For the twelve years following the passage of 687, how the United States and Britain interpreted it was a subject of controversy and tension within the international community. With hindsight, it is clear that the complexity of 687 and the inability of the international community, a decade later, to agree on whether its conditions had been implemented, and what to do if they had, implies that there should have been eight resolutions, one for each condition.[15] Still, the insistence of the US and the UK on regime change meant that the sanctions would continue indefinitely as long as Saddam Hussein held power in Baghdad.

In fact, the Hussein regime complied with all of the points of the resolution that it could. The eighth point, that Iraq would not commit or assist in carrying out terrorism, asked Iraq to prove a negative. There has been no evidence produced to show that Iraq worked with Al-Qaida, for example. And where Iraq did comply with the demands of 687, the country was damned if it did and damned if it did not. An example of this Catch-22 was an October 1994 Iraqi-Russian statement in which the former agreed to recognize Kuwait as a sovereign state. The British Foreign Secretary Douglas Hurd said the declaration was inadequate since Iraq posed a threat to Kuwait. One can conjecture that the Iraqi regime asked itself, what was the benefit of complying with the resolution's demands if no easing of the sanctions resulted?

## The Implementation of the Sanctions Regime

If the sanctions had been a naval blockade, similar to the United States' embargo of Cuba, they would have been simple to enforce. However, since Iraq was a virtually land-locked state with often undefined and porous borders, the United Nations' task of enforcing the sanctions was difficult. Rather than monitoring Iraq's borders, the decision was made to monitor goods and their sellers before the items left for Iraq. The responsibility for this monitoring fell to what became known as the '661 Committee'. Composed of the members of the Security Council, the 661 Committee had veto power over any business deal. Any member of the Committee could veto a request to export goods to Iraq or, even more insidious, force the seller up endless deadends seeking permission.

> To sell humanitarian goods to Iraq, a company would submit an application to its national mission at the UN, which would then turn it over to the 661 committee. But the 661 committee did not publish any criteria for approval, and its meetings were closed sessions at which neither Iraq nor the vendors were allowed to have representatives present to answer questions or offer information in support of the contract. The application process typically took months, sometimes as long as two years. And the committee's rulings were inconsistent – the same goods sold by the same company might on one occasion be deemed permissible humanitarian goods and on another be flatly denied without explanation.[16]

Since any nation on the 661 Committee could veto a request, or postpone a decision by asking for more information, it was extremely frustrating and costly for vendors to apply for a licence to sell goods. Further exasperating the process was the prohibition of what were called 'dual use' items: that is, things that theoretically could have more than one purpose – for example, for rebuilding the military, which was forbidden by the sanctions. Thus, spare parts for crop-dusting helicopters were interdicted because they could in theory be used to repair a military helicopter. Likewise, at one time or another, chlorine for water purification, computers, parts to repair the electrical grid, pesticides, even ping-pong balls were vetoed.[17]

With crucial health items sanctioned, for example medicine and anaesthetics, the human cost became apparent quickly. *Middle East International* reported that in 1987, Iraqi life expectancy was 65 and literacy was 89%. By 1995 life expectancy had declined to 58 years and literacy was 58%.[18] Despite these remarkable declines, it has been difficult to record the voices of those who died prematurely. This was so for two reasons: (1.) Ordinarily, research during the sanctions period consisted of fact-finding missions conducted by medical personnel or those in related fields who typically conducted surveys of clusters; for example, 200 clusters composed of 25 to 30 households. In the case of determining the impact of sanctions on child morbidity, for example, in each household all child-bearing women would be interviewed and the dates of the births and deaths of all children would be recorded. Then comparisons would be made with pre-sanction mortality rates to arrive at deductive estimates of excess deaths. (2.) Since most of the investigations during the sanctions period focused on children, especially those under age five, there are few interviews. They essentially died without voices. Furthermore, in determining the rates of death before and during the sanctions period, the killing was indirect. The deaths were not like Hiroshima where people were bombed but as Mueller and Mueller have pointed out, they were "dispersed rather than concentrated and statistical rather than dramatic".[19]

There were some exceptions to the general silence of those who died from deprivation. One was a study in 1992 which interviewed Iraqi children about the impact of the First Gulf War and the sanctions that followed.[20] More notable was a study by three editors, the International Study Team, who conducted a survey of Iraqi women and published their findings.[21] The survey team interviewed eighty women with a common questionnaire in a sample that roughly corresponded to the national demographics: 27.5% from the north; 37.5% from the centre; and 35% from the south. The extensive interviews with the eighty women give a unique insight into the human costs of the sanctions:

> How long will the sanctions continue? We are tired. We are innocent.[22]
>
> Since the beginning of the sanctions, we have not tasted chicken or meat – only flour, rice and sometimes vegetables. Our children have developed anaemia due to lack of milk. Before, when I would watch an Egyptian programme on the T.V., and hear an Egyptian say, "We are having meat for lunch today. It's an occasion," I used to laugh. But now I know that it is no laughing matter for our own turn has come.[23]
>
> Every waking moment I worry about how will I feed my eight children. It is the hardest thing for a mother not [to] be able to feed her child."[24]

The conclusions of the Study Team can be summarized:

1   As a result of the sanctions, women had to adopt traditionally male responsibilities while fulfilling their own roles.
2   The most serious crisis for women was their reduced ability to feed their families.
3   Sanctions resulted in large-scale unemployment, making female employees vulnerable to competition from males.
4   Sanctions led to household impoverishment forcing women to sell their jewellery, which made them more dependent and vulnerable.
5   Women's physical well-being was reduced by economic hardship, lack of medical care, and a decline in sanitation.
6   Marital problems increased. Women were the prime victims of familial discord.
7   Social life disappeared. There were decreased numbers of wedding celebrations, of the ability to welcome guests, or of any kind of social entertainment.
8   Women saw the lifting of the sanctions as the only hope of returning to a normal life.

There were two early attempts to ameliorate the suffering caused by the sanctions. The Security Council passed Resolutions 706 and 712 in August and September 1991. According to these early attempts to provide Iraq with humanitarian aid, Baghdad would be allowed to sell

US$1.6 billion of oil every six months. The money, however, would not go directly to the Iraqi government but would be held in an escrow account that would be administered by the UN. Vendors who sold their goods in Iraq would then present bills to the UN for repayment. The resolutions also provided that 30 per cent of the $1.6 billion would be set aside for Iraqi war reparations and another unspecified amount would be used to pay for UN costs associated with the administration of the programme. Baghdad rejected this early effort, arguing that there was not enough money permitted in the programme to make a difference, and that both resolutions violated Iraq's sovereignty.

When in 1996 the Security Council passed Resolution 986 that established a second oil-for-food programme, the sanctions were somewhat eased. This time Iraq reluctantly agreed to the programme since the amount of oil permitted to be sold increased from $1.6 billion every six months to $6.0 billion. It took some time for Resolution 986 to become operational: the first oil was shipped in 1997, and the first food arrived in March 1998. The 661 Committee members could still object, but as part of the plan, UN staff were sent to Iraq to make sure that items went where they were supposed to. If grain was sent to Iraq, the 661 Committee demanded to know the exact silo that it was being sent to, and had UN employees make sure the grain wound up where it was intended. Helicopter spare parts for civilian use were similarly monitored. A UN employee accompanied the spare parts upon their arrival in country, went to the specified helicopter and oversaw their installation and the destruction of the faulty parts. A large bureaucracy grew up to oversee this modified regime – in New York it occupied some 75 full-time employees, while in Iraq there were over four hundred UN workers and perhaps 1,300 locals employed. A British and 34-year veteran of the UN, Denis Halliday, was made coordinator of the UN effort in September 1997. Thirteen months later, he resigned in frustration so that he could openly criticize the sanctions regime, saying he did not want to be part of a programme that was fostering genocide. His successor, Hans von Sponeck also resigned in protest, as did Jutta Burghardt, head of the World Food Program in Iraq.

Even as late as July 1999, Benon Sevan, the UN's Executive Director of the Office of the Iraq Programme could complain about the impact of the 661 Committee's placing Iraq in jeopardy by its insistence on placing goods vital to the recovery of the country 'on hold':

The improvement of the nutritional and health status of the Iraqi people . . . is being seriously affected as a result of the excessive number of holds placed on supplies and equipment for water and sanitation and electricity.

- Contracts have been approved for pipes for the export pipelines to carry the oil; however, contracts for pigging these pipelines are "On Hold".
- Contracts for equipment that relate to oil exploration, well drilling . . . [and] heavy equipment vehicles needed to perform the field work . . . are also examples of contracts currently "On Hold".
- A number of contracts . . . that are for the efficient and safe operation of control rooms in pumping stations, degassing plants and crude oil treatment facilities are currently on hold "pending further technical evaluation". These goods are crucial to ensuring that other major equipment, much of it expensive, is operated within the manufacturers' recommended parameters to avoid damage through misuse and, in addition, to provide a safe working environment for operators. A contract for hydrostatic testing units, which is essential to ensure the integrity and safety of pipelines in storage tank farms, and pumping stations is also "On Hold", "due to dual use concerns".
- The Secretary General has . . . expressed concern regarding the state of the Iraqi environment. Contracts for goods that would address these types of concerns . . . are all "On Hold" . . . [or] "pending further evaluation" . . .
- A recent review of circulated contracts . . . reveal a number of examples where some goods have been approved while other complementary goods necessary to complete "Projects" are "On Hold" . . . The consequence is that these projects cannot be completed in the absence of integral parts and the contracts are often abandoned or cancelled by the purchaser.

I should like to reiterate what the Secretary-General has asked for repeatedly – it would be most helpful if the Security Council could request the 661 Committee to proceed as expeditiously as possible in its consideration and approval of applications for oil spare parts and equipment and to review further all applications placed on hold. The same applies of course for all applications submitted for other sectors covered under the approved distribution plan. There are *excessive numbers of holds being placed on essential supplies* related particularly to water and sanitation and electricity, which affects all other sectors.[25]

**What Went Wrong?**

The controversy over the sanctions regime focused almost exclusively on its impact on the people of Iraq, especially children. As mentioned earlier in March 1991 the Ahtisaari Report warned of the dire consequences to Iraqis of the massive bombing of their country. This was followed by numerous other reports issued by governmental and non-governmental agencies. UNICEF reported, for example, that the death rate for young children doubled after the imposition of the 1990 sanctions.[26] The World Health Organization stated that the sanctions had resulted in increased child malnutrition, infant mortality, and food-borne and waterborne diseases.[27] The Physicians for Human Rights, UNICEF, the World Health Organization, the International Committee of the Red Cross, the UN Food and Agriculture Organization, the World Food Program all issued similar reports. In one way or another, each warned of the impending health crisis, the re-emergence of diseases thought to have been eradicated, and the deaths that would result.

If Ms. Daponte could be forced out of the US Census bureau for asserting that 158,000 Iraqis had died during the Gulf War, the controversy that surrounded the impact of the twelve-year sanctions regime and its impact on children was even more acrid. There were several small studies that attempted to determine the effects of the war and sanctions on Iraqi civilians, including ongoing reports by the Iraqi government to the United Nations and Iraqi medical personnel claiming massive and ongoing deaths.[28]

The controversy reached the Western mainstream when a 1995 letter-to-the-editor was published in *Lancet*, the journal of the British Medical Society. The letter was authored by Sarah Zaidi of the New York Center for Economic and Social Rights, and Mary C. Smith Fawzi of Harvard's School of Public Health. The two researchers presented their findings from their study in late August 1995 of the mortality rate of children under five years of age in the city of Baghdad. Funded under the auspices of the UN Food and Agricultural Organization (FAO), the letter/article claimed that the sanctions were responsible for the deaths of 567,000 Iraqi children aged five and under.

> The data are consistent with the economic and social realities in Iraq. Food prices are high, purchasing power is low, water and sanitation systems have deteriorated, hospitals are functioning at 40 per cent

capacity, and the population is largely sustained by government rations, which provide 1000 kcal . . . per person. The moral, financial and political standing of an international community intent on maintaining economic sanctions is challenged by the estimate that since August, 1990, 567,000 children in Iraq have died as a consequence.[29]

The results of the study were picked up by major news organizations, including the *New York Times* under the headline 'Iraqi sanctions kill children'.

The most memorable fallout from the *Lancet* report was an interview with Madeleine Albright, then US ambassador to the UN under President Bill Clinton, on the CBS television news magazine, 'Sixty Minutes'. In the famous dialogue, the host, Leslie Stahl, asked Albright about the *Lancet* report and queried if that many deaths could be justified. Without disputing the figures, Albright responded that "We think the price is worth it."[30]

Elsewhere, however, the *Lancet* study came under furious attack from those who supported the sanctions, and so the death toll in Iraq quickly fell into the arena of politics. Those who supported the war insisted on a low death toll, while those who opposed the sanctions thought there must be a high death rate. The issue took a bizarre turn when scientists began to detail errors in the calculations of the 1995 report. A January 1996 letter to the *Lancet* reported that the calculations in the original report were inconsistent and suggested a lower death total.[31] This was followed in 1997 by a letter to the journal from one of the original researchers, Sarah Zaidi, reporting that a follow-up research team using the same map, survey methodology and interview questionnaire as the 1995 FAO study found that the "mortality rates estimated in 1996 were much lower than those reported in 1995, for unknown reasons."[32]

There were less well-known studies that corroborated the widespread suffering and death, for example the one that appeared in *The New England Journal of Medicine* in 1992. In that study, an international team of public health professionals conducted a survey of 271 clusters of 25 to 30 households each. The results, they wrote, "provide strong evidence that the Gulf war and trade sanctions caused a threefold increase in mortality among Iraqi children less than five years of age. We estimate that more than 46,900 children died between January and August 1991."[33]

Perhaps the two most reliable long-term studies of the rate of suffering from the sanctions are a 1999 report 'Morbidity and Mortality Among Iraqi Children' by Richard Garfield of Columbia University and a May 2000 article by Mohamed Ali and Iqbal Shah in the *Lancet*. In the 1999 report, Garfield, an expert on public health, estimated that the number of premature deaths of children age 5 and under was 227,000 between 1990 and early 1998. Ali and Shah conducted a survey for UNICEF and came to the conclusion that child mortality increased 233% between the early 1980s and the late 1990s in south central Iraq. Aided by this more recent study, Garfield revised his estimate of the number of premature deaths for children to be 350,000 through 2000.

The US and the United Kingdom governments were not altogether indifferent to the criticisms of the effects of the sanctions, and responded not by their elimination but by their modification. As noted earlier, there was the offer to institute an oil-for-food programme to be administered by the United Nations beginning in 1991. Saddam Hussein rejected the proposal to trade US$1.6 billion of oil for foodstuffs, arguing that the amount was trifling and the restrictions attached limited Iraq's sovereignty. When in 1995 the amount was raised to US$6 billion, Iraq acquiesced a year later and the first deliveries of medicine and food arrived in 1997. By 2000 the sales of oil by Iraq was nearly double that figure.

One should recognize, since the world's ire over the deaths has ordinarily been focused on the United States and the United Kingdom, that the suffering of the Iraqi people would have been ameliorated had Baghdad accepted the original 1991 offer, or had Saddam Hussein opened his country completely to weapons inspectors. It is also well to remember that there were other reasons beyond sanctions and the Ba'ath leadership. A 1999 UNICEF report mentioned, for example, a decline in breast-feeding and the reduction of investment in health care.[34] One should also note that during the same decade when child mortality was increasing in the south central area of Iraq, it was actually declining in the Kurdish-controlled area under US and UK protection. Is this an indication of the disdain of Saddam Hussein for his own people, or an indication of the largesse that the United States and the United Kingdom were bestowing on the Kurdish region under their control?

## The Iraqi Invasion of 2003 and its Aftermath

Based on the Daponte study on the Kuwait War and the Garfield study of the sanctions period, it can be reliably estimated that over 500,000 Iraqis died prematurely between 1990 and 2003, either through war or because of the sanctions. Focus on the human costs of warfare and sanctions on Iraq entered a third phase in 2003 when the Anglo-American invasion of Iraq began. Unlike the largely academic arguments that characterized the first twelve years, the debate over Iraqi deaths because of the Second Gulf War have taken on a passionate air. Those who supported the war attempt to minimize the number of deaths, while those who oppose it try to show that the level of deaths was high and therefore unacceptable.

The recent debates about the death rate were centred on two types of counting. The first, preferred by the neoconservatives, including President Bush, was a website named *iraqbodycount.org*. It tabulates the civilian toll in Iraq based on published reports of war-related deaths. In July 2008, their minimum estimate of civilian deaths was over 85,000.[35]

Probably more accurate, but certainly more controversial, was a very different estimate based on an in-country random sampling. Like the earlier cluster-based Garfield study, this one, led by Les Roberts of Johns Hopkins School of Public Health, was conducted in September 2004. Roberts' teams interviewed 30 households in 33 randomly selected clusters and asked about family composition, births and deaths since January 2002. In the words of the study, it was designed to assess "the relative risk of death associated with the 2003 invasion and occupation by comparing mortality in the 17–18 months after the invasion with the 14–16-month period preceding it."[36] So as not to appear to skew the data, a randomly chosen cluster in Fallujah was excluded.[37] The findings of the study read in part,

> We estimate that 98,000 more deaths than expected . . . happened after the invasion outside of Falluja and far more if the . . . Falluja cluster is included. The major causes of death before the invasion were myocardial infarction, cerebrovascular accidents, and other chronic disorders whereas after the invasion violence was the primary cause of death. Violent deaths were widespread . . . and were mainly attributed to coalition forces. Most individuals reportedly killed by coalition forces were women and children. The risk of death from violence in the period after the invasion was 58 times higher . . . than in the period before the war.[38]

The Roberts' Report raised a storm of criticism from those who supported the war. A spokesman for British Prime Minister Tony Blair criticized the report because it was based on extrapolation [i.e., that the health team had not interviewed every Iraqi!].[39] Others called the figures "inflated", "meaningless", or "a dart board". But the general consensus was that the study was conservatively done and the figures statistically accurate.[40] One year later, in late 2005, Richard Garfield, who was a member of the Roberts team, estimated that the death toll "couldn't possibly be less than 150,000".[41]

## Conclusion

It is not surprising to learn that the two wars with Iraq have caused hundreds of thousands of deaths on the Iraqi side, and thousands of Americans and of those allied with the United States. What is surprising is that the sanctions period, between 1990 and 2003, caused over 300,000 premature deaths of Iraqi children under five. No one has estimated the number of deaths of adults or of older children. It is sobering to report that in the face of these numbers, few voices have been raised about the relationship of the Geneva Conventions on warfare and the sanctions, or more relevantly of the 'Convention on the Rights of the Child' and the sanctions. For example, Article 6, Paragraphs 1 and 2 of the Convention state that, "Parties recognize that every child has the inherent right to life [and] . . . Parties shall ensure to the maximum extent possible the survival and development of the child."[42] Nor has much attention been paid to the relationship between the sanctions and the addition to the Geneva Conventions adopted in 1997, Protocol 1,[43] Paragraphs 52 and 54 of which are particularly relevant. Paragraph 52 reads in part: "Civilian objects shall not be the object of attack or of reprisals." Paragraph 54 reads in part: "Starvation of civilians as a method of warfare is prohibited . . . It is prohibited to attack, destroy, remove or render useless objects indispensable to the survival of the civilian population, such as foodstuffs, agricultural areas for the production of foodstuffs, crops, livestock, drinking water installations and supplies and irrigation works, . . . whatever the motive, whether in order to starve out civilians, to cause them to move away, or for any other motive."

Interestingly, if one ignores the human cost and the failure of sanctions to effect regime change, there is a case to be made that the sanctions were successful – Iraq was effectively disarmed by 2003 and had no weapons of mass destruction. But it was difficult to prove a negative. As the former chief UN weapons inspector, Hans Blix, noted: "The UN and the world had succeeded in disarming Iraq without knowing it."[44]

Still, it is legitimate to ask, were the sanctions and the two wars worth the cost? If the result has been the death of more than half a million Iraqis, a number of dead greater than has been attributed to Saddam Hussein during his three-decade-long reign of terror, can this be justified? Or did they achieve their stated goals? Certainly, the original purpose of the first Gulf War and the early period of the sanctions, to drive Saddam Hussein from Kuwait, was achieved, and one could argue that the sanctions should have been ended at that point. But then the goal of the United States and the United Kingdom morphed into 'regime change', a euphemism for removing Hussein, and the sanctions continued. The continuation of the sanctions, judged from the point-of-view of forcing Hussein from power, was a failure and should have been abandoned or refocused. The Bill Clinton administration apparently could not find the candour to admit its policies toward Baghdad were not working and so continued them despite their human cost and the slim chance of achieving regime change.

In a thorough study of the impact of sanctions worldwide, David Cortright and George Lopez suggest that a number of unintended outcomes are more common than the wished-for goals when sanctions are imposed on any country. For example, they write that if regime change is a goal, it is unlikely to be achieved. They also note that sanctions tend to enrich the powerful, that is the ones responsible for the sanctions in the first place, since they control the black market and the illicit trade. Furthermore, sanctions tend to affect the most vulnerable members of society: the poor, elderly, women and children.[45] The secret is to find the right balance whereby the goals of the sanctions are achieved with the least damage to the most vulnerable. The Institute for International Economics has studied 116 cases of sanctions between 1914 and 1990 and found that they were successful in only one-third of the cases.[46]

Only September 11 changed how Washington under President George W. Bush and Vice President Dick Cheney viewed Iraq. Seemingly desperate to make a connection between Hussein and al-Qaida, there was a concerted attempt to tie the two together in order to justify a second war against Baghdad. Motivated by what Ron Suskind calls the "1 per cent Doctrine", Cheney argued successfully that the United States could not afford to trust anyone, especially not the UN monitoring teams in Iraq. Therefore America had to go it alone if necessary.[47] When suspicion, not evidence and analysis, became the basis of American foreign policy, a second war with Iraq was assured. The sanctions ended with the beginning of the Second Gulf War.

## NOTES

1 Basra is today the second largest city in Iraq.
2 September 23, 1990.
3 The information in this section is covered in detail in David Cortright and George A. Lopez, *The Sanctions Decade: Assessing UN Strategies in the 1990s* (Boulder, Colorado: Lynne Reiner Publishers, 2000).
4 US forces made up three-fourths of the 660,000 coalition troops.
5 This statement of January 7, 1991 was widely quoted in most major newspapers the following day. The occasion for the speech was Iraq's Army Day. Saddam Hussein had earlier used the phrase 'Mother of All Battles' when referring to the Iran–Iraq War of the 1980s. The expression resonates well with Arabs because the historic 'Mother of All Battles' occurred in 636 at al-Qadisiyah when Arab forces marched out of the Arabian Peninsula and Syria and in a series of battles destroyed the Persian Empire.
6 Iraq's air force was not destroyed when, ironically, it flew to Iran.
7 R. T. Naylor, *Economic Warfare: Sanctions, Embargo Busting, and Their Human Cost* (Toronto: McClelland and Stewart, 1999). Naylor defines strategic bombing as aerial attacks on "all things that allow a nation to sustain itself", p. 319.
8 As a result, electrical production was estimated to have fallen to 4 per cent of pre-war capacity. *Iraq Situation Report for SCF (UK)* (London: Save the Children Fund). As quoted in Geoff Simmons, *The Scourging of Iraq* (New York: St Martin's Press, 1996), p. 106.
9 Ibid.
10 Or: 'shooting sheep', 'a duck hunt', 'a turkey shoot', 'a shooting gallery', and 'a massacre'.
11 David Cortright and George A. Lopez, *The Sanctions Decade: Assessing UN Strategies in the 1990s*, p. 45.
12 The Ahtisaari Report was accessed at http://www.casi.org.uk/info/undocs/s22366.html, and was issued on March 20, 1991.
13 A February 6, 2003 interview with her by *Business Week* can be found at: http://www.businessweek.com/bwdaily/dnflash/feb2003/nf2003026_0167_db052.htm
14 'Paragraph 21. *Decides* to review . . . every sixty days in the light of the policies and practices of the Government of Iraq, including the implementation of all relevant resolutions of the Council, for the purpose of determining whether to reduce or lift the prohibitions referred to therein . . .'

15 Cortright and Lopez suggest this. See David Cortright and George A. Lopez, *The Sanctions Decade: Assessing UN Strategies in the 1990s*, p. 45.

16 Joy Gordon, 'Sanctions as Siege Warfare', The *Nation*, Vol. 268, No. 11 (March 22, 1999), p. 19.

17 Also, lipstick, erasers, toothpaste, badminton rackets, epilepsy medicine, bandages, toilet paper, cloth for shrouds. Items vetoed by the 661 Committee are listed in Geoff Simons, *The Scourging of Iraq*, p. 118.

18 August 21, 1998.

19 John and Karl Mueller, 'The Methodology of Mass Destruction: Assessing Threats in the New World Order', in Eric Herring, *Preventing the Use of Weapons of Mass Destruction* (London: Frank Cass, 2000), p. 177.

20 Atle Dyregrov and Magne Raundalen, 'The Impact of the Gulf War on the Children of Iraq', Centre for Crisis Psychology, paper delivered at the International Society for Traumatic Stress Studies World Conference, Amsterdam, June 1992. One child asked, ". . . could you please tell me when the sanctions will be lifted? We lost so many things during the war . . . We have no food, we have no water . . . we don't have medicine . . . Just tell me when, because yesterday our last ration of flour was consumed . . ." As quoted in *The Scourging of Iraq*, p. 125.

21 Bela Bhatia, Mary Kawar and Mariam Shahin (eds.), *Unheard Voices: Iraqi Women on War and Sanctions* (London: Change, International Reports, 1992).

22 Ibid., p. 17.

23 Ibid., p. 19.

24 Ibid., p. 40.

25 UN Office of the Iraqi Programme, 'Briefing by Benon Sevan, Executive Director of the Iraq Programme, at the informal consultations held by the Security Council on Thursday, July 22, 1999'. Sevan was a career UN diplomat from Greek Cyprus. In 2005 he was implicated in a bribery scandal surrounding alleged kickbacks he received from Saddam Hussein designed to bypass the military restrictions imposed by the UN on the oil for food programme. In August 2005 according to a report investigating the bribery, Sevan was identified as one who took money from the Iraqi regime. Two months later, in October, he fled New York for Nicosia where he maintained he was innocent and was being used as a scapegoat by Secretary General Kofi Annan, also indirectly implicated in the scandal.

26 'UNICEF: Death Rate for Iraqi children has doubled since Gulf War', web report on www.cnn.com/world/meast/9908/12/iraq.unicef, August 13, 1999.

27 Reported in G.R. Popal, 'Impact of Sanctions on the Population of Iraq', *Eastern Mediterranean Health Journal*, Vol. 6, No. 1 (July 2000), pp. 791–95.

28 See for example the article by Karol Sikora, head of the WHO Cancer Programme, who described his visit to hospitals in Baghdad. He reported that radiotherapy equipment was unusable, and unlike the worldwide trend, stomach cancer was increasing. Breast cancer was also on the rise, and there was a threefold increase in leukemia in the southern provinces presumably linked to depleted uranium used in artillery shells entering the food chain. 'Whatever the political legitimacy of the embargo, the needless suffering of those with cancer is an unacceptable outcome', *British Medical Journal*, January 16, 1999, p. 203. Also, A. D. Niazi, 'The Humanitarian and Health Impact of War and Embargo on Iraqis', *Iraqi Medical Journal*, Vol. 47 (1998), pp. 1–4. A 2003 letter to the editor of the *Archives of Disease in Childhood* from two Iraqi physicians, L.

Al-Nouri and Q. Al-Rahim, reiterated the charges of infanticide. They cited the high incidence of wasting in children in a 2000 FAO study. The authors also lamented the ending of the national immunization programme, iodine deficiency and the rise of goitre, the closure of one-third of all hospitals, and nation-wide nutritional deficiencies for children and pregnant women.

29 *Lancet*, Vol. 346, December 2, 1995, p. 1485.

30 These comments of May 12, 1996, haunted Albright for years. When asked about her statement, she usually claimed that she was quoted out of context.

31 Carine Ronsmans and Oona Campbell, 'Sanctions against Iraq', *Lancet*, Vol. 347, January 20, 1996, p. 198.

32 *Lancet*, Vol. 350, October 11, 1997, p. 1105.

33 *New England Journal of Medicine*, September 24, 1992, Vol. 327, No. 13, pp. 931–36. Another article written almost a decade later, at the end of the sanctions period, appeared in the *British Medical Journal*. The article is a personal account written by Dr. Omeed Mubarak, the Iraqi Minister of Health, and describes his visit to the Baghdad Cancer Centre, and his frustration with the sanctions regime. "Requested radiotherapy equipment, chemotherapy drugs and analgesics are consistently blocked by United States and British advisers. There seems to be a rather ludicrous notion that such agents could be converted into chemical or other weapons." *British Medical Journal*, January 16, 1999, Vol. 318, No. 7177, p. 203.

34 UNICEF Executive Director's August 13, 1999 interview accessed at http://www.cnn.com/WORLD/meast/9908/12/iraq.unicef/.

35 The Iraqi Body count site was the favourite of those who supported the war because of the limited basis from which it drew its figures. It was a major headline in the *Los Angeles Times*, on June 25, 2006, when it reported that the Iraqi Health Ministry said at least 50,000 civilians had been killed in the second Gulf war. The story went on to note that even this figure is very low because some regions, for example the insurgent stronghold of al-Anbar, have been "grossly undercounted" and the Kurdish region does not provide figures to the Baghdad government.

36 *The Lancet*, November 20, 2004, Vol. 364, No. 9448, p. 1857.

37 Fallujah, located on the Euphrates River, was the site of a major battle between coalition forces and insurgents in November 2004. Reminiscent of Vietnam where villages were destroyed in order to save them, Fallujah was almost completely ruined. Reports suggest that 36,000 of 50,000 buildings and homes were destroyed or damaged by coalition forces. Sixty schools and 65 mosques were also destroyed. The city had, prior to November 2004, approximately 300,000 citizens. Because of the fighting, half are now internally displaced persons living with relatives or in tents. In late 2006, independent reporters and photographers were still not permitted in the city.

38 *The Lancet*, op. cit.

39 *Los Angeles Times*, 17 December, 2005.

40 See Lila Guterman's 'Dead Iraqis', *Columbia Journalism Review*, March/April 2005, pp. 6–7.

41 *Los Angeles Times*, op. cit.

42 Adopted and opened for signature, ratification and accession by General Assembly Resolution 44/25 of November 20, 1989. Entered into force on September 2, 1990.

43  Formally: Protocol Additional to the Geneva Conventions of August 12, 1949, and relating to the Protection of Victims of International Armed Conflicts (Protocol 1). Adopted on June 8, 1977 by the Diplomatic Conference on the Reaffirmation and Development of International Humanitarian Law applicable in Armed Conflicts.
44  Hans Blix, *Disarming Iraq* (New York: Pantheon Books, 2004).
45  Cited in David Cortright and George A. Lopez, *The Sanctions Decade: Assessing UN Strategies in the 1990s*, p. 14.
46  Ibid., pp. 14–21.
47  The Cheney doctrine holds that even if there is only a 1 per cent chance of an event occurring, the United States must act as though it were 100 per cent, see Ron Suskind, *The One Percent Doctrine* (New York: Simon and Schuster, 2006). Others have noted that the administration of President George W. Bush does not think but believes.

# 9

## Iraq: The Tragedy and Trauma
## of Humiliation

——

*Girijesh Pant*

After more than four years of 'liberation', Iraq today is a highly traumatized society and fragmented nation. It is passing through the worst time in its history. While the country is on the brink of losing its identity, the people are experiencing a huge sense of insecurity and uncertainty disrupting all aspects of their life. Ironically the insecurity is caused not by any dictatorial regime but by those who came to 'liberate' the country and from within. The Iraqi people are witnessing a violence that is increasingly deepening into the society. Apart from armed violence, the civilian population is facing a serious humanitarian crisis in terms of chronic poverty, denial of basic facilities and large-scale displacement, severely hurting the most vulnerable, i.e., women, children, elderly and the chronically ill. According to one estimate, "Eight million people are in urgent need of emergency aid; that figure includes over two million who are displaced within the country, and more than two million refugees. Many more are living in poverty, without basic services, and increasingly threatened by disease and malnutrition."[1] Clearly the challenge is not so much the bringing of democracy as the survival and security of the people of Iraq. This chapter attempts to provide an account of the various dimensions of the crisis faced by the people from a perspective that places people first in the nation-building project.

### The Violence

The estimates of civilian casualties since the US-led invasion of March 2003 vary drastically. According to one estimate, in the first year an average of 128 Iraqis died violently every day. The next year, an average of 115 people were killed daily, and in the third year after the war started 126 died from violence each day. In 2006 an average of 100 people were killed daily and many more were seriously injured by gunshots, shrapnel wounds and burns. In 2007 some 24,000 civilian deaths occurred according to an independent group monitoring casualties in the war-ravaged country.[2] While the World Health Organization (WHO) puts the civilian toll in Iraq at 160,000, The Iraq Body Count, a British NGO, calculated it at 47,668 during the same period.[3] Earlier, a study by Johns Hopkins had put the figure at 655,000 between March 2003 and July 2006.[4] The WHO study, however, has not taken into account the killings following the bombing of a revered Shiite shrine in Samarra, which is believed to be the worst sectarian killing, or the casualties during the latter half of 2006 and the first eight months of 2007. The violence has not only led to the killing of people, but has also been fracturing the very social fabric of the erstwhile secular Iraq, having long-term ramifications. The sectarian divide has complicated the conflict-driven context. More than half of the middle class has left the country or are fleeing, particularly professionals who have been facing serious threats from militias, insurgents and criminals.


**Displacement**

According to estimates by the United Nations High Commissioner for Refugees (UNHCR), every month 60,000 Iraqis leave their homes. Their number was estimated at 4.5 million in 2007, including 2.2 million displaced within the country. Across the borders Iraqis have been moving to Syria and Jordan.[5] Displacement has emerged as a major destabilizing factor leading to greater human insecurity. One in every six Iraqis is said to have been displaced. According to one estimate, out of the 2 million plus people who were internally displaced, half of them were forced out after February 22, 2006, the bombing of the Samarra Al-Askari Mosque. "The scale of this displacement has severely strained infrastructure and resources, creating a serious humanitarian crisis that affects both IDPs and the host communities that provide them with refuge."[6] The report further underlines: "the bombing of the Al-Askari Mosque in Samarra triggered escalating sectarian violence that drastically changed the cause and scale of displacement. Although military operations, crime, and general insecurity remained factors, sectarian violence became the primary driver for population displacement."[7] According to UNHCR, some regions experienced a ten-fold rise of population leading to overstretch on local infrastructure.[8] The trauma of the displacement is not merely physical dislocation but the sectarian dimension of the conflict has also forced many families to face separation from loved ones, as narrated below:

> "I will never believe in differences between people," the young man said. "I am a Sunni and my wife is a Shi'a. I received threats to divorce her or be killed. We have left Dora now [a once-mixed, now Sunni-dominated neighbourhood in central Baghdad]. My wife is staying with her family in Shaab [a Shi'a area] and I am staying with my friends in Mansur [a Sunni area]. I am trying to find a different house but it's difficult now to find a place that accepts both of us in Baghdad."[9]

Even prior to 2003 Iraq witnessed population displacement due to the UN-led economic sanctions, but what has acquired dangerous dimensions is the use of violent ejections of entire populations as a tool to assert political power. The central pattern of displacement is the consolidation of territory by radical armed groups. The result: the radical groups now hold sway over 'cleansed' territories, and have steadily increased their power.[10]

It has been observed that the displacement pattern varies, with sectarian violence being more pronounced in the highly mixed cities like Babil, Salah ad-Din province, Mosul, Basra and Baghdad. "In these areas, campaigns to undermine mixed neighbourhoods proceed in parallel. There tends to be less violence in areas where there is a functioning local authority – mainly the Kurdish North and the southern Shi'a towns (other than Basra)."[11]

A study carried out by Ashraf al-Khalidi and Victor Tanner has also revealed that there are different categories of sectarian displacements, like Sunni Arabs from majority Shi'a areas or Shi'as from majority Sunni areas. Furthermore, many Sunni and Shi'a Arabs forcefully settled in northern Kurdish areas during the Ba'ath regime have now been forced to leave. An important observation of the study is that, "Minority groups forced to flee from both Sunni and Shi'a areas include Kurds, Christians, Turkmen, Sabean-Mandeans, Roma and third-country nationals, especially Palestinians. The minorities are often prey to criminal gangs rather than sectarian ones, because they are viewed as having little in the way of protection, unlike the Sunni, Kurds and Shi'a."[12]

However, sectarian violence alone does not account for the massive displacement of the civilian population. Other factors like the decline of civilian law and order, the absence of basic needs and facilities, the growth of insurgencies and the US military operations have also contributed significantly in triggering it. Of late, the communities are mobilizing to face the crisis by setting up vigilance committees but in the absence of adequate resources their impact has not been very substantial. "So, in order to function, they link themselves to the bigger groups like the Shi'a Mahdi Army or the Sunni Omar Brigades. This only fuels the problem further, as the radical groups gain in power at the local level." The prognosis is alarming, "Adding to the grim picture, tribes on both sides – which were initially playing a stabilising counterpoint to the urban violence, especially in rural areas – seem to be growing restless. If open conflict erupts between tribal groups, the violence will take on an organised, popular and rural dimension that has so far, mercifully, been lacking."[13]

Reports about the situation of the Iraqi refugees in the neighbouring countries are also very disturbing. The host countries have no infrastructure and services to help them. Basic essential services, such as shelter, health, education and security, as well as specialized trauma support, are often not available. According to UNHCR,

> Roughly 50 percent of Iraqi refugees are children and some 550,000 of them are of school age. Access to education for children is, at present, severely limited. In countries that allow children to attend public schools, many children do not attend school because families cannot afford the school supplies and uniforms required. In other countries the only option for Iraqis is to send their children to private schools, but many cannot afford the tuition. In addition, some parents are reluctant to send their children to schools, as the families are in hiding due to their lack of legal status. According to UN estimates, it would cost US $78 million annually to ensure the education of these Iraqi refugee children.[14]

If Iraq is insecure for these displaced persons, then the host countries are unable to offer even basic services to the refugees.

## Infrastructure

The Iraqi infrastructure was the major target of the US invasion and of late of the insurgent attacks. Consequently it has become a major challenge to rebuild civilian life in Iraq. The country which enjoyed the best infrastructure in the region until the 1980s is now rated as the lowest in the region. Consequently the quality of life has deteriorated to such an extent that life often becomes just a question of survival. Deterioration in health care, water, power, sanitation and education has impacted the life of the people with short- and long-term consequences. It is ironic that a country that has been endowed with the Tigris and Euphrates rivers is now unable to provide drinking water to most of its people. According to a report by the United Nations Children Fund (UNICEF), "In the chaotic aftermath of the initial conflict, Iraq's main pumping stations and water-treatment plants were stripped of vital equipment by looters. Acts of sabotage damaged infrastructure even further. Municipal water became dirty and contaminated – exposing children to dangerous and health-sapping waterborne diseases."[15]

Unsafe water has been identified as one of the major causes of diseases, particularly among children. Many children in Iraq died of waterborne diseases compounded by a severe lack of medicines. UNICEF points out that mortality rates among children below five have increased from five per cent in 1990 to 12.5 per cent in 2004. It is a vicious circle as water cannot be treated due to lack of electric power and fuel for generators. Besides, as has been pointed out by the British Department for International Development, "Iraq's pipes, pumps and purifiers are often old, damaged and unreliable. In Basra, the country's second city, the situation is especially serious."[16] It says that to avoid contaminated water the people are forced to purchase water from street vendors. During summers, the water pumps are in big demand costing $10 in the local market. People have been finding it difficult to afford. "It cost us 1,000 Iraqi dinars [about 78 cents] for just 200 litres. This is enough to drink but not to wash. My children often went to school without even washing their faces."[17]

The collapse of the health care infrastructure has made civil life yet more miserable. The state-run medical supply company reportedly is unable to meet the requirements of the hospitals. Consequently, as OXFAM highlights, out of the 180 hospitals countrywide, 90 per cent lack key resources including basic medical and surgical supplies.[18] A recent report by *Medact*, an organization of health professionals that work to highlight the consequences of war, poverty and other threats to global health, has pointed out, "The health system is in disarray owing to the lack of an institutional framework, intermittent electricity, unsafe water, and frequent violations of medical neutrality. The ministry of health and local health authorities are mostly unable to meet these huge challenges, while the activities of UN agencies and non-governmental organisations are severely limited."[19] The institutional collapse brought out by the report can be well illustrated by the following reportage:

> The report tells of one young woman, Aseel, in labour for three days with no pain relief, doctor or midwife. Her family decided they would have to find the money to get her into hospital. "After parting with my first bank note to secure petrol from my neighbour, we prayed for safety during our long trip to Diwaniyah maternity hospital," said Aseel's husband. "Thankfully we arrived safely, and were greeted by the open hand of the security guard. We parted with another note to get in. It took a long time to find a midwife. Eventually a sleepy midwife answered my pleas and we exchanged papers, notes and promises to bring more notes. Amin was born the next morning."
>
> "Aseel developed a serious kidney infection and needed anti-biotics, but we couldn't get them in Diwaniyah. Amin had to be fed powdered milk diluted with tap water. There wasn't enough money to buy formula milk, so we had to make it last." Amin survived one of the toughest milestones of life – birth. By Iraqi standards his life of hardship had just started.[20]

It is rightly observed by the report that under the Geneva Convention the occupying power has a duty to protect health services even after the establishment of the interim Iraqi government in 2004. "Yet these rules and obligations have been routinely ignored."[21] Health facilities, it says, were not protected during and after the invasion. Reconstruction contracts were more often awarded to the private sector than to expert health bodies.

Baghdad reportedly receives only between two to four hours power supply daily from the state-owned electricity company. The residents have no choice but to depend upon private power generators by paying $12 per ampere or to depend on their own petrol-fuelled small generators.[22] The massive destruction of the power plants has left the country with an acute shortage of power. What is disturbing is that the ongoing violence is impeding the reconstruction efforts. According to a *Washington Post* report,

Iraq's power grid is on the brink of collapse because of insurgent sabotage, rising demand, fuel shortages and provinces that are unplugging local power stations from the national grid. Electricity Ministry spokesman Aziz al-Shimari said power generation nationally is only meeting half the demand, and there had been four nation-wide blackouts over the past two days. The shortages across the country are the worst since the summer of 2003, shortly after the U.S.-led invasion. One of the biggest problems facing the national grid is the move by provinces to disconnect their power plants from the system, reducing the overall amount of electricity being generated for the entire country. Provinces say they have no choice because they are not getting as much electricity in return for what they produce, mainly because the capital requires so much power.[23]

It is reported that in southern Tikrit there is no electricity as the plants were blasted.[24] "Two huge blasts hit Tikrit's southern power station last night, resulting in a blackout in most parts of the city . . . The blasts destroyed all the transformers in the station which reduce the voltage from 400 to 130 volts to be used for home purposes."[25] In the severe winter of 2008 when Baghdad had snowfall and temperatures falling four degrees Celsius below zero, there was no electricity for a week in eastern Baghdad.[26] While people were left to face the severe cold, the ministries merely engaged in blaming each other. The electricity ministry found fault with petroleum ministry for not supplying sufficient fuel to run the generator; the latter accuses the former of failing to provide refineries. According to an official from the ministry of power, "Oil and gas pumping from Kirkuk fields to our northern and southern plants over the past two weeks has stopped and furthermore the decision on 4 January by Turkish power provider Kartet to stop exporting electricity to Iraq is also to blame . . . Three bombs over the past two weeks have targeted the power lines that connect northern provinces with each other and with Baghdad."[27]

## Growing Poverty

Iraq is estimated to have the third largest reserves of oil yet the people of the country are facing the severe threat of rising poverty. After four and a half years, despite some recovery of the oil sector, the country remains mired in poverty, corruption and insurgent violence. The shadow economy is being manipulated by organized crime, militias and insurgents to fund attacks on infrastructure and innocent Iraqi civilians. "The shadow economy is also used extensively by the poor and women for subsistence living. The combined effect for Iraqi citizens is they have to survive in a country without adequate institutions and poor governance. The extensive shadow economy diverts funds from legitimate uses by the government such as taxes, funds for reconstruction projects, social protection, social insurance, etc."[28]

According to the Central Office for Statistics and Information Technology (COSIT), which is part of the Iraqi Ministry of Planning, 43 per cent of Iraqis suffer from "absolute poverty" that is, with an income of less than a dollar a day. This is primarily due to the fact that 50 per cent of the working population remains unemployed. Furthermore, unemployed youths are particularly vulnerable to the allure of joining the armed groups. The high casualty rates among civilian men have also contributed to poor living conditions. What is more alarming is that despite the efforts being made, people's access to food has been on the decline. A report by the World Food Programme says "over four million people in Iraq were 'food-insecure' and in dire need of different kinds of humanitarian assistance".[29] This was an increase from the estimated 2.6 million who were found to be 'extremely poor' in WFP's 2004 Baseline Survey. The problem has been compounded by the failure of the public distribution system (PDS), which was conceived during the Saddam Hussein regime to provide food to the people from the government under the UN sanctions. It includes staple items like rice, cooking oil, flour, detergent, powdered milk, sugar and white beans. According to press reports, "The amount of each item in the rations was recently reduced due to availability issues." Commenting on the system, the Office of the UN High Commissioner for Refugees observes,

> . . . of the 4 million Iraqis who cannot buy enough to eat, 40 percent don't have regular access to rations supplied by the PDS. While the system ran efficiently during Saddam's regime, and was the largest system of its kind in the world, subsequent breakdowns in infra-structure and security have caused delays and gaps in distribution.[30]

The failure of the system has affected most seriously the internally displaced people, as they have to transfer their ration card to their new locations. Reports show, "Some provinces have closed their borders to IDPs and one way to keep them out is to stop the transfer of the ration cards."[31] The infrastructure too has been contributing to the failing of PDS. The supplies are moved from Basra to Baghdad for storage in warehouses and from there transported by trucks to different regions. The centralized system has been causing delay as Oxfam reports, "food has to be transported for much longer distances than necessary".[32] Besides, the trucks have been targeted by attacks and looted on the way. Since the invasion in 2003, increasing number of people are 'food insecure', a term meaning they do not receive a minimum goal of calories each day. "The poverty that is hitting middle classes, particularly in Baghdad – they haven't seen it before," said Claire Hajaj of the UNICEF Iraq Support Centre in Amman. "What they are experiencing now is a reversal of what they are used to. The gap between how people are used to living and how they are living now – they don't have the coping mechanisms."[33]

Frequent imposition of curfews too has been eroding the purchasing power of the people, besides causing inconveniences. The price of fruit, vegetables and fuel goes up whenever a curfew is imposed. Curfews also aggravate the shortages of commodities as people start stockpiling, or turn to black marketeering. Ironically the subsidies too have been encouraging scarcity and black marketeering. It is reported that "Iraqi gas costs about 5 cents a gallon, whereas neighbouring Kuwait charges 79 cents. The difference in prices has created a thriving black market . . . smuggling has exacerbated a severe fuel shortage in Iraq . . ."[34] Along with the daily commodities, a wide range of weapons are sold. According to a report in the *New York Times*,

> The weapons are easy to find, resting among others in the semi hidden street markets here, where weapons are sold in tea houses, the back rooms of grocery kiosks, cosmetics stores and rug shops, or from the trunks of cars. Proprietors show samples for immediate purchase and offer to take orders – 10 guns can be had in two hours, they say, and 100 or more the next day. "Every type of gun that the Americans give comes to the market," said Brig. Hassan Nouri, chief of the political investigations bureau for the Sulaimaniya district. "They go from the U.S. Army to the Iraqi Army to the smugglers."[35]

The report also identifies three kinds of weapons issued to the American forces which are widely available on the black market, namely Glock and Walther 9-millimetre pistols, and pristine, unused Kalashnikovs from post-Soviet Eastern European countries.

The economy in the shadow of violence during the last four years has not been able to support the people. Consequently not only has domestic production been on the decline, but unemployment has risen to the extent that people are forced to take part in the violence. One serious consequence has been the rise of drug trafficking. The porous border has helped facilitate this. The flow of drugs into Iraq is associated with the significant increase in Iranian pilgrims visiting Shi'a shrines in Najaf and Karbala. According to officials, Karbala and Najaf are the biggest consumers of drugs. The reasons for the increase in drug use and trafficking are clear: insecurity, terrorism and lack of employment. "The number of addicts is increasing, particularly among young people from conservative families, where there are more religious restrictions," one official said. "This makes them look for another way to forget about the pressure that the society puts on them." The primary illicit drugs being used are heroin, cocaine, and marijuana, with grams of heroin or cocaine going for $20 to $30 dollars. The heroin is coming from Afghanistan and Iran and the cocaine is somehow arriving from South America. "We estimate that more than 5,000 Iraqis are consuming drugs in the south today, especially heroin, compared with 2004, when there were only around 1,500," said Dr Kamel Ali, a senior official in the health ministry's anti-narcotics program. "We fear the number could be as high as 10,000 countrywide."[36]

The extent to which the insurgency is benefiting financially or materially from the drug trade is not definite but the possibilities cannot be ruled out. As Professor Robert Looney observes, "The impact of the insurgents and criminal elements in Iraq may have significant consequences beyond their direct actions. By creating an unstable security situation while at the same time increasing the profitability of the hawala system, their actions are retarding the development of the formal banking system. The current wave of crime and insurgent activity creates, and is in turn supported by, an increasingly sophisticated criminal economy."[37]

## The Vulnerable

### Children

"The Iraqi children are paying far too high a price," said Roger Wright, UNICEF's Special Representative for Iraq. It is estimated that two million children are facing the problems of malnutrition, disease and disruption of their education. "Iraqi children were frequently caught in the crossfire of conflict throughout 2007. Insecurity and displacement continues to cause hardship for many in the most insecure parts of the country and further eroded access to quality essential services country-wide."[38] According to UNICEF, in 2007:

- Only 28 per cent of Iraq's 17 year olds sat their final exams in summer, and only 40 per cent of those sitting exams achieved a passing grade (in south and central Iraq).
- Many of the 220,000 displaced children of primary school age had their education interrupted, adding to the estimated 760,000 children (17 per cent) already out of primary school in 2006.
- Children in remote and hard-to-reach areas were frequently cut off from health outreach services.
- Only 20 per cent outside Baghdad had working sewerage in their community, and access to safe water remains a serious issue.
- An average 25,000 children per month were displaced by violence or intimidation, their families seeking shelter in other parts of Iraq.
- By the end of the year, approximately 75,000 children had resorted to living in camps or temporary shelters (25 per cent of those newly-displaced since the Samarra shrine bombing in February 2006).
- Hundreds of children lost their lives or were injured by violence and many more had their main family wage earner kidnapped or killed.
- Approximately 1,350 children were detained by military and police authorities, many for alleged security violations.

### Women

"The situation for Iraqi women since that invasion four years ago has deteriorated dramatically by every measure of daily survival: lack of access to clean water, electricity, food, education and jobs. And, as a result of the absence of personal security, women have virtually disappeared from public life in Iraq."[39]

Women are the worst victims of the present situation in Iraq. Facing sexual violence perpetuated by both the US military as well as by militant groups, their freedom has been severely restricted for security reasons. They are kept locked up in their homes by the fear of abduction and criminal abuse. According to a Human Rights Watch report entitled 'New Climate of Fear: Sexual Violence and Abduction of Women and Girls in Baghdad', the failure of the Iraqi and US-led occupation authorities has been the root cause of widespread fear of rape and abduction among women and their families. "Women and girls today in Baghdad are scared, and many are not going to schools or jobs or looking for work."[40] It is reported that "American forces have also arrested wives, sisters and daughters of suspected insurgents in order to pressure them to surrender. Female relatives have been literally taken hostage by U.S forces and used as bargaining chips. Aside from the violence related to the arrests, those women who were detained by the troops often suffer as well from the sense of shame associated with such a detention."[41] Sexual abuse is not confined simply to a few army camps, but is happening across the country. It is observed that such violence is usually kept secret. It was the *New Yorker* magazine which brought it to public domain. "The U.S. administration blamed the crimes on a few black sheep. Of course it is not true. Orders come from the top of U.S. military and civilian leaderships."[42]

Furthermore, a report by Physicians for Human Rights (PHR), a British independent organization, released in 2005 says "psychological torture has been at the centre of treatment and interrogation of detainees in Iraq". The most inhumane and damaging "techniques of psychological torture used have included sensory deprivation, isolation, sleep deprivation, forced nudity, the use of military working dogs to instil fear, cultural and sexual humiliation, mock executions, and the threat of violence or death toward detainees or their loved ones."[43]

It is not just the US forces but the terrorists and the Islamist militants too who have been posing a threat to the women. "Many women's organizations and activists inside Iraq have documented the increasing Islamist threats to women: the pressure to conform to certain dress codes, the restrictions in movement and behaviour, incidents of acid thrown into women's faces and even targeted killings. After the U.S. invasion in 2003, many women in Basra, for example, reported that they were forced to wear a headscarf or restrict their movements in fear of harassment from men."[44]

According to the Organization of Women's Freedom in Iraq, "15 per cent of Iraqi women widowed by the war have been desperately searching for temporary marriages or prostitution, either for financial support or protection in the midst of sectarian war."[45] Furthermore, the number of honour killings has gone up because of rising rape and abduction.[46] Iraqi women say that the gains won by the Iraqi women's movement in the first half of the 1900s – maintained to a large extent through the 1990s – are being rolled back. Since 2003, the US has strengthened conservative Islamic forces in Iraq both directly, by appointing reactionary clerics to the Iraqi Governing Council in 2004, and indirectly, by creating an atmosphere of chaos where such reactionary forces thrive.[47]

It is observed that in contrast to the days of Saddam Hussein when war widows were taken care of by the state, widows in Iraq today have no choice but to turn to the flesh trade. The trauma of this Iraqi mother having no means to feed her kids, forcing her to turn to prostitution, underlines the desperation:

> I'm a nice-looking woman and it wasn't difficult to find a client. When we got to the bed I tried to run away . . . I just couldn't do it, but he hit and raped me. When he paid me afterwards, it was finished for me.
>
> When I came home with some food I had bought from that money and saw my children screaming of happiness, I discovered that honour is insignificant compared to the hunger of my children.[48]

Various militant gangs are running brothels enticing women with better living conditions, particularly across the borders. The brokers argue, "Families don't want them and we are helping the girls to survive. We offer them food and housing and about $10 a day if they have had at least two clients. Our priority is virgin girls; they can be sold at very expensive prices to Arab millionaires."[49] In June 2007, the *Atlantic Review* highlighted yet another dimension by observing that loss of honour make these Iraqis good material for terrorist outfits.[50]

## Social and Family Life

The ongoing violence and accompanying fear have totally destroyed the social and family life of Iraqis previously fond of wandering in the street late at night, shopping for after dinner ice creams. Now kids find their homes have become prisons. "We are afraid to go out of it and our families do not allow us to go out of the district. We feel our houses as prisons and we wish we weren't graduated. At least we could go to school and see each other."[51] These days, children cannot go to school because their mothers feel that it is not safe.[52] Even playing in the neighbourhood or park is not seen as safe and secure. The anxiety level is so high that the family remains engaged all the time in the search for a safe and secure destination. There is very strong sense of dislocation even when a family has remained in the same habitat. The extended size of families and limited means is leading to fragmentation of families, as not all are in a position to move out.

The sense of siege is seeping across the society. Iraqis are family people and they are witnessing the disappearance of family. Families and married couples that happily lived together previously are now being forced to think in terms of their sects. The following interview illustrates the extent of the social and family trauma:

> "A 9-year-old grandson was asked at school last month whether he was Sunni or Shiite. Then, Rim, a 24-year-old niece, had her engagement broken off by her fiancé's parents because she is Sunni. She cried and cried," said her mother, Hana, sitting in a large living room with her hands folded in her lap. "Even if they come back, I will never give my daughter to them." The blow has driven her daughter to feel her Sunni identity even more intensely, she said. That, in turn, has caused a problem with an uncle, Husham, who was in prison under Mr. Hussein and is now working as a senior official in the Jafaari government. Another family member jokingly introduced him to a visitor as "the Shiite extremist". Rim stopped talking to him when he had made disparaging comments about Sunnis. "He should not talk about Sunnis like that," she said, her eyes looking straight past him. "He hates Sunnis."[53]

The American government officials think that they are accomplishing the job, the Iraqi government feels that it is acquiring the wherewithal to govern, but the people think otherwise. The quotes below sum up the trauma and humiliation of Iraqi people:

> "Americans believe their soldiers are working for the greater good. The Iraqis don't see that. They see people who are here for their

own self-interest – who drive the wrong way on roads, who stop traffic whenever they want to, who they have to be careful not to get too close to so that they won't be shot."[54]

"Now, I have a story to tell my son Haider about. It is a story that is more interesting than Titanic and the Lord of the Rings. It's even deeper in History that the story of the famous Iraqi Myth hero Gilgamesh and his first written epic that we always talked proudly about. It's the STORY OF THE IRAQI FLAG. Yes we changed the flag and all our problems were solved in a second. Now we shall not care about the electricity problem because our flag will lighten our dark night, it will warm our frozen souls, we will not even think about the thousands of the displaced families because the new flag will be their houses and it will feed their angry hungry stomachs. Now, we will be able to reconstruct our destroyed country because we will build skyscrapers, hospitals and schools made of the Iraqi flags."[55]

Clearly people in Iraq are struggling for their survival, for their honour and dignity. In this struggle the enemies are not so much from outside as from within. The unleashing of sectarian divisions and the brutalization of people's psyche has created all the right objective and subjective conditions for violence. Opinion may be divided on the political future of Iraq, the final shape of the map of Iraq, or how the oil wealth will be shared. However, there can be no doubt that Iraqi society has lost its vivaciousness and the people their voice. Perhaps in the distant future life may be restored to normality, but the schism and the scar of mutual hatred and suspicion are not going to disappear easily. The huge loss of social trust and confidence cannot be replenished by oil wealth. The tragedy and trauma of humiliation is going to loom large in the psyche of young Iraqis for years to come.

## NOTES

1 'Rising to the humanitarian challenge in Iraq', http://www.oxfam.org/en/policy/briefingpapers/bp105_humanitarian_challenge_in_iraq_0707, accessed February 12, 2008.

2 *Civilian Deaths from Violence in 2007: Iraq Body Count*, www.iraqbodycount.org/analysis/numbers/2007/, accessed on February 12, 2008.

3 Ibid.

4 'Study Claims Iraq's 'Excess' Death Toll Has Reached 655,000', http://www.washingtonpost.com/wp-dyn/content/article/2006/10/10/AR2006101001442.html, accessed on February 12, 2008.

5 The Iraq Situation website, http://www.unhcr.org/cgi-bin/texis/vtx/iraq?page=press&id=475fba5d2, accessed on February 12, 2008. Also see http://www.unhcr.org/cgi-bin/texis/vtx/home/opendoc.pdf?tbl=SUBSITES&id=470387fc2.

6 The Internally Displaced Persons Programme website, http://www.iom-iraq.net/idp.html, accessed on February 12, 2008.

7 Ibid.

8 'Iraq Displacement', on the UNHCR website, at http://www.unhcr.org/news/NEWS/452f69d74.html, accessed on February 12, 2008.

9 *Iraq Displacement Crisis: The Search for Solutions*, *Forced Migration Review* Special Issue, http://www.fmreview.org/FMRpdfs/Iraq/full.pdf, accessed on February 12, 2008.

10 Ibid.

11 Ibid.

12 Ibid.

13 Ibid.

14 NGO Statement on Regional Consequences of the Humanitarian Crisis in Iraq, International Conference on Addressing the Humanitarian Needs of Refugees and Internally Displaced Persons inside Iraq and in Neighbouring Countries, Geneva, April 17–18, 2007, http://www.unhcr.org/events/EVENTS/462777a22.pdf, accessed on February 12, 2008.

15 Claire Hajaj and Ban Dhayi, 'Lack of safe water endangers the health of Baghdad's most deprived children', http://www.unicefusa.org/site/apps/nl/content2.asp?c=duLRI8O0H&b=39306&ct=3697385, accessed on February 12, 2008.

16 'Better Basra: Getting clean water to southern Iraq', June 20, 2007, http://www.dfid.gov.uk/casestudies/files/asia/iraq-better-basra.asp.

17 Claire Hajaj and Ban Dhayi, 'Lack of safe water endangers the health of Baghdad's most deprived children', http://www.unicefusa.org/site/apps/nl/content2.asp?c=duLRI8O0H&b=39306&ct=3697385.

18 OXFAM, 'Rising to the humanitarian challenge in Iraq', Briefing Paper, July 2007, http://web.mit.edu/humancostiraq/reports/oxfam_iraq.pdf.

19 'Rehabilitation under fire, healthcare in Iraq 2003–2007', http://www.medact.org/content/violence/MedactIraq08final.pdf.

20 Ibid.

21 Ibid.

22 'Curfew in Baghdad, more financial burdens on residents', Baghdad, January 19, 2008 (Voices of Iraq), http://www.iraqupdates.com/p_articles.php/article/26361.

23 'Iraq's power grid nearing collapse', http://www.washingtonpost.com/wp-dyn/content/article/2007/08/04/AR2007080400547.html, accessed on February 12, 2008.

24 'Blackout in Tikrit after power plant blown up', http://www.iraqupdates.com/p_articles.php/article/25425.

25 Ibid.

26 'IRAQ: Population hit by acute power outage, shortage of petroleum products', http://www.irinnews.org/Report.aspx?ReportId=76337.

27 Ibid.

28 'Gaining Control of Iraq's Shadow Economy', http://stinet.dtic.mil/oai/oai?&verb=getRecord&metadataPrefix=html&identifier=ADA474397.

29 'Iraqi Food Rations Program Besieged by Breakdowns, Delays', http://www.pbs.org/newshour/indepth_coverage/middle_east/iraq/july-dec07/foodrations_10-23.html.

30 Ibid.

31 Ibid.

32 'Rising to the humanitarian challenge in Iraq', http://www.oxfam.org/en/files/bp105_humanitarian_challenge_in_iraq_0707.pdf/download.

33 'Iraqi Food Rations Program Besieged by Breakdowns, Delays', http://www.pbs.org/newshour/indepth_coverage/middle_east/iraq/july-dec07/foodrations_10-23.html.

34 'Iraq Fuel Subsidies Create Thriving Black Market and Shortages', http://economistsview.typepad.com/economistsview/2005/08/iraq_fuel_subsi.html.

35 'Black-Market Weapon Prices Surge in Iraq Chaos', http://www.nytimes.com/2006/12/10/world/middleeast/10weapons.html

36 'Iraq: Officials Complain of Rising Drug Use, Trafficking', http://stopthedrugwar.org/chronicle-old/429/iraq.shtml.

37 Robert E Loony, 'The business of insurgency: the expansion of Iraq's shadow economy (organized crime)', *The National Interest*, online 22-SEP-05, http://goliath.ecnext.com/coms2/gi_0199-4840867/The-business-of-insurgency-the.html, accessed on February 12, 2008.

38 UNICEF, 'Little respite for Iraq's children in 2007', http://www.unicef.org/infobycountry/media_42256.html.

39 'U.S.-Occupied Iraq: Women suffer untold violence', http://www.worldproutassembly.org/archives/2007/03/usoccupied_iraq.html.

40 Ibid.

41 Nadje Al-Ali, 'Iraqi Women – Four years after the Invasion', http://www.fpif.org/fpiftxt/4055.

42 Ghali Hassan, 'Iraqi Women under Occupation', http://www.countercurrents.org/iraq-hassan090505.htm.

43 'Abu Ghraib–One Year Later: Comprehensive Report Documents Use of Psychological Torture by US Forces', http://physiciansforhumanrights.org/library/news-2005-05-12.html.

44 Ibid.

45 'Organization of Women's Freedom in Iraq Summer Report 2007', http://www.madre.org/media/OWFI2007.pdf.

46 Ibid.

47 Ibid.

48  Afif Sarhan, 'Sex for Survival', http://english.aljazeera.net/NR/exeres/36B04283-E43F-4367-90BB-E6C60CB88F76.htm.
49  Ibid.
50  'More Terrorism to Expect due to "Lost Honor" of Iraqi Sunnis?', http://atlanticreview.org/archives/688-More-Terrorism-to-Expect-due-to-Lost-Honor-of-Iraqi-Sunnis.html, accessed on February 12, 2008.
51  'We feel our house as prisons', blog entry dated 18-1-2008 at http://121contact.typepad.com/my_weblog/women_of_peace/index.html, accessed on February 12, 2008.
52  'Middle-Class Family Life in Iraq Withers Amid the Chaos of War', http://www.nytimes.com/2005/10/02/international/middleeast/02families.html.
53  Ibid.
54  Michael Massing, 'As Iraqis See It', *New York Review of Books*, Vol. 55, No. 1, January 17, 2008, http://www.nybooks.com/articles/20934.
55  'Is that all?', blog entry dated January 26, 2008 at http://washingtonbureau.typepad.com/iraq/.

# Chronology

*Stuti Bhatnagar*

## Arab–Israeli War, 1948–49

| | |
|---|---|
| November 28, 1947 | UN General Assembly endorses partition of Palestine |
| May 14, 1948 | State of Israel is proclaimed |
| May 15, 1948 | Armies of Egypt, Iraq, Lebanon, Trans-Jordan and Syria invade Israel |
| May 20, 1948 | General Assembly Committee appoints Count Folke Bernadotte as mediator for Palestine |
| May 29, 1948 | Jewish Quarter in the Old City of Jerusalem falls to the Arab Legion. Security Council calls for a four-week ceasefire within 72 hours |
| June 11, 1948 | Four-week truce commences |
| July 8, 1948 | Arab League refuses to renew truce, fighting resumes and Israel makes territorial gains on all fronts |
| July 15, 1948 | Security Council orders another truce; Israel and Arab countries accept it |
| July 18, 1948 | Second truce begins |
| September 17, 1948 | Count Bernadotte is assassinated in Jerusalem and is succeeded by Ralph Bunche |
| October 19, 1948 | Security Council calls for an immediate ceasefire |
| October 22, 1948 | Israel and Egypt agree on a ceasefire |
| November 16, 1948 | Security Council calls for armistice talks |
| December 11, 1948 | General Assembly establishes the Palestine Conciliation Commission, which reaffirms the |

|  | decision on Jerusalem and calls for repatriation or resettlement of refugees |
|---|---|
| January 7, 1949 | Fighting ends in Sinai. Israeli forces withdraw from Sinai following British ultimatum and US pressure |
| February 24, 1949 | Israel and Egypt sign Armistice Agreement |
| March 23, 1949 | Israel and Lebanon sign Armistice Agreement |
| April 3, 1949 | Israel and Jordan sign Armistice Agreement |
| May 11, 1949 | Israel is admitted to UN membership |
| July 20, 1949 | Israel and Syria sign Armistice Agreement |

## June War of 1967

| May 19, 1967 | At the request of Egypt, United Nations Emergency Force (UNEF) is withdrawn from the Sinai Peninsula and the Gaza Strip |
|---|---|
| May 22, 1967 | Egypt imposes a naval blockade against Israel on the Straits of Tiran |
| June 5, 1967 | Israel air-force attacks Egyptian and Syrian air bases and ground forces advance into Sinai. Jordan launches an attack on Israel. |
| June 6, 1967 | IDF advance in Sinai, West Bank and Jerusalem |
| June 7, 1967 | Israel captures Jerusalem and completes the conquest of West Bank and Gaza Strip |
| June 8, 1967 | IDF reaches the Suez Canal, completing occupation of the entire Sinai Peninsula. Egypt accepts the UN call for a ceasefire |
| June 9, 1967 | President Nasser resigns but withdraws his resignation under public pressure |
| June 10, 1967 | Israel occupies Golan Heights and Syria accepts ceasefire |
| November 22, 1967 | UN Security Council unanimously adopts Resolution 242 |

## October War of 1973

| | |
|---|---|
| October 6, 1973 | In a surprise attack against Israel, Egyptian forces cross Suez Canal and Syrian forces attack Golan Heights captured by Israel in 1967 |
| October 7, 1973 | Syrian attack is contained |
| October 8, 1973 | Israeli counter-offensive in Sinai fails |
| October 10, 1973 | Syrian forces are driven back in Golan. Israel stabilizes new battle line in Sinai |
| October 12, 1973 | IDF advances to within 28 miles of Damascus |
| October 13, 1973 | IDF repels Jordanian and Iraqi forces fighting with Syrians in the Golan Heights |
| October 15, 1973 | US begins a massive military air lift to Israel |
| October 15, 1973 | Israeli forces cross Suez Canal and establish bridgehead on the western banks of the Canal |
| October 17, 1973 | Sadat proposes a ceasefire |
| October 17, 1973 | Arab oil-producing states announce a 10 per cent reduction in oil production and impose a total embargo on the United States and the Netherlands |
| October 20, 1973 | Saudi Arabia halts oil exports to the United States |
| October 20, 1973 | Israel expands its bridgehead on the west bank of the Suez Canal, besieging Third Egyptian Army |
| October 22, 1973 | UN Security Council adopts Resolution 338 |

## Civil War in Lebanon

| | |
|---|---|
| April 13, 1975 | Gunmen kill four Phalangists during an attempt on their leader Pierre Gameyel's life in Beirut. In retaliation the Phalangists attack a bus carrying Palestinian passengers across a Christian neighborhood, killing about twenty-six of the occupants |

| | |
|---|---|
| December 6, 1975 | The killing of four of its members leads the Phalange to set up roadblocks throughout Beirut and many Palestinians and Muslims passing through the roadblocks are killed immediately. Phalange members take hostages and attack Muslims in East Beirut. Pro-Muslim and Palestinian militias retaliate with force, increasing the death toll to 600 civilians and militiamen |
| January 18, 1976 | About 1,000 people are killed by Christian forces in the Karantina Massacre |
| January 20, 1976 | Palestinian militias kill around 300 Christians in Damour, a Lebanese Christian town, in retaliation for the Karantina Massacre |
| June 1976 | President Suleiman Frangieh calls for Syrian intervention |
| 1976 | Syrian troops enter Lebanon, occupying Tripoli and the Bekaa Valley |
| August 12, 1976 | Christian forces manage to break through the defences of the Tel al-Zaatar refugee camp in East Beirut. About 2,000 Palestinians are killed. |
| October 1976 | Syria accepts Arab League proposal that gives Syria the mandate to keep 40,000 troops in Lebanon as the bulk of an Arab Deterrent Force |
| 1977 | In East Beirut, Christian leaders of the National Liberal Party (NLP), the Kateeb Party and the Lebanese Renewal Party join the Lebanese Front. Their militias, the Tigers, Phalange and Guardians of the Cedars, enter into a loose coalition known as the Lebanese forces, to form a military wing for the Lebanese Front |
| March 1977 | Lebanese National Movement leader Kamal Jumblatt is assassinated |

| | |
|---|---|
| March 14, 1978 | Israel launches Operation Litani against Lebanon, occupying areas south of the river Litani |
| March 19, 1978 | United Nations Security Council adopts Resolution 425 that calls on Israel to withdraw from Lebanon and establishes the United Nations Interim Force in Lebanon (UNIFIL) |
| March 23, 1978 | UNIFIL forces arrive in Lebanon and set up headquarters in Naqoura |
| April 19, 1978 | South Lebanese Army shells UNIFIL headquarters killing eight UN peacekeepers |
| April 2, 1981 | Syrian army attacks ancient Lebanese city of Zahle |
| June 3, 1982 | Members of the Abu Nidal Organisation attempt to assassinate Shlomo Argov, Israeli Ambassador in London. In retaliation, Israel launches an aerial attack on PLO and PFLP targets in West Beirut leading to 100 casualties |
| June 5, 1982 | UN Security Council adopts Resolution 508 calling all parties to cease military activities within Lebanon and across the Lebanese–Israeli border |
| June 6, 1982 | Under an operation code-named Peace for Galilee Israel invades Lebanon and attacks PLO bases |
| July 21, 1982 | Israel Defence Forces (IDF) intensify aerial bombardment of neighbourhoods in East Beirut |
| August 20, 1982 | A multinational force lands in Beirut to oversee the PLO withdrawal from Lebanon |
| August 23, 1982 | Bashir Gemayel is elected President of Lebanon |
| September 14, 1982 | Bashir Gemayel is assassinated |
| September 16–19, 1982 | Massacre of Palestinian refugees in Sabra and Shatilla |

| | |
|---|---|
| April 18, 1983 | A suicide attack at the US Embassy in West Beirut kills 63 persons |
| May 17, 1983 | Israel and Lebanon sign a peace agreement that conditions Israeli withdrawal on the departure of Syrian troops from Lebanon |
| August 1983 | Israel withdraws from the Chouf District (southeast of Beirut) |
| October 23, 1983 | A suicide bombing targets the headquarters of the US and French forces in Beirut, killing 241 American and 58 French servicemen |
| February 1984 | US forces withdraw from Lebanon |
| March 5, 1984 | Lebanese government cancels the May 17 Agreement |
| June 1, 1987 | Rashid Karami, head of government of national unity, is assassinated |
| 1988 | Violence flares up between Amal and Hezbollah and the latter seize control of several Amal-held parts of the city and emerge as a strong force in the capital |
| September 1988 | President Amine Gemayel's term of office expires and Lebanese Armed Forces Commanding General Michel Aoun takes over as Acting Prime Minister |
| March 14, 1989 | Aoun launches 'war of liberation' against the Syrian forces and their Lebanese militia allies |
| January 1989 | The Arab League appoints a committee comprising Algeria, Kuwait, Morocco and Saudi Arabia to formulate solutions to the conflict in Lebanon |
| October 1989 | Taif Agreement is signed, marking the beginning of the end of fighting in Lebanon |
| November 4, 1989 | Taif Agreement is ratified and Rene Mouawad is elected as President |
| November 22, 1989 | President Rene Mouawad is assassinated |

| | |
|---|---|
| August 1990 | Lebanese Parliament endorses constitutional amendments embodying some of the political reforms envisioned at Taif. The National Assembly is expanded to 128 seats and is divided equally between Christians and Muslims |
| October 13, 1990 | Syrian forces attack Presidential Palace in Baabda. Michel Aoun surrenders |
| March 28, 1991 | Lebanese Parliament passes Amnesty Law which pardons all political crimes committed prior to its enactment |
| May 1991 | With the exception of the Hezbollah, all militias are dissolved |

## Islamic Revolution in Iran

| | |
|---|---|
| January 1978 | Students and religious leaders in the city of Qom protest against a story in the official press attacking Ayatollah Khomeini. The army is sent in and several demonstrating students are killed |
| February 18, 1978 | Violence erupts in Tabriz in clashes between the army and people protesting against the death of students in Qom in January |
| March 29, 1978 | In renewed protests across the nation, luxury hotels, cinemas, banks, government offices and other symbols of the Shah regime are attacked |
| May 1978 | Government commandos burst into the home of Ayatollah Kazem Shariatmadari, and shoot dead one of his followers right in front of him. Shariatmadari abandons his quietist stance and joins the opposition to the Shah. |
| August 20, 1978 | Cinema Rex in Abadan is set on fire by Islamic Militants, killing over 400 people |

| | |
|---|---|
| September 8, 1978 | The Shah introduces martial law in several cities and bans all demonstrations |
| September 8, 1978 | Army uses force on peaceful protestors against imposition of martial law at Zhaleh Square in Tehran. The incident comes to be known as Black Friday. |
| September 24, 1978 | Iraq seizes the house of Ayatollah Khomeini in Najaf |
| October 3, 1978 | Khomeini leaves Iraq for Kuwait but is refused entry at the border |
| October 6, 1978 | Khomeini leaves for Paris and establishes a base in the Parisian suburb of Neauphle-le-Chateau |
| December 2, 1978 | During the Islamic month of Muharram, over two million people fill the streets of Tehran's Shahyad Square (later known as Azadi or Freedom Square) and demand the removal of the Shah and return of Khomeini |
| January 12, 1979 | Khomeini establishes the 'Revolutionary Council' to manage the unfolding developments |
| January 16, 1979 | The Shah and the empress leave Iran at the demand of Prime Minister Shapour Bakhtiar |
| February 1, 1979 | Ayatollah Khomeini returns to Tehran to a rapturous greeting by several million Iranians |
| February 4, 1979 | Khomeini appoints Mehdi Bazargan as interim Prime Minister |
| February 9, 1979 | Fighting breaks out between loyal Immortal Guards and pro-Khomeini rebel Homafaran of the Iran Air Force. Khomeini declares jihad on loyal soldiers who did not surrender. Revolutionaries and rebel soldiers begin taking over police stations and military installations, distributing arms to the public |
| February 11, 1979 | Supreme Military Council declares itself "neutral in the current political disputes in |

order to prevent further disorder and blood-shed". Shapour Bakhtiar resigns as Prime Minister

## Palestinian Intifada

| | |
|---|---|
| December 4, 1987 | Shlomo Sakal, an Israeli plastics salesman, is stabbed to death in Gaza |
| December 8, 1987 | Four Palestinian refugees from Jabalya Camp are killed in a traffic accident caused by an Israel Defence Force truck in Gaza. Riot breaks out in Jabalya and Israeli soldiers kill an 18-year-old Palestinian leading to further riots leading to a popular uprising or intifada. |
| December 22, 1987 | The United Nations Security Council condemns Israel for violating the Geneva Conventions |
| 1988 | Palestinians initiate a nonviolence movement to withhold taxes. When time in prison doesn't stop the activists, Israel crushes the boycott by imposing heavy fines while seizing and disposing of equipment, furnishings, and goods from local stores, factories and even homes. |
| April 19, 1988 | A leader of the PLO, Abu Jihad, is assassinated in Tunis |
| November 1988 | UN General Assembly condemns Israeli actions against Palestinian civilians |
| July 6, 1989 | The first suicide attack occurs inside Israel's borders, against bus 405 in Tel Aviv. The incident comes to be known as the Tel Aviv Jerusalem bus 405 massacre and claims the lives of 14 civilians, wounding 30 more. |

## Kuwait War

| | |
|---|---|
| August 2, 1990 | Iraq invades Kuwait and later that day UN Security Council adopts Resolution 660 identifying Iraq as an aggressor and demanding immediate Iraqi withdrawal to positions occupied till August 1, 1990 |
| August 7, 1990 | US troops move into Saudi Arabia and get ready to launch Operation Desert Shield |
| August 8, 1990 | Iraq declares parts of Kuwait to be extensions of the Iraqi province of Basra and the rest to be the 19th province of Iraq |
| December 29, 1990 | United Nations Security Council adopts Resolution 678 and authorizes a coalition attack to implement Resolution 660 and to evict Iraqi forces from Kuwait. January 15, 1991, is set as the deadline for an Iraqi withdrawal. |
| January 17, 1991 | Coalition forces launch Operation Desert Storm |
| January 23, 1991 | Iraq dumps 400 million gallons of crude oil into the Persian Gulf and causes the largest oil spill in history |
| January 29, 1991 | Iraq attacks and briefly occupies Saudi city of Khafji |
| February 22, 1991 | Iraq agrees to Soviet ceasefire proposal but coalition rejects the agreement and gives Iraq 24 hours to start withdrawing troops |
| February 24, 1991 | Coalition ground forces enter Iraq |
| February 26, 1991 | Iraqi troops begin retreating out of Kuwait, setting fire to Kuwaiti oil wells as they leave |
| February 27, 1991 | US President George Bush declares ceasefire and the liberation of Kuwait |

**Iraq War**

| | |
|---|---|
| March 20, 2003 | US and UK launch Operation Iraqi Freedom |
| April 9, 2003 | Baghdad falls to US forces |
| April 13, 2003 | The town of Tikrit comes under coalition control |
| April 15, 2003 | Coalition partners claim the war is effectively over |
| May 16, 2003 | Paul Bremer is nominated as Civil Administrator and creates the Coalition Provisional Authority (CPA) as transitional government |
| July 13, 2003 | The Iraqi Governing Council is established under the authority of the US Coalition Provisional Authority |
| July 22, 2003 | Uday and Qusay Hussein, Saddam Hussein's sons, are killed in Mosul |
| August 7, 2003 | Truck bomb kills 19 outside the Jordanian embassy in Baghdad |
| August 19, 2003 | Truck bomb at the UN headquarters kills the top UN envoy, Sergio Vieiro de Mello, and 21 others |
| August 29, 2003 | Influential Shiite cleric Ayatollah Mohammed Baqr al-Hakim is killed in a car bomb blast as he leaves his mosque after Friday prayers. At least 84 others are killed |
| October 16, 2003 | UN Security Council issues Resolution 1511, which envisions a multinational force and preserves Washington's quasi absolute control of Iraq |
| October 26, 2003 | Coalition authorities lift a nighttime curfew on Baghdad's 5 million residents that has been in place for six months since the city fell to US forces |
| November 12, 2003 | A suicide truck bomb detonates at the Italian military HQ in Nasiriyah, killing 19 Italians (17 of them soldiers) and 14 Iraqis |

| | |
|---|---|
| December 13, 2003 | Coalition forces capture Saddam Hussein on a farm near Tikrit |
| February 1, 2004 | Two suicide bombers kill 109 and wound 235 at two Kurdish buildings in the northern Iraqi city of Arbil |
| March 2, 2004 | Almost 200 are killed in a series of bomb blasts in Baghdad and Karbala at the climax of the Shi'a festival of Ashura |
| March 8, 2004 | Signature of the provisional Iraqi constitution |
| March 31, 2004 | Fighting continues between Iraqi insurgents in Fallujah and the American forces |
| April 4–August 2004 | Violent clashes take place between coalition forces and the followers of the Shi'a cleric Muqtada al-Sadr |
| April 18, 2004 | Spain pulls out its troops from the multi-national force in Iraq |
| June 1, 2004 | The Iraqi Interim Government led by Prime Minister Iyad Allawi assumes functions. Ghazi al-Yawer is designated as head of the Iraqi state |
| June 8, 2004 | The UN adopts Resolution 1546 on the transfer of sovereignty from the Coalition Provisional Authority to the Iraqi Interim Government |
| June 28, 2004 | US-led Coalition Provisional Authority formally transfers sovereignty of Iraqi territory to the Iraqi interim government, two days ahead of schedule |
| January 30, 2005 | Elections are held for the Iraqi legislature. The Shi'a list obtains absolute majority ahead of the Kurds |
| January 31, 2005 | Iraq elects a Transitional Government to draft a constitution |
| April 6, 2005 | Kurdish leader Jalal Talabani is elected as President of Iraq |

| | |
|---|---|
| April 7, 2005 | Ibrahim al-Jaafari is nominated as the Prime Minister of Iraq |
| October 2005 | Constitutional referendum is held |
| December 2005 | The Iraqi National Assembly is elected |
| February 22, 2006 | The Al-Askari Mosque is bombed, sparking a wave of sectarian violence |
| December 30, 2006 | Saddam Hussein is hanged after being found guilty of crimes against humanity by an Iraqi court |

## Al-Aqsa Intifada

| | |
|---|---|
| September 28, 2000 | Israeli opposition leader Ariel Sharon visits the mosque compound of the Temple Mount in the Old City of Jerusalem. He is accompanied by a Likud Party delegation and surrounded by hundreds of Israeli riot police |
| September 29, 2000 | Following Friday prayers, riots break out around the Old City of Jerusalem during which five people are shot dead by Israeli security forces and 200 others are wounded after Palestinians throw rocks over the Western Wall at Jews and tourists below |
| September 29, 2000 | Riots and demonstrations break out in the West Bank |
| October 1, 2000 | General strike and demonstrations begin across northern Israel |
| October 8, 2000 | Thousands of Jewish Israelis participate in acts of violence in Nazareth and Tel Aviv |
| October 12, 2000 | Two Israeli reservists who entered Ramallah are arrested by the Palestinian Authority police. An agitated Palestinian mob enter the building and beat the soldiers to death. |
| February 2001 | Ariel Sharon is elected as the Prime Minister of Israel through a special election to the Prime Ministership |

| | |
|---|---|
| May 7, 2001 | IDF naval commandos capture the vessel *Santorini*, which was sailing towards Gaza |
| June 1, 2001 | A Hamas suicide bomber detonates himself in the Tel Aviv coastline Dolphinarium dancing club, killing 21 Israelis, mostly high-school students |
| January 2002 | The IDF Shayetet 13 naval commandos capture the *Karine A*, a large boat carrying weapons presumably for the Palestinian militants |
| April 2002 | 30 Israeli civilians are killed in a suicide bombing at Park Hotel in Netanya. The incident comes to be known as the Passover Massacre |
| April 2002 | Israel launches Operation Defensive Shield to apprehend Palestinian militant groups |
| April 2–May 10, 2002 | A stand off develops between armed Fatah militants and the IDF at the Church of the Nativity in Bethlehem. IDF snipers kill 7 people inside the church and wound several others. The stand-off is resolved by the deportation of 13 Palestinian militants identified by Israel to Europe. |
| April 3–11, 2002 | As part of Operation Defensive Shield, Israeli forces launch an attack on the Palestinian refugee camp at Jenin, leading to the death of 52 Palestinians |
| March 13, 2003 | Yasser Arafat appoints Mahmoud Abbas as Palestinian Prime Minister |
| May 20, 2003 | Israeli naval commandos intercept the vessel *Abu Hassan*, on course to the Gaza Strip from Lebanon |
| June 2003 | Hamas and the Islamic Jihad unilaterally declare a *Hudna* (truce) – a halt to all attacks against Israel – for a period of 45 days |

| | |
|---|---|
| August 19, 2003 | Hamas coordinates a suicide attack on a crowded bus in Jerusalem, killing 23 Israeli civilians including 7 children |
| October 4, 2003 | A suicide bombing takes place in Maxim restaurant in Haifa, claiming the lives of 21 Israeli civilians |
| October 5, 2003 | IAF warplanes bomb an alleged former terrorist training base at Ain Saheb, Syria |
| February 2, 2004 | Israeli Prime Minister Ariel Sharon announces his plan to transfer all the Jewish settlers from the Gaza Strip |
| March 22, 2004 | An Israeli helicopter gunship kills Hamas leader Sheikh Ahmed Yassin |
| April 17, 2004 | Yassin's successor Abdel Aziz al-Rantissi is killed by an IDF helicopter gunship strike |
| May 11–12, 2004 | Palestinian militants destroy two IDF M-113 APC's, killing 12 soldiers and mutilating their bodies |
| May 18, 2004 | IDF launch Operation Rainbow with the stated aim of striking the terror infrastructure of Rafah, destroying smuggling tunnels and stopping a shipment of SA-7 missiles and improved anti-tank weapons. 40 Palestinian militants and 12 civilians are killed during the operation. |
| September 29, 2004 | A Qassam rocket hits the Israeli town of Sderot and kills 2 Israeli children |
| September 29, 2004 | IDF launch Operation Days of Penitence in the north of the Gaza Strip, aimed at removing the threat of Qassam rockets |
| October 16, 2004 | Operation Days of Penitence ends, leaving more than 100 Palestinians dead |
| October 21, 2004 | The Israeli Air Force kills Adnan al-Ghoul, a senior Hamas bomb-maker and the inventor of the Qassam rocket |

| | |
|---|---|
| November 11, 2004 | Yasser Arafat dies in a military hospital in Paris |
| December 9, 2004 | Five weapons smugglers are killed and two are arrested on the border between Rafah and Egypt. Leader of the Popular Resistance Committees Jamal Abu Samhadana is injured by an Israeli air-strike |
| December 10, 2004 | Israeli soldiers fire at Khan Younis refugee camp, killing a 7-year-old girl |
| December 12, 2004 | Explosives are detonated in a tunnel under an Israeli military-controlled border crossing on the Egyptian border with Gaza, near Rafah. The attack claims the life of 5 Israeli soldiers, wounding ten others and causing damage to several structures in the area |
| January 9, 2005 | Mahmoud Abbas is elected as the President of the Palestinian Authority |
| February 8, 2005 | President Abbas and Prime Minister Sharon declare a mutual truce between Israel and the Palestinian National Authority at the Sharm al-Sheikh Summit |
| February 9–10, 2005 | A barrage of 25–50 Qassam rockets and mortar shells hit the Neve Dekalim settlement |
| February 10, 2005 | Israeli security forces arrest Maharan Omar Shucat Abu Hamis, a Palestinian resident of Nablus, who was about to launch a bus suicide attack in French Hill in Jerusalem |
| February 13, 2005 | Mahmoud Abbas enters into talk with the leaders of the Islamic Jihad and Hamas, for them to rally behind him and respect the truce |
| June 2005 | Palestinian factions intensify bombardment over the city of Sderot with improvised Qassam rockets |
| July 12, 2005 | A suicide bombing in the coastal city of Netanya kills 5 people |

| | |
|---|---|
| July 14, 2005 | Hamas starts to shell Israeli settlements inside and outside the Gaza Strip with dozens of Qassam rockets, killing an Israeli woman |
| July 15, 2005 | Israeli resumes its 'targeted killing' policy, killing 7 Hamas militants and bombing about 4 Hamas facilities |
| February 4, 2006 | Israel launches a series of attacks against Islamic Jihad and al-Aqsa Martyr's Brigades Qassam rocket launcher squads and kills 9 Palestinians. The air strikes come after Qassam rockets hit southern Ashkelon and Kibbutz Carmia, and seriously wound a 7-month-old baby |
| April 17, 2006 | A suicide bomber in Tel Aviv kills 11 people and injures 60 |
| June 8, 2006 | Jamal abu Samhadana, the leader of the Popular Resistance Committees, is assassinated along with three other PRC members in an Israeli air strike |
| June 9, 2006 | Seven members of the Ghalia family are killed on a Gaza beach. The cause of the explosion remains uncertain but in response, Hamas declares an end to its commitment to a ceasefire declared in 2005 and announces the resumption of attacks on Israelis |
| June 25, 2006 | A military outpost is attacked by Palestinian militants and a gunbattle follows that leaves 2 Israeli soldiers and 3 Palestinian militants dead |
| November 26, 2006 | A truce is implemented between Israel and the Palestinian Authority |

**Second Lebanon War**

| | |
|---|---|
| July 12, 2006 | Hezbollah abducts two Israeli soldiers in the border village of Zar'it |

| | |
|---|---|
| July 13, 2006 | Hezbollah launches rockets at Haifa, hitting a cable car station and a few other buildings |
| July 13, 2006 | Israel attacks civilian infrastructure in Lebanon, imposes an air and sea blockade of Lebanon. and bombs the main Beirut–Damascus highway |
| July 14, 2006 | IDF bombs Hassan Nasrallah's offices in Beirut |
| July 23, 2006 | Israeli land forces cross into Lebanon in Maroun al-Ras area |
| July 25, 2006 | IDF engage Hezbollah forces in the Battle of Bint Jbeil |
| July 26, 2006 | Israeli forces attack and destroy UNIFIL post, killing all four UN observers |
| July 27, 2006 | Hezbollah ambush Israeli forces in Bint Jbeil and kill eight soldiers |
| July 28, 2006 | Israeli paratroopers kill 26 of Hezbollah's commando elite in Bint Jbeil |
| July 30, 2006 | Israeli airstrikes hit an apartment building in Qana and kill 28 civilians, 16 of which are children |
| July 31, 2006 | Israeli military and Hezbollah forces engage in the Battle of Ayta ash-Shab |
| August 4, 2006 | Israel targets the southern outskirts of Beirut |
| August 5, 2006 | Israeli commandos carry out night-time raid in Tyre |
| August 11, 2006 | The United Nations Security Council unanimously adopts Resolution 1701 to end the hostilities |
| August 17, 2006 | The Lebanese army begins deployment in Southern Lebanon |
| September 8, 2006 | Israel lifts the naval blockade of Lebanon |
| October 1, 2006 | Israeli troops are withdrawn from Lebanon |

# Index